D1084261

University of London Historical Studies

VIII

UNIVERSITY OF LONDON HISTORICAL STUDIES

I. HUGH TINKER. *The Foundations of Local Self-Government in India, Pakistan and Burma.* 1954.

II. AVROM SALTMAN. *Theobald, Archbishop of Canterbury.* 1956.

III. R. F. LESLIE. *Polish Politics and the Revolution of November 1830.* 1956.

IV. W. N. MEDLICOTT. *Bismarck, Gladstone, and the Concert of Europe.* 1956.

V. JOHN LYNCH. *Spanish Colonial Administration, 1782–1810: The Intendant System in the Viceroyalty of the Rio de La Plata.* 1958.

VI. F. H. W. SHEPPARD. *Local Government in St. Marylebone, 1688–1835.* 1958.

VII. R. L. GREAVES. *Persia and the Defence of India, 1884–1892.* 1959.

VIII. M. J. SYDENHAM. *The Girondins.* 1961.

IX. M. E. HOWELL. *Regalian Right in Mediaeval England.* 1961.

THE GIRONDINS

JEAN PIERRE BRISSOT

THE
GIRONDINS

BY

M. J. SYDENHAM

UNIVERSITY OF LONDON
THE ATHLONE PRESS
1961

Published by
THE ATHLONE PRESS
UNIVERSITY OF LONDON
at 2 Gower Street, London WC1

Distributed by Constable & Co. Ltd
12 Orange Street, London WC2

Canada
University of Toronto Press

U.S.A.
Oxford University Press Inc
New York

Printed in Great Britain at
THE CURWEN PRESS LTD
PLAISTOW E13

PREFACE

ONE of the great episodes of French history, both in drama and in consequence, is *la Chute des Girondins*, the Fall of the Girondins. Although many men perished in the proscription which inaugurated the Terror in France in 1793, it is of Vergniaud and the other orators from the Gironde that the Frenchman thinks first. To him, the Fall of the Girondins signifies the silencing by the Revolutionary Tribunal of the twenty-one men who were accused as 'the accomplices of J. P. Brissot', their cool courage in the Conciergerie and their final praises for the Republic as the tumbrils carried them and the corpse of their colleague Valazé, who had chosen to die by his own hand, towards the scaffold.

Since for those familiar from childhood with this dramatic story the name 'Girondins' may have much emotional significance but yet suggest only the names of a limited number of deputies, the French are perhaps less likely than others to suppose that Robespierre's path to power was ever blocked by anything like a large political party. Nevertheless, French interpretations of the history of the Revolution, often influenced by prejudice, have often been distorted also by an over-casual use of the name 'Girondins' as a convenient collective term, while in English histories of France the expression 'Girondin party' appears almost as a matter of course. In consequence, the history of the period 1792-3 is almost invariably written in terms of party warfare, with particular policies allocated to Robespierre and the Montagnards on the one hand and to a Girondin party on the other.

This book is an attempt to collate and interpret the mass of material in the form of judicial documents, pamphlets, correspondence, memoirs, and so on, which exists concerning the so-called Girondins. It begins with a review of the various theories which have been suggested about them by the historians of the French Revolution, compares these with the views they

and their accusers expressed at the time of their trial, and shows
that proscription by the Montagnards was in reality so haphazard a process that no credence can be given to deductions
about the political unity of its victims. There follows an attempt
to ascertain the origins, the real nature and the ultimate extent
of the supposed party by the examination of developments from
1791–2.

The book represents an abridgement of work approved by the
University of London for the award of the degree of Doctor of
Philosophy. By grouping together some of the more detailed
references I have tried to achieve a combination of convenience
to the student and a minimum of distraction to the eye of the
more general reader; and since the book is designed principally
for English readers, I have endeavoured to use English trans-
lations, or near equivalents, for some French terms. Thus
reference is normally made to Department and to Memoirs
rather than to the French *Département* and *Mémoires*, although
more technical terms, such as *appel nominal*, remain in the original. Similarly, since the spelling of the names of some deputies
often varies considerably from one contemporary document to
another, I have retained in text and footnotes a commonly
accepted form even where this differs from the formal one given
in the final list of the first appendix.

To prepare a work of this sort for publication is to become
aware of the dependence a writer has upon the help of other
people. I am very greatly indebted to many who have assisted
me from time to time in a wide variety of ways, and I should
like to express here my warm and sincere appreciation of all
that they have done. More particularly, I would gratefully
acknowledge the assistance I received from the Central Research
Fund of the University of London and the clear criticism and
constructive comments of Mr. Alun Davies of the London School
of Economics. Above all, however, my thanks are due to Professor
Alfred Cobban of University College London, whose kindness
and helpfulness have encouraged me to attempt, over the years,
to produce work of which his scholarship might approve; and
to my wife, who has been my most constant critic and colleague.

M.J.S,

CONTENTS

B

LIST OF PLATES

A map of Western France showing the
distribution by *Départements* of the deputies
from that area who have been said to
have been Girondins appears on page 184

LIST OF ABBREVIATIONS

A.N.	Archives Nationales
B.M.	British Museum
B.N.	Bibliothèque Nationale
Brissot	*Mémoires de J. P. Brissot*, ed. Perroud. Paris, 1904
Jacobins	Aulard, *La Société des Jacobins, Recueil des Documents.* Paris, 1889–97
Journal	*Journal des Débats de la Société des Amis de la Constitution séante aux Jacobins*
Kuscinski	Kuscinski, *Dictionnaire des Conventionnels.* Paris, 1917
La Vie chère	Mathiez, *La Vie chère et le mouvement social sous la Terreur.* Paris, 1927
Madame Roland	*Mémoires de Madame Roland*, ed. Perroud. Paris, 1905
Moniteur	*Réimpression de l'Ancien Moniteur.* Paris, 1854
Mortimer-Ternaux	Mortimer-Ternaux, *Histoire de la Terreur, 1792–1794.* Paris, 1868–81
Procès-verbal	*Procès-verbal de la Convention nationale.* Paris, 1793
Proscription	Perroud, *Recherches sur la Proscription des Girondins 1793–1795.* Paris, 1917
Tuetey	Tuetey, *Répertoire général des sources manuscrits de l'histoire de Paris pendant la Révolution française.* Paris, 1890–1914
Valazé	Nicolle, *Valazé, député de l'Orne à la Convention.* Paris, 1933
Vergniaud	Lintilhac, *Vergniaud, Le drâme des Girondins.* Paris, 1920

CHAPTER I

The Girondins in History

THE French Revolution was an event of such magnitude that few historians have been able to combine an adequate survey of its whole course with a just appreciation of its detail. In the nineteenth century historians tended to treat it on a grand scale, compressing great events into small compass and subordinating personalities to the rise and fall of parties. During the last fifty years historians have subjected particular aspects of the Revolution to such detailed research that a clear appreciation of the whole has, perhaps temporarily, become increasingly difficult to achieve. This is particularly a consequence of the fact that monographic studies, exhaustive within their own limits, have tended to follow certain well-trodden paths, while other lines of research, of at least equal significance, have been generally neglected.

The picture that results is therefore a rather unbalanced one, and neither general histories nor monographic studies have so far produced any adequate investigation of the deputies in the Convention who are commonly called the Girondins. Those who have written the history of the Revolution as a whole have most often been interested in the rise of the Jacobins and the events which culminated in the triumph of Robespierre in June 1793. This concentration of attention has magnified the distortions caused by the tendency to treat all Robespierre's opponents as if they were a united party, and to identify them with policies which are really deduced from the historians' own interpretations of the whole course of the Revolution rather than from a study of what the so-called Girondins said or did. On the other hand, for more detailed researchers the career of Robespierre has become so symbolic of the triumph and atrophy of the Revolution that the fate of his opponents has tended to be treated as a side-issue, and therefore neglected.

Successive historians have thus put forward a series of contradictory generalizations about these opponents of Robespierre. Radical writers have regarded them as men who unconsciously served the royalist cause, moderates have seen them as liberal republicans or as constitutional monarchists, and those of royalist sympathies have thought them indistinguishable in violence and ambition from the Jacobins. At the same time, even hostile writers, catching the echoes of the Girondins' oratory and considering the drama of their downfall, have been tempted to colour history with romance and so have made them in some sort legendary figures—symbols, perhaps, of the persistent weakness and repeated failures of moderation in France.

Two consequences have followed from this prolonged variation of view. One is the general acceptance of the belief that the Convention, summoned in the early autumn of 1792 to provide France with another new constitution but primarily concerned with domestic disorganization and the imminence of foreign invasion, was from its inauguration distracted by the strife of two opposing parties, the Girondins and the Jacobins or Montagnards,[1] strife which was only ended when in the spring of 1793 the triumph of the Jacobins cleared the way for the effective reorganization of France. The second consequence is that confusion still prevails about the nature of the Girondin party and the reasons for its conflict with the Jacobins. A complete reassessment of the position through a detailed investigation of the deputies concerned is therefore necessary.

As a preliminary, a brief review of the views of the historians may serve to illustrate the present confusion in greater detail and to indicate the way in which historical writing is influenced by changing circumstances. This will be limited to the work of French historians and, since every French historian of the Revolution has been compelled to consider the Girondins and to come to some conclusion about them, it will be further limited to the work of major historians and to those others who have given particular attention to the supposed Girondin party.

---

[1] No distinction is made in this chapter between the Jacobins and the Montagnards, and the name Girondins is used without prejudice to future argument.

I

One of the first historians of the Revolution was Toulongeon. When in 1801 he published his *Histoire de France depuis 1789* he was obviously unhappy about the Girondins. He repeatedly explained that he used the name because it was the contemporary one—a view that, as will be seen, is open to doubt—and he stressed the Girondins' proud independence and their failure to vote as an organized group. He also asked his readers to remember that sub-divisions in the party, concealed at the time, became clear later. He found difficulty in distinguishing the Girondins from the Montagnards, whom he represented as concealing themselves among the Girondins until the revolution of 10 August 1792. At the same time Toulongeon, himself a monarchist, spoke of the Girondins as constructive constitutional monarchists, who only became republicans after the abolition of the monarchy, and who even then, in contrast to the revolutionary party, attempted to establish a republic by legitimate methods and with all proper constitutional forms.[1]

Toulongeon's cautious approach is echoed, though in vaguer phraseology, in the *Considérations* of Madame de Staël, which were published posthumously in 1818. She, too, was a constitutional monarchist, and she tended to treat as a single party all those who criticized the Court in the Legislative Assembly. Thus at first she disparaged the Girondins as republicans, but she subsequently praised them for their conduct in the Convention, where, unlike Toulongeon, she thought them monarchists, men who died for their attempt to save the life of the King.[2] She then implied that the alteration in their attitude was a consequence of their own ambition, and concluded that their existence and their elimination were equally harmful to France.[3]

During the period of the Restoration, when it seemed possible that the *ancien régime* might yet be re-established, there appeared the important histories of the Revolution by Mignet and by Thiers, and in each the Girondins were portrayed in a light

---

[1] Toulongeon, *Histoire de France depuis 1789*, ii, particularly pp. 9, 242, 252.

[2] Although the theme is not developed here, successive stages of the Revolution often evoke changing attitudes in the work of individual writers.

[3] Madame de Staël, *Considérations sur les principaux événemens de la Révolution française*, ii, particularly pp. 28–30, 38, 88.

favourable to the writer's political views. Mignet's work is a
plea for constitutional monarchy. He accepted the Girondins as
a well-defined political party, possessing all the virtues of the
middle class. They were constitutional monarchists at heart,
although circumstances compelled them to become republicans.
Their brief period of nominal authority revealed them as
idealists who hated violence and endeavoured to establish constitutional government in impossible conditions. The imminent
danger of successful invasion in 1792 made the triumph of the
multitude essential, and when on 10 August the Jacobins, the
leaders of the new movement, became the real rulers of France,
the Girondins had to pay the price of their weakness.[1]

Thiers's history of the Revolution, written almost simultaneously with that of Mignet, had the same political purpose
and reached similar conclusions. Thiers, too, regarded the
Girondins as but superficial republicans, their attitude being
but a consequence of their distrust of the King. Their conduct
at the time of the August insurrection convinced him that
'Monarchy was not an unbearable prospect to them . . . they
would have accepted a constitutional monarchy with adequate
safeguards'. He emphasized the virtues he found in the Girondins, their humanity, their courage and their talents. In his
view they were, above all else, moderates and liberals, men
'desiring liberty in the means as well as in the end, wanting
security for their enemies, deliberation in the administration of
justice, and absolute freedom of commerce'. He praised these
opinions, but concluded with Mignet that Girondin weakness
had seriously compromised the security of France, and so of
liberty itself, in 1793. Although in all this Thiers, like Mignet,
treated the Girondins as a definite party, he added the qualification that they could hardly be distinguished from the Jacobins
before 10 August 1792, and that they were never closely organized. The party, he believed, was united more by political
circumstances—Jacobin pressure and popular envy—than by
any harmony of principle.[2]

---

[1] Mignet, *Histoire de la Révolution française depuis 1789 jusqu'à 1814*, i, 221, 276, 294,
317–19, 406.
[2] Thiers, *The History of the French Revolution*, i, 207, 214, 257, 353–4, and ii, 75–9,
135, 379.

II

After the expulsion of Charles X in 1830 a distinct change of attitude towards the Girondins is apparent. In 1834, to Buchez and Roux, the compilers of the forty-volume *Histoire parlementaire de la Révolution française*, who regarded *fraternité* as the real heritage of the Revolution, they had all the appearance of counter-revolutionaries, and their power was 'illegitimate in the strictest sense of the word' because it was an obstacle to the development of an egalitarian society.[1] A less important study by Tissot was even more hostile and echoed every accusation made by the Jacobins.[2]

In the 1840's, growing dissatisfaction with the rule of Louis Philippe and the bourgeoisie was accompanied by a new series of studies of the Revolution with an appropriate political message to unfold. The first and most immediately influential of these was the *Histoire des Girondins* by Lamartine. It is now customary to decry this famous book. It is undoubtedly untrustworthy—Dr. Gooch has described it as 'the most worthless and the most eloquent of books'—and, equally certainly, it is a political pamphlet on a grand scale. Lamartine wrote well. He used his imagination, supported by extensive quotations from newspapers, to present a lively and colourful picture of the Revolution, one which would reawaken popular interest in it and suggest the deficiencies of Louis Philippe's *régime*. He achieved his purpose. Nevertheless, his conclusions are no more politically biased than those of many other writers whose credit as historians is justifiably much higher.

So far as later historians are concerned, Lamartine's influence was rather negative than positive. No important historian accepted his scholarship, and many have attacked him as the creator of the legendary Girondins—liberals, moderates and idealists. This seems a mis-interpretation of his work, for these ideas are those of earlier historians, and not of Lamartine. In fact he held no brief for the Girondins, although he deplored the destructive violence of their opponents. If he created a legend

[1] Buchez and Roux, *Histoire parlementaire de la Révolution française*, xxv, preface.
[2] Tissot, *Histoire de la Révolution française depuis 1789 jusqu'à l'Empire*, v, 17–20.

he did so inadvertently, by dramatizing their downfall at a time when, as he himself suggested, Frenchmen were finding only tedium in the pettifogging politics of their middle-class monarchy.

To Lamartine, as to earlier writers, the Girondins were a party. After a temporary union with the Jacobins in the struggle with the monarchy, they separated from them again in the Convention, where they appeared as a disciplined group with a party headquarters at Madame Roland's, a system of propaganda through the Girondin press, and a definite plan of campaign—to secure control of the executive by organized voting and by infiltration into the Committees. The only distinctions he allowed amongst them were those of youth and age, of ardour and caution.[1]

As a party, the Girondins represented for Lamartine the bourgeoisie—'triumphant, restless, eloquent, wishing single-handed to conquer and exploit liberty, power and the nation'. He showed them attacking the church, the aristocracy and the monarchy, and inciting the nation to war, as steps on their road to power. When they had attained this, they fell, because they had the weaknesses of their class—greed, timidity and indecision. One begins to speculate whether all those who have talked about Lamartine idealizing the Girondins have ever read him. Admittedly he repudiated the 'liberal monarchist' views put forward by Mignet and Thiers. The Girondins, with few exceptions, were for him whole-hearted republicans, but their republic was not that which the French people—in Lamartine's view—wanted. Dominated by the antiquated conception of a classical republic, an aristocracy founded on slavery, they were unable to conceive the republic of the future, based on equality and democracy. In contrast to the Jacobins, who wished to transform society and establish such a fraternal republic, the Girondins wished to change the form of government alone. Their ideal was that of the Senate and People of Rome, an aristocracy of talent and a people well-governed but excluded from political power, which would be exercised by the Girondins themselves. Some of them, indeed, would have liked to

---

[1] Lamartine, *Histoire des Girondins*, iii, 113-14, 128, 241. Dr. Gooch's comment occurs in his *History and Historians in the Nineteenth Century*, p. 228.

establish a federal republic, in which the Departments of France would have been controlled by local oligarchies.[1]

From this interpretation of the Girondins Lamartine concluded that they were an obstacle to the progress of the Revolution and of France, and he left his readers to make the obvious comparison with the Orleanist monarchy. A similar conclusion was reached, though by a different route, in the second study of the Revolution to appear in the 1840's, that of Michelet. Lamartine had written to propagate a political programme; Michelet did so to teach the corresponding political philosophy. His basic belief was faith in the natural goodness of the people, whose emancipation from the artificial restrictions imposed upon them by clericalism and social privilege was required by reason and justice alike. The Revolution, which attacked both the church and the monarchy, was therefore Justice incarnate, a great uprising of the whole people to cast off their ancient shackles and to build a new society.

Against this background the Girondins were portrayed by Michelet as true men, sincerely patriotic and republican. 'Personally innocent', they were exculpated from almost every charge ever brought against them. They were not compromised by their relationships with Louis, Lafayette or Dumouriez, they were not federalists, and their attacks upon the church and their demand for war in 1792 were very creditable to them.

But despite their brilliant gifts, 'the true spirit of the Revolution was not to be found in them'. Their policy in 1793 was 'blind and futile', endangering the security of France. Once the republic had been attained, their weaknesses became apparent, and with no other great principles to spur them on, inertia and incapacity marked their conduct. Then, their personal antipathies led them to alienate other revolutionaries, particularly Danton, and to attack Paris. They also showed an increasing tendency to favour the bourgeoisie. In the political disunity which followed, they found themselves the unwilling representatives of middle-class self-interest in the towns, and of the conservative apathy of the peasantry. Unwittingly they encouraged local resistance to the new national government, and

[1] Lamartine, *op. cit.*, i, 239–40, 371–2, 413, ii, 263, and iii, 113, 124–7, 240, 251, 272.

this in turn rapidly became the mark of royalism and counter-revolution. It was this, according to Michelet, that was their 'true and only crime'. Republicans in theory, their practice led to royalism. Their removal was therefore an imperative necessity, although the Terror which followed was to prove fatal to the Revolution.[1]

So Michelet saw the Revolution as the failure of a brave experiment in republicanism, the men and not the system being at fault. This conclusion is underlined by a view of the Girondins as a party which appears to be unique. He considered that the party was only clearly perceptible as an entity, distinct from the Jacobins, in its earliest days, when the war policy and the struggle with the monarchy gave it a true *raison d'être*. After 10 August 1792 its only cohesive force was fear of the Jacobins. Distracted by provincial rivalries and by the individual brilliance of its leaders, it rapidly split up into factions and coteries, and eventually disintegrated completely.[2]

The work of a third republican writer of this period represents a still more radical approach to the Revolution. Louis Blanc's *Histoire de la Révolution française* is a serious and well-documented study, and as he was a convinced socialist his opinions led him towards an economic interpretation of the Revolution. As might be expected, his judgement upon the Girondins is severe. The best that he can say for them is that they were sincere republicans, who stood up bravely to the church, to the monarchy and to Europe. This virtue, however, was more than offset by their two great faults, ambition and individualism. Although he granted that their ambition was vicarious, followed for the sake of posterity, Louis Blanc still considered it excessive. The Girondins' attempts to retain power led them to devote every effort to the elimination of their rivals and to neglect the public interest at a time of crisis. Although they claimed to stand for freedom of conscience, their implacable intolerance towards their foes, the patient and moderate Jacobins, made them appear almost as a new aristocracy. Even more culpable was their failure to grasp the paramount

---

[1] Michelet, *Histoire de la Révolution française*, iv, 48–50, 108, 236, 274, 325, 330, 340, 349, 364–6, 470 and v, 36, 48–52, 182, 252, 350–2, 363, 509–11, 533–5, 585, 612.   [2] *Ibid.*, v, 38–41.

importance of social obligations. Their Constitution was little more than an instrument for the promotion of an unlimited individualism. They supported unrestricted freedom of commerce and they regarded property rights as absolute and sacred, not as relative and social. 'Their true fault was to have as their social doctrine Liberty without Equality.'

For Louis Blanc all other charges against the Girondins were insignificant compared with this one. Like previous writers, he also assumed that they were a party, though a rather pathetic one. They were 'small men in high office', 'a bizarre mixture of exalted patriotism and ambition, of magnanimity and intrigue, of fantasy and prudence'.[1]

III

If Louis Blanc, Lamartine and Michelet were hostile to the Girondins it was because they regarded them as faint-hearted republicans who had not dared to go far enough along each writer's chosen road. Succeeding writers were to be much more hostile, for the contrary reason. During the Second Empire, Cassagnac, one of the first of the ultra-royalist historians, portrayed all revolutionaries as public enemies. His lead was followed after the Commune of 1871 by Edmond Biré and by Hippolyte Taine, who condemned democracy outright. The Girondins suffered accordingly.

Like his predecessors, Cassagnac identified the Girondins with the bourgeoisie, which, seen from above, seemed still more evil. In the past it had supported the foreigner against Henry IV, and Condé against Louis XIV, for the sake of power; in the nineteenth century 'this turbulent and egotistical element' had overthrown its chosen dynasty for the same reason. The Girondins, whose only principle was ambition, had been true representatives of these 'insatiable place-hunters'. Cassagnac interpreted the whole history of the Legislative Assembly on these lines, and the Girondins were made responsible for all the disasters and misfortunes of France. A vast plot to gain control of the ministry had been succeeded by a final violent effort to

---

[1] Blanc, *Histoire de la Révolution française*, vii, 5–6, 85, 247, 255, 303–5, 375, and viii, 255, 450–1, 480.

impose Girondin rule on a conquered King, and in the process
all constituted authority was destroyed. The culmination of this
plot came in the September massacres, 'coldly resolved and
organized, executed and paid for by the *de facto* government
which had gained power by the Revolution of 10 August'. The
Girondins were therefore 'the most deadly party in France',
whose blind and insatiable ambition had paved the way for the
horrors of the Terror.[1]

Obviously Cassagnac made no effort to distinguish the
Girondins from the Jacobins. The only distinction he allowed
between them was that between principals and auxiliaries: the
Girondins controlled the Jacobins until they fell before them.
But Cassagnac was also interested in repudiating the idea that
the Girondins were morally worthy of being called a party, and
for this particular purpose he relied not on his usual royalist
sources but on material published by the Jacobins at the height
of their campaign for power, much of which is certainly un-
reliable. He also used curious reasoning. In his view, the
Girondins lied when, at their trial, they denied their unity, and
because they disavowed each other they were unworthy of
respect; yet at the same time he accepted as truth their denial
of any concerted policy. Consequently he could condemn them
for the lack of both the elements he considered essential to a
political party—personal honour, and political principles.[2]

Cassagnac's theme was echoed by the more scholarly historian Edmond Biré in a series of articles first published in 1880.
Biré denied that the revolutionaries were divided in the
Legislative Assembly. They might have had leaders and followers, but any other sub-division was 'purely imaginary', a
contradiction of all documents and facts. From this beginning
Biré proceeded to discredit the legend of the liberal Girondins
for the period of the Convention as Cassagnac had done for that
of the Legislative Assembly. He found that 'all their law rested
on the single foundation of denunciation'. Lusting for power,
they were responsible for the trial of the King, for the policy of
revolutionary war and for the creation of the instruments of the

---

[1] Cassagnac, *Histoire des Girondins et des massacres de septembre*, i, introduction and
1–2.
[2] *Ibid.*, i, 3–26, 270, 305, 319.

Terror. He concluded that their sole motive was coldly-calculated self-interest.[1]

A more intellectual condemnation of the Revolution appeared in the work of Hippolyte Taine. Taine was not a royalist, but a radical who was convinced by the events of 1871 that anarchy lurks beneath the surface of modern societies and is only held in check by strong government and the social hierarchy. In his history of the Revolution he therefore rejected the idea of democracy and damned the Revolution itself as a vast conspiracy by the worst elements in French society to destroy the political and social organization created and controlled by a rational but apathetic majority.[2]

Taine's description of the Girondins is what might be expected from this. At first quite indistinguishable from the Jacobins, and so utterly disreputable, the Girondins later appear in the Convention as 'the most estimable of republicans'. They were then educated believers in an ideal society, which was to be based on a known, established law, as opposed to the anarchy of Jacobinism, unrestricted popular sovereignty, and the power of the mob of Paris. But if the Girondin had the watchword 'Law, not bloodshed', if he attempted 'to muzzle the beast', if he failed because he was 'too civilized for his foes', he was still basically a Jacobin 'who knew no scruples where his abstract utopia was concerned'. He was a member of a party, but it was one which was unable to act collectively.[3]

During the period of the Second Empire no important justification of the Girondins appeared. They were defended only in a history by Quinet and in a new edition of a little-known work by Guadet. Quinet, a political exile, wrote without reference to sources. A Protestant and a republican, his account of the Revolution was an indirect attack upon Napoleon III and the Catholic church. Because he regarded the Terror as leading directly to the First Empire, he was sympathetic to the Girondins, whose fall marked for him the failure of the Revolution and the permanent exile of liberty from France. Although he regarded the Girondins as a party he hardly distinguished it

---

[1] Biré, *Légendes révolutionnaires*, 111–16, 127, 139, 144–8.
[2] Taine, *Les origines de la France contemporaine: La Révolution*, ii, 9, 45 and *passim*.
[3] *Ibid.*, ii, 106–9, 145, 189, 382–6, 432.

from the Jacobins. Both had the same aim, a republic, the same
interests and the same enemies. Their division was fundamentally due to their lack of a common faith. Consequently mis-
understandings developed, fostered by ambition and by fears
of insidious royalism. The Montagnards falsely supposed that
the people could be forced to be free, and so they struck down
the party which was the last bulwark against tyranny.[1]

Family loyalty made Guadet, the nephew of the deputy of
the Gironde in the Convention, still more sympathetic towards
his uncle's friends. He wrote because he considered that too
many historians had merely repeated the libels of 1793. His
analysis of the characteristics of the party is fairly commonplace,
the Girondins appearing as moderate statesmen capable of
saving France. Their only ambition was that of service, and the
federalism with which they were charged was 'nothing but a
phantom conjured up to animate Paris against them'. His view
of the composition of the party is more original: he believed
that in reality party unity was unknown in 1793, and that the
deputies of the Gironde thought and acted as individuals. If
they ever acted together, their alliance was 'as mobile as events'
and 'could only be said to exist when it was actually in operation'. According to Guadet it is history which tends to group
men together. All those involved in the fall of the deputies of the
Gironde had wrongly been treated as Girondins themselves, and
since the deputies of the Gironde had at different times fought
both the monarchy and the mob, all had indifferently been
damned by material drawn from demagogic or reactionary
sources.[2]

IV

After 1880 the histories of the Revolution take on a different
character. The comparative stability of the Third Republic, the
foundation in 1886 of the chair of the History of the French Revolution at the Sorbonne, and the influence of such great

[1] Quinet, *La Révolution*, i, 422–4, 436, 445–56, and ii, 18–19.
[2] Guadet, *Les Girondins* (1828 and 1861), i, 507–14. Similar emphasis upon the
individualism of the deputies who were proscribed appears in Mortimer-Ternaux,
iv, 100, and vii, 428 ff., and in Wallon, *Histoire du Tribunal révolutionnaire de Paris*,
Ch. ix.

historians as Sorel, Aulard, Mathiez and Lefebvre, made scholarship and the study of original sources more important than literary merit or propaganda value.

Sorel was primarily concerned with the European scene, but since the deputies of the Gironde were amongst those who were influential when war with Austria began in 1792 his assessment of them has importance. Indeed, his dictum that 'the Girondins wanted war, regarding war as the road to power' has become classical.[1] The phrase, taken from its context, is misleading in that it implies that the war policy was a distinctive characteristic of the Girondins. Sorel in fact believed that the Girondins, fearful lest peaceful constitutional rule should destroy their prestige, desired war in order to identify the monarchy with the enemies of France, and that the Jacobins were equally war-like for other reasons. Ambition and bellicosity were thus for Sorel equally characteristic of both the Girondins and the Jacobins, and he despised both factions for their amateur diplomacy, condemning both alike for 'mingling the noblest struggles that a people has ever undertaken with the most shabby and atrocious jealousies that have ever divided men'. Both had the same hates and ambitions, which united them so long as both were out of power. Nor was the conflict between them a consequence of Girondin moderation, for their love of liberty and their repudiation of *raison d'état* was the result of policy rather than of principle. Personal rivalry was for Sorel the fundamental cause of the discord, and in the quarrels it caused the Girondins were distinguished only by political incompetence. Their conduct of the war and their attitude in the trial of the King both demonstrated this incompetence, and their inclination towards federalism was the supreme manifestation of it.

Sorel's attitude towards the composition of the Girondin party reflected his belief in the importance of personalities. He explained that he used the name Girondins only because it was customary to do so, not because it was contemporary, and that the members of the group had no true bond of union. Political expediency, similarities of character and common hatreds alone held the coterie together.[2]

[1] Sorel, *L'Europe et la Révolution française*, ii, 395.
[2] *Ibid.*, ii, 300, 314–17, 341, 395, 565, and iii, 70–4, 411.

C

Aulard, whose conclusions were published in 1901 and 1906, also agreed that the name Girondin was not, in its wider sense, a contemporary one, but one made popular by later writers, particularly Lamartine. But where Sorel saw only a coterie, Aulard saw a definite, though not a completely successful, attempt to organize a political party in the English fashion. He did not admit the existence of any recognized party leader, but he considered that the deputies proscribed in June 1793, with their sympathizers, had the appearance of a compact group and almost that of a party. Indeed, he subsequently compiled a list of 163 men who could be regarded as Girondins.[1]

Aulard was concerned almost exclusively with political ideals and was an apologist of republican democracy and of the bourgeoisie. In spite of the rather rigid party organization he ascribed to the Girondins, he saw little difference between them and the Jacobins. Even contemporaries, he asserted, could not divine the true cause of their quarrels. Both were equally patriotic and equally republican. Republicanism, indeed, was the first bond of the Girondin party. The Girondins, too, were even more democratic than their opponents. All were at heart agreed upon the social-economic question, and on the Constitution they had 'no doctrinal difference of opinion'. Aulard, however, believed that the Girondin party had two distinctive principles. One of them was a toleration of true religion after the church had been subjected to state control, a toleration alien to the dogmatic deism which Robespierre would have imposed upon France. The other was federalism. Aulard was convinced that after the establishment of the republic the Girondins felt that they represented the people of France, whereas the Jacobins represented only the mob of Paris. Because of this they felt it their duty to protect the provinces against Paris and the centralizing tendencies of the Jacobins. Aulard deplored 'this secret inclination of the Girondins towards federalism' as anti-national at a time when France was consolidating herself as a nation. He also deplored what he regarded as the incompetence of the Girondins, but he remained attracted to them and praised their leaders as the flower of revolutionary

---

[1] Aulard, *Orateurs de la Législative et de la Convention*, i, 144–55, 164.

France, representing 'all that was best, most selfless and most human in French politics'.[1]

Very different were the views of Jean Jaurès, perhaps the greatest of French socialist statesmen, whose *Histoire socialiste* (*1789–1900*) began to appear in 1901. Fundamentally an idealist, he, like Michelet, saw the Revolution primarily as a mighty upsurge of the human spirit. Breaking the bonds of feudalism and clericalism, Frenchmen had shown Europe the way to political self-government and had begun to advance towards prosperity and a democratically-controlled economy when their further progress was prevented and their achievements compromised by bitter factious strife about trivialities. For this the Girondins were for Jaurès wholly responsible. He believed that when the ancient monarchy had at last been overthrown and the Convention met in September 1792, they, the leaders of France, were given a moment of great opportunity, when it would have been easy for them to have associated themselves with every vital section of progressive opinion in a co-operative effort to establish the democratic republic and to aid other nations to achieve their independence; the tendency towards disorder could have been controlled, and economic and social progress promoted throughout France. The great crime of the Girondins was that they failed to grasp, failed perhaps even to perceive, this opportunity. Guided only by petty pride and rancorous resentments, they abused their power to persecute their critics, and in so doing they stimulated antagonisms and disorders which ultimately ruined the Revolution. For Jaurès their distinction from the Montagnards was thus self-evident: they were clearly an exclusive set of selfish and vindictive men, intriguers who had neither the vision nor the sense of reality which marked the Montagnards; and they naturally acquired a clientele of wealthy speculators and reactionaries.[2]

Whatever may be thought of this interpretation, Jaurès's success in relating the potentialities of the Revolution to the social and economic trend of twentieth-century thought, as well

---

[1] *Ibid.*, i, 192–6, 200–2, 215–16. See also Aulard, *Histoire politique de la Révolution française*, ii, 100, 176–81, 314.

[2] Jaurès, *Histoire socialiste, 1789–1900*, particularly vol. vi (*La Gironde*), pp. 116–21, 172, 176–7, 192, 194, 318.

as his searching reviews of the economic aspects of the Revolution, certainly inspired his most influential successor in this approach, Albert Mathiez, whose explanation of the conflicts in the Convention was as economic as Aulard's had been political.

So far as party organization is concerned, Mathiez, in an isolated study of the Girondins, denied Aulard's assertion that they ever approached effective unity. To him this conception seemed irreconcilable with the Revolutionary belief that the existence of sectional interests must obscure a true understanding of the General Will. The group, he thought, was 'essentially unstable' and could not be credited with any political principles. But like other historians who have had similar doubts, Mathiez in most of his writings habitually treated the Girondins as a party. He wrote of them as united by class interest and economic ideas, and distinguished them from the Jacobins in social rather than in political terms.

To Mathiez, the Girondins represented the property-owning commercial classes, whereas the Jacobins represented the lesser bourgeoisie, the skilled artisans and the prosperous workmen. They had no remedy for economic difficulties except repression. For him, their true characteristics were political incompetence and a wholly negative social policy. He looked doubtfully upon Aulard's contention that they were sincere republicans, emphasizing the fact that they differed with the Jacobins before the fall of the throne. He asserted that the Girondin Constitution was really designed to strengthen the bourgeoisie everywhere, decentralization being simply an incidental consequence of this.[1]

Although no subsequent French historian except Professor Georges Lefebvre has written with a breadth of vision and grasp of detail comparable to that of Aulard and Mathiez, the work of two lesser writers should be mentioned here. The history of Gaxotte, published in 1928, represents an attempt to reconcile the familiar royalist interpretation of the Revolution with the results of modern research. Here, the Girondins were credited with a list of principles which was little more than the glacial debris of a hundred years of history. They were democratic,

---

[1] Mathiez, *Girondins et Montagnards*, pp. 3–13, 90–2, and *La Révolution française*, ii, 48, 67, 140, 150, 192, 221. See also *La Vie chère*, p. 29 ff.

radical republicans, cultured and anti-clerical. They were bourgeois free-traders, men with a horror of the mob and a longing for established Girondin government. They were also incompetent provincials, who disliked Paris and who were convinced that the Revolution had attained its apogee. Royalism alone was not ascribed to them.[1] By contrast, a modern biographer of Vergniaud, Lintilhac, has asserted that the Girondins had no common programme and were at no time a party or even a coalition. Their so-called unity, he claimed, was a myth inspired by Jacobin propaganda, stamped on the public imagination by a simultaneous proscription and accepted without adequate investigation by later historians.[2] This view, a reversion by a modern writer to an attitude hitherto only explicitly adopted by Guadet in the nineteenth century, is the more interesting since Mathiez's doubts about the real stability of the party have recently been repeated by Lefebvre.

Lefebvre has effected some reconciliation between the apparently conflicting views of Aulard and Mathiez.[3] Although he too finds it necessary to use the terms 'Girondins' and 'Montagnards' in speaking of the history of 1792 and 1793, and so tends to suggest the presence of parties in the English sense, he explains that the deputies 'fought in dispersed order' and had no real programme or effective organization. Nor does he think that any real difference of principle divided them. The origin of their conflict is ascribed to differences of character and temperament, which grew greater as personal antipathies became embittered by mutual recrimination. The Girondins, whose tastes and contacts led them to respect wealth and to worship free-trade, lost touch with the people, and in their struggle against Jacobin centralization they tended to encourage local autonomy and particularism. Thus personal differences led, according to Lefebvre, to political quarrels which in turn gradually identified the Girondins with provincial resistance to Paris and with bourgeois resistance to the disturbing progress of the Revolution. Ultimately and inevitably they became the unwitting defenders of reaction, and they were then eliminated

[1] Gaxotte, *La Révolution française*, ii, 34–5.
[2] *Vergniaud*, preface.
[3] Lefebvre, *La Révolution française*, pp. 225–6, 256, 273.

as a matter of national necessity. Fundamentally, however, their conduct was shallow and superficial, their faults springing from their weakness of character.

V

Any further analysis of the works of less important historians would involve tedious repetition of views already sufficiently explained. Clearly, the history of those whom historians call the Girondins has often been written to serve some political purpose or has been influenced by particular prejudices. The critics of the restored Bourbons praised them as liberal monarchists, the opponents of Louis-Philippe praised them as republicans but attacked them as feeble and self-centred politicans, and subsequently royalist and even disillusioned republican writers have reviled them as revolutionaries. Tissot, Lamartine, Sorel and Aulard accepted federalism as a distinct feature of their policy, but Michelet, Louis Blanc and Mathiez denied this, Lefebvre afforded it a place of subsidiary importance, and other historians said little about it. Other allegations which the principal historians were also concerned to accept or to deny were the supposed Girondins' liberalism, their royalism, their support for the economic interests of the bourgeoisie, and their personal ambition and incompetence.[1] There is here a common ground of controversy, but practically no agreement.

Political prejudices have in fact both created and destroyed the Girondin legend. Nineteenth-century writers were not concerned with a single cumulative theory, steadily developing as knowledge widened, but with the destruction of earlier ideas. Of their work there remains not one broad-based building, but simply a series of demolitions. Indeed, the constant collapse of exclusive interpretations of what is called Girondin policy suggests that no single explanation is valid since no predominant characteristic really existed.

Moreover, in many writers there appears considerable uncertainty about the very existence of a Girondin party. The early caution of Toulongeon on this point gave way to the

---

[1] Their anti-clericalism has evoked some historical comment, but little controversy.

Girondin legend, which included a disciplined party. Seen most clearly in Lamartine, and accepted with qualifications by Thiers and Mignet, this conception evoked a strong but ineffective protest from Guadet, whose work is little known. During the reaction which followed, the Girondins were practically identified with the Jacobins, and the existence of a separate party was questioned first by the illogical arguments of Cassagnac and then by the scholarship of Biré. Later, Aulard revived the party theory, which was developed in terms of economic interests by Mathiez and then qualified by Lefebvre. Most writers have found it convenient to treat these deputies as a distinct group, but only Mignet, Lamartine and Louis Blanc accepted the existence of the party without qualification.

So incoherent does the 'Girondin party' appear, when we have emerged from this welter of historical interpretations, and so elusive is its policy, that there is some temptation to look with interest upon the unusual and little-heeded view of Guadet and Lintilhac that historians have created a Girondin party which never really existed. But this is merely another assertion. What is needed to restore coherence to the question is a complete reassessment of the facts. This book is an attempt to sift the evidence relating to the so-called Girondins, and the only condition asked of the reader is the effort provisionally to suspend judgement on two questions: whether there was or was not something that can be called a Girondin party, and whether it had or had not something that can be called a policy. The evidence which can best be considered first is that which has probably contributed most to obscuring the truth about events during the early months of the Convention—the explanations put forward both by the Montagnards and by their victims in the weeks immediately following the Montagnard seizure of power.

CHAPTER II

The Creation of the Legend of the Girondin Party

THE PROPAGANDA OF THE MONTAGNARDS

THE most useful sources from which an impression of the final form of the Montagnard picture of the so-called Girondins can be obtained are the reports which were presented to the Convention about them on 8 and 15 July and 3 October 1793, and the account of their trial before the Revolutionary Tribunal. The political situation should, however, first be explained.

When on 2 June 1793 the twenty-nine deputies who have since been regarded as the leading Girondins were arrested, their arrest was legally valid.[1] On the previous 1 April a decree had ended parliamentary immunity and had sanctioned the arrest of any deputies against whom there existed strong presumptions of complicity with the enemies of liberty, equality and republican government. Nevertheless, the measure was clearly a revolutionary one. Some individual deputies had indeed been arrested previously on particular charges, but now for the first time a substantial number were placed under guard without any official accusation. Moreover, their arrest was effected by force. A minority in the Convention, supported by the Sections of Paris, over-awed and over-ruled the majority of the deputies. This act was represented as a manifestation of the sovereignty of the people, no constitution being then in existence, but it was nonetheless an act of violence, and the name Revolution has ever since commonly been applied to it.[2]

---

[1] The names of those concerned in this and subsequent occasions are reviewed in Chapter III.

[2] The event is usually referred to as the Revolution of 31 May, that being the day on which the Convention was first invested by the Sections.

The presence in Paris of the excluded deputies was necessarily a source of grave embarrassment to the new *de facto* government. They remained the legally elected representatives of their Departments, which were temporarily deprived of any share in the counsels of France. In the Convention their friends spoke on their behalf, and a considerable body of opinion seemed ready both to support them and to condemn the events of 2 June. Most serious of all, many deputies left Paris to raise forces in the provinces to defend the Convention against the Jacobins and the Mountain, so that France, already beset by foreign armies, was further racked by yet more civil strife. In fact the provincial revolts were royalist in origin and object, the fate of the detained deputies being little more than an incidental complication, but as the situation deteriorated Montagnard opinion about these deputies hardened, and the reports made about them by the Committee of Public Safety became increasingly hostile and severe.

I

At first the Committee, which was then dominated by Danton, appears to have hoped that national unity could be restored by procrastination and leniency. The first report, made by Barère on 6 June, was markedly moderate in tone.[1] Although individual Montagnards had spoken of the arrested men as conspirators, foes of liberty and plotters of federalism,[2] Barère implied that their faults were personal rather than political. He alleged that they were half-hearted revolutionaries, ever intriguing to gratify their personal ambitions or to score off personal opponents. Their predominance had caused discord in the Convention and had aroused antagonism between Paris and the provinces, but now that harmony had been restored the events of 31 May and 2 June should be forgotten. This plea for unity was accompanied by an evasion of the practical problem presented by the exclusion of the arrested men: their fate was for France to decide, and in the meanwhile the Convention should send hostages to the Departments as a guarantee of its good faith.

[1] *Moniteur*, xvi, 583–6.   [2] *Moniteur*, xvi, 569, 572.

During the next month, however, the situation grew worse, not better, and a change of emphasis in the Montagnard attitude became apparent. The accused were more heavily guarded and were transferred to state prisons.[1] An official 'Address to the French People' implied that in pursuit of their own interests they had neglected the public welfare and exposed the state to the danger of foreign conquest.[2] In the Convention Robespierre alleged that the troubles France had had during the past three years, particularly the civil war in the Vendée, sprang from the activities of a handful of conspirators; and the agitation by the friends of the accused men was countered by a Montagnard demand for a full revelation of their crimes.[3]

The second report, presented by Saint Just on 8 July, has the appearance of an attempt to satisfy both sides and to justify some severity without exciting further controversy by harshness.[4] In this report, Saint Just accepted the idea of the conspiracy. He alleged that from the first meeting of the Convention the existence of a monarchical party had been apparent; it had supported the cause of liberty in trivial matters but had counselled inaction at all times of crisis. Saint Just nevertheless admitted and even insisted that distinctions should be drawn amongst the accused. Brissot, he said, had had no real accomplices, although some men had weakly followed his lead; as the principal plotters had revealed their guilt by escaping from Paris, the others should be pardoned lest error be confused with crime. In accordance with these arguments rather than with his earlier assertions, Saint Just asked the Convention to exonerate most of those who had been arrested and to outlaw only the nine men who had already fled from Paris. The contradiction between the hypothesis of a malevolent conspiracy and the relatively moderate recommendations can be explained by the political necessities of the situation: to be lenient might be to reconcile the friends of the accused, yet it was necessary to

---

[1] They had at first been simply under supervision.

[2] *Moniteur*, xvi, 762.

[3] *Moniteur*, xvi, 598, 738, 749.

[4] *Moniteur*, xvii, 146–50, 153–8; *Procès-verbal*, xv, 502. Baudot says that according to Cambon the committees had agreed as a matter of principle that none of the deputies should be brought to trial: Baudot, *Notes historiques sur la Convention nationale*, p. 103.

insist upon the reality of the conspiracy in order to justify the Montagnards' actions in seizing power and silencing their opponents.

According to Saint Just, the first object of the conspirators was the preservation of the monarchy. In the Legislative Assembly the guilty deputies had attacked the Court only to screen their assaults upon republicanism. They had opposed the revolution of 10 August and temporarily vitiated it by securing the suspension, instead of the deposition, of the King. In the Convention, too, they had laboured to keep royalism alive, particularly by their subterfuge of an appeal to the people during Louis's trial, and they had even provoked a widening of the war in the hope that patriotism would rally round the throne. After the King was dead, they had joined Dumouriez in a treasonable attempt to crown the Duke of Orleans. Their final plot, to seize Paris in the name of the Dauphin, had only been prevented by the popular insurrection which had brought the Montagnards to power. In all this, Saint Just suggested only one redeeming feature: he implied that the accused were constitutional monarchists, who had repudiated Louis because they regarded him as identified with absolutism.

The other activities of the conspirators were, for Saint Just, subordinate to their royalism. Their plan, he claimed, was to divide and dominate, to sanction disorder so that a restoration would be easy and justifiable. They had therefore opposed the establishment of any permanent form of government, and used their influence to stifle every constructive proposal put forward by the Mountain. They had caused discord by denouncing imaginary dictators, by exaggerating the importance of the September massacres and by demanding a provincial guard for the Convention. Using as an excuse the unrest they had themselves excited, they had then led an unnecessary campaign for repression, discovering imaginary plots and persecuting the leaders of the people. In this way, the Departments had been alienated from Paris, and property owners had been frightened into fomenting local resistance to the authority of the Convention. The conspirators were therefore responsible for all the divisions of the Republic.

II

Since Saint Just spoke on this occasion for the Dantonist Committee of Public Safety, his views may be regarded as representative of moderate Montagnard opinion as it was at the beginning of July 1793. Yet within a week the policy of compromise was jettisoned. On 10 July control of the Committee passed to the supporters of Robespierre,[1] and three days later Marat was murdered, an event which quite destroyed the Montagnards' sense of proportion. It was generally assumed that the friends of the imprisoned deputies were responsible for the assassination. Saint André, the President of the Convention, told the assembly that 'Those who have endlessly prated to us of their principles, of their respect for law and order and for peace, have now lent themselves to the most horrible of crimes.'[2] It was in this atmosphere that Billaud Varenne rose next day, 15 July, to present a new report and a new decree to the Convention.[3]

Where Saint Just had made a comparatively rational appeal for moderation, and had attempted to prove his assertions, Billaud Varenne tried by violent language and revolutionary arguments to justify more repressive measures. Conspiracy, he said, was so difficult a crime to prove that reliance must be placed on a plain moral judgement. This moral proof of the detained deputies' guilt was to be found in full in the similarity of their past conduct with that of such recognized counter-revolutionaries as Lameth and Barnave, as well as in the disasters that had come upon France while they were influential. Finally, the existing disorders were conclusive evidence of a previously concocted master-plan. By such arguments as these Billaud Varenne justified his proposal that all the arrested deputies, as well as others who were equally guilty, should be formally indicted for treason, and when his decree was eventually accepted on 28 July the number of those involved had grown even greater. The effect of his speech, therefore, was to make the alleged conspirators appear a larger and a more coherent group than that envisaged by Saint Just.

---

[1] Aulard, *Recueil des actes du comité de salut public*, v, 224, and 'Le Comité de salut public', *La Révolution française*, xviii (1890), p. 22.

[2] *Moniteur*, xvii, 127.   [3] *Moniteur*, xvii, 198–201, 207–8, 225–6, 230–2.

The characteristics which Billaud Varenne ascribed to the group were also broader. Like Saint Just, he regarded the conspirators as inveterate royalists, and he repeated many of his predecessor's accusations with new refinements of detail. But where Saint Just had condemned them for inertia, Billaud Varenne alleged that they had deliberately planned to surrender France to its enemies so that a restoration might be effected from abroad. Moreover, where Saint Just had spoken of the revolts in the Departments as mere manifestations of provincial feeling, which the accused had shrewdly exploited in order to discredit the Republic, Billaud Varenne regarded them as a consequence of a deep-laid federalist plot. Thus the accused deputies and their associates now became a numerous and coherent band of conspirators, at once royalists, federalists and traitors to their country.

III

On 28 July the decree first proposed by Saint Just was finally accepted, with the important difference that many more deputies were accused.[1] This made necessary the preparation of an official *acte d'accusation*, a detailed recital of the case for the prosecution before the Revolutionary Tribunal. During the delay which ensued, pressure for a speedy trial began in a different quarter. Early in September the extreme element in the Jacobin Society called for the condemnation of the conspirators, and forced the appointment of a committee to draft a model *acte d'accusation*. After further agitation this Jacobin committee was compelled on 2 October to present its proposals for consideration by the Society.[2] These consisted of sixteen charges against Brissot personally and supplementary charges against the other deputies, who were all accused of supporting him in a conspiracy against the Republic and the sovereignty of the people. The charges are remarkable as an attempt to prove that the conspiracy had begun even earlier than had previously been

---

[1] The charge of federalism was also reiterated at this time at the trial of Charlotte Corday.

[2] For these debates, see *Moniteur*, xvii, 613, 693, 707, and xviii, 43–4, 57–8; and *Jacobins*, v, 391, 405, 439.

alleged. Brissot and his associates were blamed for the appointment of Roland's Ministry in the spring of 1792 and for the
troubles in the West Indies in the previous autumn; they were
accused of aiding and abetting Lafayette in 1792 and of bringing
about the 'massacre' on the Champ de Mars in July 1791.

The debate which followed is also of interest, for two speakers
suggested that speedier results might be obtained if Brissot alone
was accused. This proposal, which would have made the theory
of the great conspiracy untenable, roused passionate opposition.
Hébert reminded the members that French law allowed any
number of persons to be convicted for a single crime, and
another member of the Society argued that the condemnation
of Brissot necessarily implied that of all his associates. The draft
charges were eventually referred back to the committee as
'over-detailed', and any further action was anticipated by
Amar, who presented the official indictment to the Convention
on the following day, 3 October.[1]

This began with the formal charge against the accused in its
final form: 'There has been a great conspiracy to destroy the
unity of the Republic, a vast plot to conquer and enslave the
French people.' Like the earlier reports, the indictment reviewed
the history of the Revolution, in which Amar professed to find
proof of four separate plots by the conspirators. The first of
these was an attempt to deliver France to the Prussians in the
summer of 1792: discord was to be created by the encouragement of financial speculation and the hoarding of food, Paris
was to be discredited and abandoned as the enemy advanced,
and finally the Duke of Brunswick was to be crowned as king of
France. The failure of this plan Amar found in the Prussian
defeat at Valmy, after which the evacuation of France by the
invaders was arranged by Dumouriez, Carra and Sillery. Next
came an effort to prevent Louis's execution: the conspirators
concealed proofs of the King's duplicity, delayed his trial,
attempted to excite unrest by an appeal to the electoral assemblies, and tried to win a reprieve. Frustrated, they attempted to
revenge themselves by organizing an indiscriminate assassination
of republicans in January and March 1793. A third plan again
envisaged the destruction of the Republic by military defeat:

[1] *Moniteur*, xviii, 200–6, 212–13, 220–2.

the war was deliberately extended and disaster invited by an attempt to invade Spain at the very moment when Dumouriez's desertion and the revolt in the Vendée were anticipated. Finally the plotters had come into the open, advocating federalism and inciting rebellion throughout France.

In all this Amar spoke of the conspirators as a united group. He referred to secret meetings in which they concocted their schemes, and asserted that although some charges applied only to individual deputies, that of conspiracy was common to all. If those concerned had occasionally appeared to be divided, that was only deliberate deception; if they had sometimes diverged, they had always reunited to encompass the ruin of France. Amar's unequivocal attitude is the more interesting as the number of the accused men had again risen considerably: his indictment involved thirty-six more deputies than Saint Just had proposed to proscribe.

Indeed, at this point the number of the accused was almost doubled again. After Amar had ended his speech, a demand was made for the indictment of some seventy-five other deputies who had signed a written protest against the original arrests on 2 June. Amidst murmurs, Robespierre intervened, saying that the Convention should not seek to multiply the numbers of the guilty, but should deal only with the leaders of the conspiracy and should leave the Committee of General Security to distinguish between the minor accomplices.[1] He carried his point, and the seventy-five were simply placed under arrest—a fact which did not prevent them from being confused with the others in the rapidly hardening conception of a large and united party of conspirators.

The final phase of the Montagnards' attack occurred when those of the accused who were actually in custody appeared before the Revolutionary Tribunal on 24 October 1793.[2] There were only twenty-one of them and the scales of justice were weighted heavily against them from the outset. Every witness was hostile, many being leading members of the Commune of Paris.

---

[1] *Moniteur*, xviii, 37–8. For Robespierre's later protection of the seventy-five deputies, see *Proscription*, pp. 152–67.

[2] *Moniteur*, xviii, 225–68, and *Le Procès de J. P. Brissot et ses complices* (Paris, 1793), B.M., R.97.35.

The President of the Tribunal, as well as individual jurors, also joined in the attack. In spite of this, even the doctored account of the trial which appeared in print suggests that the accused might have raised dangerous doubts about the reality of the conspiracy if the proceedings had not been brought to an abrupt end after Robespierre and Barère had hurried *ad hoc* legislation through the Convention.[1]

To the case for the prosecution, Amar's *acte d'accusation*, the long perorations of witnesses like Hébert and Pache, Chaumette and Chabot add little of interest. These men blamed the accused for innumerable episodes in the history of the Revolution, placing particular emphasis upon their hostility to the Commune and repeating the general charges of royalism and federalism. The ironic allegation that Brissot had opposed the creation of the Revolutionary Tribunal is the sole suggestion of anything approaching that moderation which later historians found so characteristic of the 'Girondin party', and two or three incidental accusations of incompetence in economic and social affairs are lost amidst endless political vituperation. On the other hand, several witnesses elaborated the charge that the accused had held meetings in secret, and suggested that they had procured the appointment of all kinds of officials, from ministers downwards. Indeed, an inordinate lust for power seems to be the motive most commonly ascribed to the accused by these witnesses.

On 30 October the Tribunal pronounced further evidence to be superfluous and declared that all the accused were guilty. One deputy, Dufriche-Valazé, stabbed himself. The remainder were guillotined next day.

IV

Any historian who approaches the Revolution through Montagnard sources is bound to find ample evidence to suggest that those whom the Montagnards drove from the Convention were royalists or federalists, dominated by ambition but completely

---

[1] In the report of the trial published at Amar's instigation, the answers of the accused and their pleas in their own defence are reduced to the briefest of reported speech. The legislation enabled the President of the Court to end proceedings as soon as the jury were sufficiently enlightened, and so to prevent speeches for the defence from being heard.

incompetent—for treason is often but another name for failure, particularly in times of crisis. Historians may not all have been influenced in this way, but the characteristics they have tended to ascribe to their Girondins are all present in the Montagnards' attacks, which were trumpeted abroad to discredit all who were associated with the opposition to the Mountain. Of the principal charges, federalism was the one which most influenced later writers—for ambition and incompetence are assumptions easily made about any group of politicians, and the constitutional royalism ascribed to the so-called Girondins in the nineteenth century was very different from the reactionary attitude attributed to the accused by Amar.

On the other hand, the later picture of the Girondin as a bourgeois, interested primarily in the preservation of property and free trade, does not clearly appear in these Montagnard attacks. The Girondin of later tradition, liberal, law-abiding and moderate, appears in Montagnard eyes as an unscrupulous anarchist. Indeed, royalist historians could easily use Montagnard material to portray their Girondins as Terrorists—but the Montagnards would not have accepted the substitution. For them, the Terrorist was essentially efficient, a restorer of order and national unity, a conception which was the very antithesis of their view of the men they proscribed.

Fundamental to all these various assumptions about the characteristics of the supposed Girondin party is the hypothesis on which they all depend—the existence of a coherent group whose members were acting in unison. In respect of this theory a steady development is apparent. Where Saint Just had demanded the outlawing of only nine men, and had found reason to suspect five more, Amar obtained an *acte d'accusation* against forty-six, and arrested some seventy-five others. Moreover, where Saint Just had tried to draw distinctions between his few, asserting that some were guilty but others merely misguided, Amar and the Revolutionary Tribunal insisted that all those whom they accused were equally guilty, each having responsibility for the crimes of all. The attitude behind this assumption is as obvious as its expediency. For the revolutionary, all opposition is necessarily counter-revolutionary and preconcerted, and if all could be accused as conspirators, all could be

D

convicted on a single capital charge. Thus potentially dangerous truths about the conduct of individual opponents of the Mountain need not be investigated, and a divided nation need be no further distracted by awkward political arguments. The Montagnards clearly propagated in their own interest the idea that the deputies from the Gironde and their sympathizers constituted a considerable and closely united group of conspirators.

Indeed, as the political situation in France deteriorated in the summer of 1793, so the destruction of the reputation of the accused deputies became not merely expedient, but even an imperative necessity to the Montagnards, who sacrificed them in order to preserve the widest possible measure of unity amongst their supporters. Inconsistencies in the accusations ceased to matter, and the accused deputies were charged at once with royalism and federalism, and even with a superficial sort of republicanism. Apparently they had reviled the Duke of Orleans in order to enhance his popularity, and instigated the attack upon the Tuileries in June 1792 in order to save the King—an attack for the failure of which they were yet alleged to be responsible. Their very votes for the execution of the King were represented as evidence of their machiavellian sympathies for the Crown. Charges such as these were scarcely susceptible of proof, and the Montagnards did not seriously attempt to substantiate them, although a few letters were produced at the trial. The true value of the accusations is apparent in the words of Billaud Varenne at the conclusion of his report: 'Let us strike down these misguided men, these traitors to their office. The vengeance of the people and the security of the State demand that this conspiracy should be snuffed out with the lives of the conspirators themselves.' Of Brissot and his associates it might well be written, as *The Times* wrote of those accused during more recent political trials: 'Any precise charges against them were engulfed in the greater need to satisfy State and party needs.'[1]

THE APOLOGIA OF THE ACCUSED

An account of how the accused deputies appeared in their own eyes in the summer of 1793 must be less coherent than the

[1] *The Times*, leading article of 26 September 1949.

interpretation of their actions which the Montagnards tried to impose. Since they were not permitted to present their full defence in open court, their apologia must be pieced together from a multiplicity of sources, the fragmentary records of their final failure. The story of these miscellaneous memorials might be made a saga in itself. Prepared speeches of defence were flung hopelessly upon the court-room floor. Police proceedings, protests and declarations of policy were lost in local archives. Memoirs, written in garrets and prison-cells, concealed in crannies and even hurled into a cesspool, were smuggled away by faithful friends or exposed and suppressed by the stern commands of *commissaires*. Much of this material has been recovered, but many gaps remain.[1]

Moreover, whereas the accusers spoke as one, the accused, being many, answered with many voices. Accused of conspiracy, they strove to assert their innocence as individuals and to deny the existence of the unity which had been ascribed to them.

I

The deputies who were proscribed by the Montagnards naturally emphasized the obvious weaknesses in the charges made against them. They called upon their accusers to produce documentary proof or the evidence of eye-witnesses to support their allegations. They pointed out the incompatibility of federalism with royalism. They challenged the anachronisms implicit in the accusations: even if they had hesitated to disown Dumouriez or to depose the King, they were no more guilty than others who had also failed to foresee the future. Many asserted that it had been their duty to express their opinions freely, and maintained that if this right were to be circumscribed all freedom was at an end. Some denied the competence of their accusers

---

[1] Something of the story of these documents is indicated in the prefaces to the memoirs which have been used for this section of this Chapter—except where particular references are given—as follows: *Brissot*, ii, 229–69, 272–7, 315, 327–32, 340, 342–52; *Madame Roland*, i, 40, 65, 85–91, 128; *Valazé*, p. 207; *Mémoires de Buzot* (ed. Guadet, 1828), pp. 6, 39, 46–8, 57, 140, 169–76 and (ed. Dauban, 1866) pp. 23, 30, 60, 98; *Mémoires de Barbaroux*, pp. 119–21, 167; *Mémoires de Louvet*, pp. 53–61; and *Mémoires de Pétion*, pp. 105, 119–21.

and claimed that they were the victims of violence, who were
being persecuted for resisting the same political power which
had now assumed the trappings of justice in order to condemn
them.[1]

They claimed that they had long been the real defenders of
liberty in France. On 10 August 1792 they had supported the
popular cause and legalized the insurrection by suspending the
King, and by summoning the Convention they had inaugurated
the Republic. Unhappily control of Paris had fallen into the
hands of a few fanatics, who had defied the authority of the
Assembly. In the streets liberty had become licence, leading to
massacre, and the men responsible for this had striven to seize
power in order to avoid the scaffold, distracting and intimi-
dating the majority of the Convention with the aid of ruffians
whom they euphemistically called the sovereign people.[2]

To redeem this situation it was necessary to force the Commune of Paris and the deputies of the Mountain to acknowledge the legitimate authority of the majority of the Convention.
Thus, in Brissot's phrase, the restoration of order became 'true
Revolutionary policy'. The accused deputies had been fighting
for just, humane and constitutional government and for the
liberal administration of established law.[3]

They had fought also to maintain the unity of France, for
the same violent minority which threatened freedom had also
pursued a policy presaging the disruption of the Republic. The
Commune of Paris had gained privilege after privilege, flouting
the authority of the Convention and enhancing its own powers
until it threatened to dominate the whole of France. The danger
that the Departments, unjustly deprived of their due share in
national affairs, might secede from the Republic had thus

---

[1] e.g., the *Interrogations* of Ducos, Duprat, Lacaze and Lehardi, A.N., w.292.204,
Part 5, Nos. 4, 8, 13, 18; the *Défense de Vergniaud*, A.N., w.292.204, Part 3 No. 24;
La Défense de C. E. Dufriche-Valazé (Paris, 1793), B.M., F.1023.17, p. 34; and J. B.
Salle, *L'Ancien comité de salut public* (Caen, 1793), B.M., F.R.57.47.

[2] e.g., Ducos, *Sur les principales époques de ma vie politique*, A.N., w.292.204, Part 3,
No. 32; Bergoeing, *La longue conspiration des Jacobins* (Paris, 1795), B.M., F.353.11;
and *Lettre de Rabaut St. Etienne* (Paris, 1795), B.M., F.1004.6.

[3] e.g., J. P. Brissot *à ses commettans* (Paris, 1793), B.M., F.674.2; *Déclaration de Salle
du 3 juin 1793* (Paris, 1793), B.M., F.853.16; *Le dernier crime de Lanjuinais* (Rennes,
1793), B.M., F.1008.17; and the *Interrogations* of Fauchet and Birotteau, A.N.,
w.292.204, Part 5, No. 23 and BB³. 30, dossier 2.

become acute, and the accused had laboured to prevent that catastrophe. They had tried to keep the Departments informed of events in Paris, and they had endeavoured to associate them with national responsibilities by devising a departmental guard for the Convention and by calling for a referendum to decide the fate of the King.

This effort to establish a truly unified Republic, in which every Department would participate in national decisions, had failed. Agents of the Commune of Paris, it was alleged, had fostered class hatred throughout France, threatening rights of property. Simultaneously the Montagnards had tried to curtail that commercial freedom on which general prosperity depended. The Departments had been goaded into final revolt when the Convention fell under the domination of the forces of disorder. This was why some at least of the deputies, considering that the Convention had become a tool in the hands of tyrants, had attempted to call a national crusade to liberate the oppressed people of Paris and to restore national unity by force of arms.[1]

Since they wrote in captivity or in concealment, the proscribed deputies could not but acknowledge that they had failed. Their unscrupulous opponents had misrepresented their every action, saddling them with responsibility for all the disasters that disorder had brought upon France. To such men and such methods they had succumbed. Too talented and too honest—or, as some of them said, too weak—to meet slander with slander, they had hesitated too long to meet force with force, and an undiscerning people, unprepared for republican responsibilities, had lacked the strength of soul to strike out sturdily in their defence.[2]

While these arguments appear generally in the apologia put forward by the accused deputies, the commonest assertion in these accounts is a denial of all collaboration with the others. Some asserted that they were being made responsible for actions which had actually been taken with the full approval of the

---

[1] On this question of the relationship between Paris and the provinces, as the accused saw it, see, e.g., the *Interrogations* of Vergniaud and Lauze-Deperret, A.N., w.292.204, Part 5, Nos. 14 and 10, or such pamphlets as *Charles Barbaroux . . . aux citoyens de Marseille* (Caen, 1793) and *Opinion de J. Pétion* (n.d.), B.M., F.981.19 and F.666.4.

[2] See particularly *Mémoires de Buzot* (ed. Guadet), *passim*.

whole Assembly, and indeed of the whole of France. Vergniaud, Brissot and Lasource, for example, argued that the decision to suspend the King had been endorsed by the Legislative Assembly as the most that could be done within the limits of the constitution, and the responsibility was therefore shared by all its members.[1] Brissot, who justified his part in the declarations of war against Austria and England on the same grounds, pleaded that he had acted under orders as the spokesman of the Diplomatic Committee and the servant of the Assembly.[2] As Ducos wrote of the deputies of the Gironde in the Legislative Assembly: 'The only coalition which existed was that formed of every patriotic deputy who was there.'[3]

On the other hand, they emphatically denied that they were personally united in anything save friendship and mutual regard. Their relations, in Vergniaud's words, were relations of 'friendship and regard for one another'.[4] Their opinions and their actions were their own, and their association together in proscription was merely the result of the Convention's compliance with the demagogues' demand for the expulsion of twenty-two deputies. Louvet dismissed the number as a mere shibboleth. Pétion, amongst others, asserted that the alterations made in the list of accused men during the debate on 2 June proved that it was devoid of meaning, and several deputies echoed the contemptuous words of Ducos: 'A glance at the votes we gave on any important question will soon show how far we were from any sort of unity.' The clearest single statement of this general attitude occurs in the speech which Dufriche-Valazé proposed to make in his own defence: 'First they accuse one of us of one thing; then they proceed to disregard both time and circumstance and to contrive by an ingenious use of ambiguous phrases to charge all the others with the same offence.'[5]

[1] *Défense de Vergniaud*, A.N., w.292.204, Part 3, No. 24; *Interrogation* of Lasource, A.N., w.292.204, Part 5, No. 19; and *Brissot*, ii, 321–2.

[2] *Brissot*, ii, 289, 311.

[3] Ducos, *Notes pour ma défense*, A.N., w.292.204, Part 3, No. 29.

[4] *Défense de Vergniaud*, A.N., w.292.204, Part 3, No. 24.

[5] Louvet, *Mémoires*, i, 87; *Opinion de J. Pétion*, B.M., f.666.4; a separate page in the hand of Ducos, A.N., w.292.204, Part 3, No. 33, and the comparable *Interrogation* of Duprat, *ibid.*, Part 5, No. 18, or Gensonné, *Moniteur*, xviii, 257; *Défense de Dufriche-Valazé* (above, p. 32, n. 1).

In their own eyes, then, the accused deputies were no more than a group of friends and acquaintances who all believed in certain general principles which were also accepted by the majority of their colleagues: property must be preserved, liberty safeguarded and national unity maintained. These principles they had tried to uphold against the forces of disorder and disruption, but they had acted as individuals, not as members of a party. They were, above all, patriots, whose record of opposition to the monarchy and to the Mountain proved their sincere attachment to the Republic and to France.[1]

II

That Brissot and his friends were linked only by some ties of friendship, or by mutual regard and common general principles, seems more probable than the allegation that they formed a group of counter-revolutionaries, closely united in conspiracy, and their reactions to this allegation tend to confirm the probability. For the accused, proscription proved a searching test of character. Some men openly defied their accusers as agents of an illegitimate authority, some sought to justify their own conduct without incriminating their friends or compromising with their beliefs, and some tried to prove their loyalty to the Mountain.[2] But only one, an obvious craven, acknowledged the existence of any conspiracy.[3]

At their trial, their reactions were similar. When the first witness had been heard, each of the accused rose in turn to point out that, whatever the truth of the allegations, nothing had been said to inculpate the speaker personally. Their perplexity is indicated by Vergniaud's reply to the accusation of complicity in Dumouriez's betrayal of the Republic: 'Is this

[1] e.g., Gensonné, *Protestation*—see A. Vermorel, *Œuvres de Vergniaud*, p. 200; Lasource, *Lettres au Président de la Convention* (Paris, 1793), B.M., F.981.15. For statements of the poverty of the accused, see e.g., *Lettre écrite par Salle* (Bordeaux, 1793), B.M., F.980.4 and Madame Brissot's claim for compensation after Thermidor, A.N., F⁷.4443. No. 199.

[2] *Interrogations* of Carra, Ducos, Gensonné, Boyer-Fonfrède and Vergniaud, A.N., w.292.204, Part 5, Nos. 22, 13, 14, 7 and 21; also, *Précis de la défense de Carra* (Paris, 1793), B.M., F.1022.4.

[3] Jacques Boilleau. See, e.g., *Interrogation*, A.N., w.292.204, Part 5, No. 9, and *Justification* (Paris, 1793), B.M., F.1000.1.

charge supposed to apply to all the accused? I cannot tell.'
Their preoccupation with their innocence as individuals is still
more apparent in the notes which both Vergniaud and Ducos
drafted as they listened to the succession of hostile witnesses:
'None of the statements made by Pache can possibly concern
me'; 'The witness Hébert has not even mentioned my name'.[1]
Reactions such as these have a ring of truth. They may be
contrasted with the comment of the magistrate who examined
Lauze-Deperret and who assumed that as all those who had
voted for an appeal to the people in Louis's trial had planned to
destroy the Republic, 'no one who had voted in favour of the
appeal could possibly have been ignorant of the schemes of
the conspirators'.[2] In this matter the statements made by the
accused deputies sound the more simple and the more sincere.

It is also significant that similar denials of unity were maintained later, when circumstances were more favourable to the
opponents of the Mountain. After the fall of Robespierre in
July 1794 many of those who had been ostracized in 1793
demanded rehabilitation. This caused considerable embarrassment to the leaders of the Convention, who were perforce less
concerned with abstract justice than with calculating the effects
of an influx of displaced deputies upon the delicate balance of
forces which existed in the depleted ranks of the Assembly.[3]
Rehabilitation therefore came but slowly, and those who sought
it had initially to plead their cause with caution. The deputies
who had been imprisoned for signing the 'Protest of the
Seventy-five' were considered first, and the pamphlets which
they wrote as apologia all emphasized the purity of their
motives, their abhorrence of faction and their innocence of any
knowledge of the supposed conspiracy.[4] A few writers were
more outspoken: Petit—a deputy accused for signing a letter

---

[1] *Moniteur*, xviii, 226; Ducos, *Notes sur les dépositions* and *Notes pour ma défense*,
A.N., w.292.204, Part 5, Nos. 18 and 29.

[2] *Interrogation* of Lauze-Deperret, A.N., w.292.204, Part 5, No. 10.

[3] The re-admissions first of the deputies who had protested and then of those who
had been outlawed were in fact successive stages in the campaign waged by the
reactionaries after Thermidor against the survivors of those who had directed the
Terror. See G. Lefebvre, *Les Thermidoriens*, pp. 34, 56–7, 63–4.

[4] See the letters written by these deputies from their prisons, which are more
fully considered in the following chapter, and F. Rivaud, *Les Conspirateurs démasqués*
(Paris, 1794–5), B.M., F.R.64.15.

to his constituents similar in content to that of the seventy-five—
wanted to know whether 'we must now believe that there used
to be a Girondin faction simply because Robespierre once
asserted that there was, and had those whom he called its
members executed?'[1] This and the analogous arguments written
by others are tendentious, but they are nevertheless consistent
with the earlier statements of the accused. Certainly there was
not at this time any attempt to glory in the name of Girondin.
Indeed, when in December 1794 these deputies were finally
allowed to re-enter the assembly, their admission was apparently
facilitated by a gentleman's agreement to refrain from referring
to the past. As Dusaulx, who acted as their spokesman, put it,
'We have left our resentments behind in our dungeons'.[2]

A more strident note was struck when other deputies, who
had been fugitives and outlaws since 1793, took courage to
emerge from their places of concealment and to press for reinstatement in their turn. Now it was argued that the ending of
the Terror ought necessarily to imply the emancipation of its
first victims.[3] The 'conspiracy' was still strenuously denied—
Lanjuinais referred to it as 'a chimera . . . something invented
to distract attention from a conspiracy only too real'[4]—but
some men, like Marie-Joseph Chénier, hailed the dead as
heroes, 'the martyrs of 31 May, proscribed in a time of shame
and madness',[5] and some, like Isnard, extolled themselves as
those who had dared to defy the tyrant Robespierre on the very
morning of his triumph.[6] The readmission to the Convention in
March 1795 of such men as Isnard, Lanjuinais and Louvet,
which marks the assembly's repudiation of 31 May 1793, may
also mark the fact that to have been proscribed in 1793 was
becoming for some sections of opinion a proof of patriotism and
that the title 'Girondin' was acquiring an honourable significance. The tacit acceptance by many deputies of this assumption

[1] M. E. Petit, Le Procès de 31 Mai (Paris, 1794–5), B.M., 935b.13.10.
[2] Moniteur, xxiii, 705, and Mathiez, La Réaction Thermidorienne, p. 123.
[3] Moniteur, xxiii, 588 (Penières) and 618–19 (Isnard).
[4] Adresse de Lanjuinais à la Convention nationale (Paris, 1794–5), pp. 8–9, B.M.,
F.985.3, and cp., e.g., Moniteur, xxii, 745 (Mollevaut) and 747 (Defermon).
[5] Moniteur, xxiii, 637. Cp. Penières, ibid., 188 and 637.
[6] Moniteur, xxii, 748. Cp., e.g., Deverité, Réclamation d'un . . . patriote opprimé
(Paris, 1794–5), B.M., F.1025.8.

of an earlier political association has certainly contributed to the concealment of the truth about 1793,[1] for few others, if any, had the courage shown by Lebreton, who refused 'to recognize as a deputy of the Gironde anyone save those who indisputably belonged to the delegation elected by that Department'.[2]

[1] Thus Mathiez, writing of the Constitutional Committee of the Year III, mentions the deputies Creuzé-Latouche, Baudin, Lépaux, Daunou, Lanjuinais and Louvet as 'former Girondins, often in accord'. Mathiez, *La Réaction Thermidorienne*, pp. 282–3.

[2] R. P. F. Lebreton, *Réponse à quatre pages d'impression, distribuées par Dufay, sous le titre: Sur les vingt-deux députés et autres connus sous le nom de la Gironde* (Paris, n.d.), B.M., f.r.63.23. Since the pamphlet is undated it is possible that Lebreton may have been writing soon after the fall of Robespierre and so concerned simply to repudiate the past.

CHAPTER III

The Traditional Party Examined

THE conception of the Girondins as a large and integrated party, apparently derived in part from Jacobin propaganda, has been fostered also by the deceptive ease with which a list of 'party supporters' can be compiled from the names of those whom the Montagnards proscribed.

This method was adopted without reserve by Morse Stephens, for whom 'the only way to get a true idea of the leaders and the rank and file of the Girondin party' was 'from an examination of the proscription lists drawn up against them'.[1] Aulard and Claude Perroud both acted on the same principle. Mathiez, on the other hand, did not accept these lists as adequate criteria of party allegiance, and pointed out that only a careful examination of the deputies' actions and votes could provide any valid basis for classification.[2] He did not, however, attempt to draw up a list in this way himself, but tended rather to use the name 'Girondin' loosely, and sometimes applied it even to members of the Convention who are not generally so called.[3]

The use of the proscription lists to establish *previous* party membership is in fact essentially unsound. It either presents a picture of a party at the very time when it had for all practical purposes ceased to exist—if, indeed, it had ever existed at all—or it simply confuses opposition to the Mountain at one time with opposition to it at another. Nevertheless, the lists at least indicate the extent of the traditional party, and so their growth and subsequent consolidation may usefully be reviewed.[4]

---

[1] Morse Stephens, *A History of the French Revolution*, i, 522.

[2] Aulard, *Orateurs de la Législative et de la Convention*, i, 155; *Proscription*, p. 5; Mathiez, *Girondins et Montagnards*, p. 3.

[3] He refers, e.g., to Cloots as being a Girondin in September 1792, and to Barère as being one in February 1793: *La Vie chère*, pp. 67, 159.

[4] All those deputies who have been named as Girondins by historians who have accepted proscription as an adequate criterion of party loyalty are included in this

The most convenient starting point is the first purge of the Convention on 2 June 1793. On that date Couthon proposed the arrest of the twenty-four deputies named in a petition which Hassenfratz had presented for the Commune of Paris on the preceding evening,[1] as well as all twelve deputies in the Commission of Twelve[2]—a committee appointed by the Convention to investigate reports of impending insurrection in Paris—and of two executive ministers, Clavière and Lebrun. During the debate which followed, Marat secured the addition of two names and the withdrawal of three, and Levasseur and Legendre each successfully moved the exemption of two others.[3] Eventually twenty-nine deputies were placed under guard pending a report upon their conduct.[4]

Throughout the next three months the arrest or impeachment[5] of individual deputies continued. Of these events the two decrees of 28 July and 3 October provide a useful, though not a complete, synopsis. As we have seen, the increasing severity of the Montagnard accusations was on each of these occasions accompanied by a corresponding increase in the number of those accused. Thus the decree presented to the Convention on 28 July affected many more deputies than those arrested on 2 June. Saint Just's lenient proposal on 8 July had suggested the outlawing of nine, and the retention as suspect of five, of the original twenty-nine.[6] The decree of 28 July outlawed eighteen deputies and retained eleven as suspect,[7] while it ignored eighteen others who had either fled from Paris or had been

---

review, but men casually referred to as members of the supposed party are not. Omissions are thus possible, but as the comprehensive list which emerges is longer than that given by any individual historian, it is unlikely that any deputy of consequence is omitted.

[1] Appendix A, List I.   [2] Appendix A, List II.

[3] Rabaut St. Etienne and Boyer-Fonfrède were named by Hassenfratz, but were also members of the Commission. Boyer-Fonfrède being exempted from arrest, the arrest of Rabaut increases the number of those proscribed by one only. Marat added Louvet and Valazé, but excluded Ducos, Dusaulx and Lanthénas; Levasseur excluded Isnard and Fauchet; Legendre excluded Boyer-Fonfrède and St. Martin Valogne. *Moniteur*, xvi, 553-4, *Proscription*, p. 38.

[4] Appendix A, List III.

[5] Terminology: the word impeachment is used for the French *Décret d'arrestation*; the word proscription is deliberately used loosely, as it has been in the past, and includes attacks which were not followed by any official ostracism.

[6] Appendix A, List IV.   [7] Appendix A, List V.

arrested individually.[1] It includes six names which were not among those on the list of 2 June, and so brings the total of those purged from the Convention to thirty-five. Others again were proscribed by Amar on 3 October, when forty-six deputies were impeached on the general charge of conspiracy. Seventeen of these had already been included in the earlier lists, and it is also customary to exclude Philippe-Egalité, the Duke of Orleans— one at least whose earlier Montagnard affiliations are obvious. Thus twenty-eight additional names appeared on this occasion.[2]

In addition to the impeachment of these deputies, Amar also obtained an order for the arrest of all those others who had signed the then unpublished protest of 6 and 19 June against the first violation of the Convention on 2 June. The confusion that has existed about this protest is shown by Morse Stephens's description of it as 'that signed by seventy-four or seventy-five deputies of the Right, which is known as the Protest of the Seventy-Three'.[3] It was in fact signed by seventy-five deputies, of whom ten had already been included in earlier lists.[4] The addition of the other sixty-five to the twenty-eight new names on Amar's list and to the thirty-five named on 2 June and 28 July gives a total of 128 deputies.

This figure yet falls short of the total given by the historians, who regard others as Girondins although they were not included in the official proscription lists. Aulard included in his list the names of twenty-seven deputies who signed letters to their Departments in protest against the events of 31 May and 2 June. The deputies in question are those who signed what it will be convenient to call the Somme, the Aisne, the Haute Vienne, the Maine et Loire and the Morbihan protests.[5] But Aulard fails to mention Boucheroux, a signatory of the Aisne protest; and as Condorcet, Deverité and Lesterp-Beauvais have already been included in the list of those accused by Amar on 3 October these three names must be deducted from his twenty-seven. He also names a further eleven deputies for miscellaneous reasons.[6] His total of additional names thus becomes thirty-five, and the

---

[1] Appendix A, List vi. [2] Appendix A, List vii.
[3] Morse Stephens, *A History of the French Revolution*, ii, 523.
[4] Appendix A, List viii. [5] Appendix A, List ix.
[6] Appendix A, List x(a).

inclusion of these brings his estimate of Girondin party membership to 163.[1]

More recently, Perroud has estimated the number of those
he calls Girondins to be 191, although he admits that some
thirty of these must be considered as rather remote fellow-
travellers.[2] Unlike Aulard, Perroud did not include in his list
the deputy Dupin, who withdrew his signature from the Aisne
protest, and so he adds in reality a further twenty-nine names.
One of these is that of Boucheroux of the Aisne, whom Aulard
had omitted, and three others are those of men who signed
another letter of protest to their Department, that of the
Hautes Alpes.[3] Many of the other twenty-five had either protested orally in the Convention or had resigned from it during
the first months of Montagnard power.[4]

Finally: in the opinion of the English historian, Morse
Stephens, the Girondin party had a total strength of 183
deputies.[5] This is a lower figure than that of 192 already
reached here, but Morse Stephens included eight new names in
his list, giving no specific reasons for doing so.[6] The addition of
these eight gives a total of 200 here,[7] of whom the names of
162 are accepted by Aulard, Perroud and Morse Stephens,
while thirteen others are accepted by two of these historians and
the remaining twenty-five are accepted by one only. Some of
the 200 are admitted to have been men of little importance in
the Convention, but the inclusive list nevertheless represents an
historical judgement: scholars of repute have agreed that
between 160 and 200 members of the Convention may legitimately be called 'Girondins'. So positive an assertion as this
cannot be accepted without further examination. This will in

---

[1] Aulard, *Orateurs de la Législative et de la Convention*, i, 155. He had previously
accepted a still higher figure: see his *Histoire politique*, p. 393.

[2] *Proscription*, 6–21 and p. 21 footnote: '*La poussière d'un parti.*'

[3] Appendix A, List ix. I. Caseneuve and Serre, who also signed this letter, have
already been included amongst those who signed the protest of the seventy-five.

[4] Appendix A, List x(*b*).

[5] Morse Stephens, *op. cit.*, i, 522.

[6] Appendix A, List x(*c*).

[7] Appendix A, List xi. The 200 were all deputies in the Convention. Men like
Roland, who were associated with the deputies of the Gironde but who were not
deputies themselves, will also be referred to here, but men who were deputies in the
Legislative Assembly, but not in the Convention, will not be considered.

the first place be confined to political considerations, since it is from these that the assertion itself is derived.

The first question that ought to be asked is one that has hitherto been completely neglected in practice: is the fact that a deputy was proscribed by the Montagnards after 2 June 1793 in itself sufficient proof that he had been a member of a Girondin party before that date? If it is not, then a similar question must be asked about the particular reasons for his proscription, and about any other reasons historians have given for his inclusion in their lists.

The answer to the main question is a simple negative. If the fact that a man was proscribed by the Montagnards is to be regarded as proof that he was a Girondin, then the word Girondin is nothing more than a term of negation, applicable to all those who in any way incurred the Montagnards' displeasure. While this may possibly prove to be the only meaning that can be attached to the name, it does not provide any reason why the 200 deputies named by the historians should be regarded as a distinct party. Still less acceptable is the totalitarian doctrine that all opponents of a dominant party must of necessity be counter-revolutionaries, whose actions are by hypothesis preconcerted. That the Jacobins did their best to propagate this idea cannot excuse its disregard of individuality, of time and of circumstance.

Moreover, the assumption that all who opposed the Revolution of 2 June, by which the twenty-nine deputies were arrested, must have been their associates and supporters before that date is also fundamentally unsound. It disregards the essential fact that a revolution had taken place, in which a minority had triumphed over a majority and legal forms had been beaten down by armed might. Many deputies, perhaps even some who would have welcomed Montagnard leadership if it had been brought about by other means, may have been alienated from the Mountain by the methods which were employed on that occasion. Proscription for subsequent hostility to the Mountain need not imply previous support for the arrested men: it may equally well indicate a sincere and disinterested dislike of a *coup d'état* and of the violation of the Convention, the sacrosanct assembly which embodied the sovereignty of the people. After the insurrection, support for its victims and opposition to those who had triumphed by force naturally became synonymous, but resistance after the event is no criterion of earlier association with a hypothetical Girondin party.

For these reasons proscription alone cannot be accepted here as any proof of party membership, and the particular reason for the classification of the 200 deputies must be considered in greater detail.

I

As the majority of the twenty-nine deputies who were arrested on 2 June may be more conveniently considered in subsequent chapters, this part of the inquiry will be principally concerned with the others, and these will be dealt with according to the reasons for their proscription, without regard for any chronological order.

Of those who have been called Girondins because they signed some written protest against the events of 31 May and 2 June, the largest single group is that of the seventy-five whose arrest was decreed on 3 October. The document which they signed was found amongst the papers of Lauze-Deperret, the friend of Barbaroux and the most likely author of it, when he was arrested for his alleged collusion with Charlotte Corday. During the Terror it remained unpublished, but after Thermidor Amar was ordered to retrieve it from the files of the Revolutionary Tribunal, and it was then printed by order of the Convention.[1]

Since this protest is representative of other similar documents, its main points are worth summarizing. By their signatures, the seventy-five deputies agreed that to fail to condemn the violation of the Convention would be to condone a crime. They therefore explained that a long series of attacks upon the Convention had culminated on 2 June. On that day armed citizens and soldiery had been assembled and organized, the Convention besieged, the deputies menaced by artillery and compelled to order the arrest of thirty-two of their number.[2] By this

---

[1] *Moniteur*, xxii, 300, 385; *Proscription*, pp. 53–5; Loiseau, *Réponse aux objections* (Paris, 1794), B.M., f.r.63.34.

[2] The figure 32 is a common contemporary error for 29.

outrage those responsible had gained control of the national executive and the national resources, of the armed forces and of the capital. The Convention itself had become a mere instrument for these men, and was unable to restrain their excesses or to control their autocratic agents in the departments of France. The seventy-five asserted that these events were a violation of the rights of man and an insult to the majesty of the people. They considered it their duty to denounce a situation which it was beyond their power to restore, and to declare to the whole nation that they themselves had ceased to take any part in the proceedings of the Convention.

These sentiments were obviously hostile to the Mountain. The references to a long-standing plot against the Convention, to conspiracy and to dictatorship, all imply acceptance of the belief that the leaders of the Mountain had long planned to seize power after eliminating all who opposed them. But this does not indicate that all who accepted this belief had previously supported the twenty-nine deputies who were under arrest. The course of events certainly seemed to substantiate this view of Montagnard methods, and many who had not previously accepted it may well have done so after the Montagnards had actually seized power.

The importance of this protest as a criterion of party loyalties therefore seems to have been exaggerated. All that can be said with confidence is that some of those who signed it may have previously sympathized with the men arrested on 2 June. To be more specific is difficult, for most of the deputies concerned took no further action in the matter, and they were not allowed to state their case when they were themselves arrested on 3 October. Some supplementary evidence can, however, be drawn from their appeals for release from prison, which were published after Thermidor by the deputies at the Port-Libre, the Carmes and the Ecossais prisons.[1] These must be used with care, because only thirty deputies could sign them and because they were obviously designed to present their case in its most

---

[1] *Les représentans du peuple détenus à la maison d'arrêt des Ecossais; des Carmes; à Port-Libre* (Paris, 1794), B.M., F.1023.16, F.848.16 and F.843.17; see also: *Cambon plaidant la cause de ses 73 collègues détenus* (Paris, 1794), B.M., F.844.11, and *Jacques, de l'intérêt des comités* (Paris, 1794), B.M., F.845.9.

E

favourable light. Nevertheless, they have significance: like the original protest, the cause these pamphlets plead is that of the Convention as a whole rather than that of any particular group.

All three pamphlets asserted that the deputies' only offence was to sign the document found amongst Deperret's papers, and that no other charge had been, or could be, made against them. While this is not true of all the seventy-five, some of whom were in fact arrested on other charges, it is certainly true of the majority of them. The exact nature of that document was therefore an important issue, and the deputies tried to establish the fact that it was not even a protest, but merely a declaration, a simple narrative of what had happened on 31 May and 2 June, such as they were in duty bound to render to their constituents.

Some inconsistent and pusillanimous arguments follow: the declaration was never published; they thought that it had been destroyed; they had continued to co-operate in the work of the Convention after 2 June. Some assertions of independence are, however, of interest. The deputies imprisoned in the Carmes, for example, maintained that before their imprisonment they hardly knew each other at all: 'Guided by conscience alone, we assiduously preserved our independence of mind. Our decisions were taken without regard for party passion or factional interest, and we remained as impervious to these as to the threats of the mob.'

The thirty deputies also repeated the story of the Montagnards' plots against the Convention, and inveighed against Robespierre and the Terror. This is of course no real evidence of their feelings eighteen months earlier. Denunciation of Robespierre was fashionable after Thermidor, and the story of a Montagnard conspiracy against the Convention seemed even more credible after the Terror than in June 1793. On the other hand, the wording of the pamphlets tends to confirm the view that the violation of the Convention was a matter of greater concern to those who protested than was the arrest of this deputy or that. The Port-Libre pamphlet, for example, emphasized that the insurrection had been aimed at 'the national parliament as a whole' and that mob-law seemed to endanger the very existence of parliamentary government. The deputies at the Carmes asserted that the enemies of the Convention had intended 'to annihilate it by massacring every man in it', and referred to the insolent menaces of the popular leader, Hanriot, 'who gave his illegitimate orders in the name of the Will of the People—but did so at the point of the bayonet and with the backing of cannon'. From the Ecossais, too, came a similar condemnation of those 'who have dared to compel the national parliament to expel many of its members, men whose conduct could only be called in question by the people of France as a whole'.

These phrases, like those in the original protest, accord too well with the contemporary belief that the Convention alone could represent the sovereignty of the people, and make known the general will, to be dismissed as mere platitudes. Neither the pamphlets nor the original protest, therefore, provide adequate support for the assumption that these seventy-five deputies were associated with any particular party before 2 June 1793.

The same argument, that a protest after an illegal act is no criterion of earlier association with its victims, applies equally to the five departmental protests which historians have taken as sufficient evidence that those who signed them were Girondins. Of these protests, only the letters sent to their departments by the deputies of the Aisne, the Hautes Alpes and the Somme are known in full, and although these three differ in emphasis, they are very similar in substance, and they correspond closely with the protest signed by the seventy-five.[1] Each was introduced as a straightforward account of the events which led to the arrest of the twenty-nine, and each told the story of those events, carefully distinguishing the people of Paris from the agitators responsible for the rising. Each asserted that the decree of arrest was an outrage, brought about by force and in direct contravention of all legal forms. Each condemned the violation of the Convention as sacrilege, as an insult to the sovereignty of the people and a menace to the freedom and unity of the nation. In particular, the Aisne and the Somme letters censured the unlawful character of the whole proceedings, while the Hautes Alpes letter deplored the tumultuous and chaotic conditions which

---

[1] The Somme and the Aisne letters are available in Mortimer-Ternaux, vii, 546 ff., and the Hautes Alpes letter is in Wallon, *La Révolution du 31 mai et le fédéralisme en 1793*, i, 484–8.

had prevailed in the Convention on 2 June. The deputies of the Somme concluded by disassociating themselves from the *coup d'état*, and the others called upon their constituents to consider what measures they should take to restore the situation.

Of another letter, written by the deputies of the Haute Vienne, only one sentence is known, and that written by deputies of the Maine et Loire is known only from references to it.[1] But it is not likely that either of these was different in kind from the other three, which are so similar. This assumption is supported by the fragment of the Haute Vienne letter which said that the insults suffered by the Convention must end republican confidence in it. La Revellière-Lépaux's reference to the Maine et Loire letter in his memoirs suggests that it was more outspoken than the protest signed by the seventy-five, but there is no reason to suppose that it was distinct in form or general content.

Interesting as they are, these letters are no more a proof of party membership than the declaration of the seventy-five. They may suggest that their authors had discovered that the people, seen in the flesh, were less attractive than philosophy had taught, but they were not alone in this view in the Convention. Moreover, even if every allowance is made for the conditions in which the Montagnard executive committees were working during the strenuous summer of 1793, their failure to prosecute the writers is significant. Of the five letters, signed in all by thirty-two deputies, three were denounced, yet only one, that to the Haute Vienne, brought arrest to the five deputies who signed it.[2] Proscription by itself proves very little, but immunity from it may well indicate the unimportance of the episodes which sometimes occasioned it.

Again, if all the thirty-two deputies who signed these letters were to be accepted as Girondins, others, whom historians have not noticed, would also have to be included in a lengthening and apparently endless list. Four deputies who were on mission in Brittany, for example, were much perturbed by the news from Paris, and reported that 'the outrages perpetrated against

---

[1] Mortimer-Ternaux, vii, 553–4, and La Revellière-Lépaux, *Mémoires*, i, 150.

[2] The Somme letter was denounced by St. André on 14 June (*Moniteur*, xvi, 644, 648); that of the Haute Vienne by Gay Vernon on 28 August (*Moniteur*, xviii, 458, and *Procès-verbal*, xix, 139); and that of the Aisne by André Dumont on 30 June (Mortimer-Ternaux, vii, 553, and A. N., F⁷.4443, Plaque 5, No. 282).

the Convention, and the weakness it has shown in the face of force' had caused grave disquiet in that part of France—a spontaneous opinion which was much modified before it was reported to the Convention late in June.[1] Another account of the insurrection, written to the people of the Department of the Manche on 5 June, and expressing that same abhorrence for the violation of the Convention which is so characteristic of all the other protests, was signed by no fewer than ten deputies, whom no one has ever thought of calling Girondins.[2] In fact, all that any of these letters really show is that a great many deputies were profoundly shocked by what had happened on 2 June, and felt it their duty to inform the Convention or their constituents of it.

The protests which were made by individuals, either in writing or from the benches of the Convention, similarly do not in themselves reveal anything more than this general dislike of violence and resentment of Montagnard domination, unless it be the personal courage of some of the otherwise obscure men who opposed it. Casenave, for example, told the Convention that he had been so shocked by the attack upon it that he had been physically ill and had had to retire to bed. Dechezeau boldly proclaimed that the *coup d'état* was a tragedy, and sent a signed copy of this opinion to the Committee of General Security. He survived one denunciation, only to be arrested and executed after he had resigned his seat, but while he lived he continued to assert that he had never favoured any party and that he was persecuted for daring to speak the truth.[3] Some deputies, too, protested because they felt that there would be no peace in France until the twenty-nine had been tried in open court. Devars, for example, called for a report about the

---

[1] The deputies concerned were Cavaignac, Gillet, Merlin (of Douai) and Sévestre. See Wallon, *La Révolution du 31 Mai*, i, 400, *Moniteur*, xvi, 723, 752, and Mortimer-Ternaux, viii, 463.

[2] J. Poisson, Ribet, Sauvé, Pinel, Bonnesoeur, Engerran, J. M. Hubert, Laurence (one of the seventy-five), Regnauld and Bretel. See *Les députés de la Manche: A nos commettans* (Paris, 1793), B.M., F.R.64.11. A further *Compte rendu* (Paris, 1793), B.M., F.1205.10, which I have not been able to identify, expresses the same view as the others; written on 7 June, it was left unsigned.

[3] CASENAVE: Mortimer-Ternaux, vii, 570. DECHEZEAU: *Moniteur*, xvii, 165, 198; *Procès-verbal*, xviii, 285, cp. *Moniteur*, xxiii, 252-4, 370; see also G. *Dechezeau à ses commettans, . . . à Billaud Varenne, . . . aux membres composant le comité de sûreté générale* (Paris, 1793), B.M., F.833.21, F.1023.3 and 4; and the *Précis des faits* which accompanies his widow's petition in 1795 (Paris, 1795), B.M., F.986.14.

arrested men in order to pacify the Departments. But the absurdity of assuming that all such men were previously 'Girondins' is shown by the application of the reasoning to Guyomer: his 'protest' consisted of a cry that the arrest of Couhey was outrageously tyrannical—and Couhey had been sent to prison for three days for daring to applaud a proposal that every deputy ought to present himself for trial by a tribunal composed of his constituents.[1]

The suggestion put forward by Perroud that resignation from the Convention is a form of protest and therefore another indication of earlier support for a Girondin party is equally unconvincing. The most that can be said is that this may be true of some individuals, and the facts do not suggest that it is likely to apply to many. Thus Daubermesnil, who forfeited his seat by unauthorized absence, was subsequently exonerated by the Committee of Public Safety, which accepted his plea of ill-health. Larroche was even excluded from the Convention by mistake, for the decree of 16 April, dismissing all deputies who were absent without reason, was applied to him although he had been granted leave of absence. Confusion of this sort ought to discourage any hasty assumption that other deputies' pleas of domestic troubles were merely the excuses of plausible liars.[2]

Even those deputies who openly resigned for political reasons cannot on that account be assumed to have been Girondins. Mennesson's attitude, that constant quarrelling was sapping the strength of the Convention and that he was not prepared to remain in an assembly which could neither command confidence nor enforce the law, is not incredible. Again, Duplantier of the Gironde resigned, as he said, in order to disassociate himself from any responsibility for the revolt at Bordeaux—and for doing so he was defended as a true patriot by the Montagnard Paganel, but attacked by his 'Girondin' colleague Ducos.[3]

Most of those who resigned, however, did so in mid-August 1793, and the only one who was then compelled to remain in the

---

[1] DEVARS: *Moniteur*, xviii, 24. GUYOMER and COUHEY: *Moniteur*, xvii, 46, 79, 86–7 and 164.

[2] DAUBERMESNIL and LARROCHE: Kuscinski and *Moniteur*, xxiv, 184.

[3] MENNESSON: *Moniteur*, xvi, 570, *Procès-verbal*, xviii, 92, and *Déclaration du citoyen Mennesson* (Paris, 1793), B.M., F.1019.13. DUPLANTIER: Kuscinski and *Moniteur*, xvi, 579.

Convention was Moreau, who could not find a substitute to take his seat. That so many deputies should resign at one time is easily explained, without reference either to a protest or a party. The Convention had been convoked in order to provide France with a constitution, and many deputies undoubtedly felt that their duties were over when the Montagnard constitution had been officially approved and fêted on 10 August. Moreau, in fact, said so quite explicitly on 16 August.[1]

A number of other deputies were proscribed for known or suspected participation in the provincial risings which followed the Montagnard seizure of power. At the time the very suspicion of this was damning, and ever since there has been a not unnatural temptation to regard such extremism as a clear indication of established party allegiance. While it may have been so in some cases, the general argument is again unsound, the difference between armed resistance and the more passive protests against Montagnard domination already considered being only one of degree. Moreover, detailed evidence shows that the deputies in question were proscribed for a variety of reasons, apparently bearing more upon the immediate situation than upon past history.

Some of these deputies, for example, fled from Paris soon after the *coup d'état*, and were punished on that account. Their motives for doing so, so far as they can be ascertained, seem to vary considerably. If Meillan, at whose house several of those who feared arrest had taken refuge on 2 June, really left the city, as he said, to tell the provinces the truth about events, other men, like Couppé, Cussy or Giroust, appear to have been wholly concerned with their own safety at a time when widespread massacres were almost hourly expected. Moreover, the provincial revolts certainly provided an opportunity for dissidents of every sort to strike a blow at the Montagnards, and some of the deputies concerned—particularly, perhaps, Delahaye—may with some justice be suspected of outright royalism.[2]

---

[1] MOREAU: *Procès-verbal*, xix, 2, and *Moniteur*, xvii, 409.
[2] MEILLAN: *Mémoires*, pp. 52, 65. COUPPÉ: Kuscinski, *Moniteur*, xvii, 15, 45, and *Biographie bretonne*; CUSSY: Kuscinski. GIROUST: *Proscription*, p. 293. DELAHAYE: *Moniteur*, xxiv, 205, *Delahaye . . . à la Convention nationale* (Paris, 1794), B.M., F.1000.11,

The fear of massacre, which made some men leave Paris, was moreover matched by the Montagnards' acute sense of the national emergency, at times almost approaching pure panic. Thus four deputies, Forest, Michet, Patrin and Vitet, were apparently arrested for no other reason than the fact that Lyons, one of the centres of revolt, was in their Department. All four were exonerated on investigation after Thermidor.[1] Equally, any suspicion of inefficiency by deputies entrusted with missions to the provinces was ruthlessly punished as deliberate counter-revolution. Some, like Brunel and Rouyer, who were in the provinces before 2 June, were proscribed for their dilatoriness in returning to the Convention. Others, like Lesterp-Beauvais and Antiboul, who were sent out at a later date—a fact which itself suggests that they were not then distrusted—suffered for their subsequent incompetence. Antiboul was captured by rebels, and apparently submitted to save his skin; Lesterp failed to prevent the seizure of an arms depôt at Lyons. Both men were eventually guillotined with the 'conspirators' arrested on 2 June, although the association seems quite fortuitous.[2] Such instances show clearly the standards of instant obedience, inflexible resolution and unfailing efficiency that were demanded of the Convention's representatives on mission, but they show little else.

Two even more obvious examples may be cited to emphasize the major point. Girard, included in Morse Stephens's list, failed to return from a mission in 1794, but the real reason for this appears to have been that he had been found wandering and deranged, and had been arrested as a vagrant. In the same year Marc Bernard was executed at Paris for assisting the rebels at Marseilles: guilty or innocent, he could not possibly have been a member of any group in the Convention before 2 June,

---

Proscription, p. 282 (cp. Lefebvre, La Convention, ii, 6), and J. Loth, Les Conventionnels de la Seine inférieure, pp. 257–66.

[1] Procès-verbal, xvi, 6, Moniteur, xvii, 108 and xviii, 647, and Proscription, p. 263.

[2] BRUNEL and ROUYER: Kuscinski; Moniteur, xvii, 22, 259, and xxii, 305; Mémoire adressé par Rouyer, and Brunel à ses collègues (Paris, 1794), B.M., F.1002.9 and F.844.7. See also Rouyer's letter to Louis XVI, Moniteur, xiv, 639. LESTERP-BEAUVAIS and ANTIBOUL: Moniteur, xvi, 515, and xvii, 452, 458, 488 and 601; Procès-verbal, xx, 168–70; Rapport du citoyen Lesterp-Beauvais, A.N., F⁷.4443, Plaque 10, No. 619. In their interrogations both these men emphatically denied all association with the Brissotins: A.N., w.292.204, Part 5, Nos. 2 and 3.

since he only took his seat as the substitute of the proscribed Barbaroux in the following August.[1]

II

So far it has been possible to consider deputies by groups according to the reasons for their proscription. Various individuals who cannot be so classified may now be briefly discussed together. In general, the majority of these appear to have been so insignificant that no clear reasons for their inclusion in the lists of either the Montagnards or the historians are now apparent. Thus seven of the forty-six deputies accused by Amar on 3 October 1793 had not previously been charged with any specific offence, and for these men lack of evidence prohibits comment on the general charge of conspiracy. For other men named by particular historians what evidence is available would appear to be of the flimsiest kind. For example, Chiappe was named by Perroud because he called for a vote of confidence in the deputies accused by the Sections on 15 April: it is true that Barbaroux once referred to him as a friend, but Perroud does not point out that Chiappe's brief interjection on 15 April was his only recorded comment on national affairs in the Convention. Nor does there seem any valid reason for the inclusion of M. J. Chénier, who was also named by Perroud. His 'poems in praise of the Girondins' may be regarded as one with his alleged persecution by Robespierre, which is now regarded as a Thermidorian legend.[2]

Moreover, here as elsewhere, there appear individuals whose supposed affiliation with an earlier 'Girondin' party can be confidently denied. Saladin, who was impeached on 21 August, was probably connected with Philippe-Egalité, the Montagnard Duke of Orleans, and was by his own account a Montagnard

---

[1] GIRARD: Kuscinski. BERNARD: *Moniteur*, xviii, 471 and xix, 217–9; *Précis de la conduite civique du citoyen Bernard* (n.d.), B.M., F.1023.10. Much the same is true of three of those proscribed for signing the protest of the seventy-five. Blanqui, Dabray and Massa only took their seats as deputies for the newly-constituted Department of the Alpes Maritimes on 25 May, one week before the Revolution. See Kuscinski, and *Dabray . . . à qui de droit* (Paris, An X), B.M., F.845.8.

[2] CHIAPPE: *Moniteur*, xvi, 198; Mortimer-Ternaux, xviii, 471. CHÉNIER: *Moniteur*, xxiii, 637; *Madame Roland*, i, 187; and M. Guillame, 'Marie Joseph Chénier et Robespierre', *La Révolution française*, xliii (1902), p. 348.

himself until 2 June, a statement confirmed by Deverité's reference to him soon afterwards as 'our latest convert'. The position of Dulaure is similar. As editor of the *Thermomètre du Jour* he had indeed been invited to Madame Roland's salon, and even accepted a small subsidy from Roland as Minister of the Interior, but he nevertheless criticized the leaders of the Convention impartially, and although he condemned the arrests on 2 June he did not support the victims until Madame Roland —who described him on 8 June as a Montagnard—persuaded him to publish her account of her interrogation later in the month. He himself believed his arrest to be the work of Hébert and Desfieux, his personal and professional enemies.[1] This, if true, is but one of several examples of the part played by individual vindictiveness in the growth of the proscription lists,[2] which increasingly appear to contain the names of a miscellaneous selection of unfortunates.

All save two of the deputies who remain to be considered were proscribed on 2 June itself, or for their actions before that date. (The exceptions, Lanthénas and Bancal des Issarts, were also named by historians in respect of earlier conduct.) It is not therefore possible to argue that they were attacked for opposing the *coup d'état*. Nevertheless, a short survey of some individual records soon suggests that even here proscription is no proof of previous party allegiance.

The records of Rebecquy, Manuel, Kersaint, Lanthénas and Bancal des Issarts, for example, show something of the fundamental instability of relationships in the Convention.[3] Rebecquy

---

[1] SALADIN: *Moniteur*, xvii, 457–8; Mortimer-Ternaux, vii, 570; *Saladin . . . sur le décret du 21 août* (1793) and *Saladin au Peuple français* (Paris, 1795), B.M., F.1031.2 and 1. DULAURE: *Madame Roland*, i, 54–9; Dulaure, *Mémoires*, introduction and 289–91; J. A. Dulaure, *Physionomie de la Convention, Du fédéralisme en France, Observations à mes commettans* ((Paris, 1793), B.M., F.R.61.28, F.1103.3 and F.1000.9; C. Perroud, 'Le premier ministère de Roland', *La Révolution française*, xlii (1903), p. 520; and Boudet, *Les Conventionnels d'Auvergne: Dulaure, passim*, particularly pp. 87–98.

[2] The case of Richou is perhaps comparable. Seemingly something of a time-server, he was denounced by Duroy mainly on account of a supposed seditious letter, and it seems that Duroy later discovered that his charge was unfounded, but concealed the fact for his own advantage. See *Moniteur*, xvi, 550, and the two pamphlets called *Richou . . . à ses collègues*, B.M., F.36.32 and F.1025.7.

[3] REBECQUY: *Moniteur*, xvi, 93. KERSAINT: *Moniteur*, xv, 235, 243, 255, 267, and Paganel, *Essai historique*, iii, 71. MANUEL: *Jacobins*, iv, 623. BANCAL: *Henri Bancal . . .* ,

resigned on 9 April, and Kersaint and Manuel did so in January, when the execution of Louis XVI seemed certain. As Manuel was not excluded from the Jacobin Society until 26 December 1792, his association with those who opposed the Mountain was obviously short-lived. Conversely, Lanthénas abandoned his friends the Rolands and began to favour the Mountain late in 1792, so earning the contemptuous protection of Marat on 2 June, when he was dismissed as being 'too chicken-hearted to be worth worrying about'. At that time Bancal des Issarts was a prisoner of the Austrians, to whom he had been handed by Dumouriez in early April. He was another of the Rolands' friends, but even more than most deputies he took pride in his political independence.

The trial and execution with the so-called conspirators of three other deputies—Duprat and Minvielle from Marseilles, and Sillery of the Somme[1]—is another example of fortuitous association. Two of them, indeed, were already under arrest before the Convention itself was purged. Both the younger Duprat and the elder Minvielle were friends of Barbaroux, and both were ultimately proscribed on 30 July for their supposed complicity in the rebellion at Marseilles. Their quarrel with the Jacobins, however, had begun in Avignon as a family quarrel between Duprat and his elder brother, and when Minvielle arrived at the Convention at the end of April, as the substitute of Rebecquy, he was at once involved in a scuffle with the elder Duprat, now a Jacobin deputy. He was first placed under a guard, then exonerated on 16 June, and then rearrested on 30 July as 'implicated in the intrigues of the others'. As for Sillery, he had actually been denounced on 1 April by Lasource, who was himself arrested on 2 June, and was arrested on 4 April

à ses collègues (Paris, 1793), B.M., F.1022.9, and F. Mège, *Le Conventionnel Bancal des Issarts*, p. 59 and *passim*. For LANTHÉNAS, see Chapter IV, below.

[1] MINVIELLE and DUPRAT: Minvielle was under guard, but free to attend debates, from 29 April to 16 June, when he was exonerated from blame for the incident on 29 April. His final arrest was as one 'implicated in the activities of those already arrested'. See *Moniteur*, xvi, 260–4, 662, xvii, 270, and xviii, 265; A.N., F⁷.4443, Plaque 5, No. 360; and the pamphlets *Jean Duprat à Jean Etienne Duprat*, *Jean Etienne Duprat . . . à Jean Duprat, Minvielle . . . à la Convention nationale*, *Minvielle aîné . . . à Duprat aîné* (Paris, 1793), B.M., F.1012.16, F.40.25, F.1027.7 and R.568.5; also, *Mémoires de Barbaroux*, 99, 171. SILLERY: *Moniteur*, xvi, 25, 60–1, 79–80, and xvii, 59, 309, 342.

as an accomplice of Orleans and Dumouriez. That he should later have been tried and executed with the very men who first demanded his arrest, and should then be accepted by historians as a member of their 'party' is more than ironic: it is an example of the confusion that must arise if history is read backwards, and a party which is assumed to have existed in 1792–3 is sought for amongst the victims of the Terror in 1793–4.

No reason is now apparent why Audrein's name should have appeared on the list drawn up by the Central Revolutionary Committee on 31 May: he was not arrested, nor was he attacked on any later occasion. The appearance of the forthright English Radical, Tom Paine, amongst the proscribed deputies is more comprehensible, if a little incongruous.[1] Granted French citizenship, he was elected to the Convention by several Departments, of which he selected the Pas de Calais. He was undoubtedly friendly with some of those arrested in June. When they died, loneliness and disillusionment drove him to seek oblivion in drink, and he took little part in politics until he was arrested in January 1794. Unable to speak French, he was never an active member of any group in the Convention. As he told Danton in May 1793 'I have no personal interest in any of these matters, nor in any party disputes. I attend only to general principles.'

Even the deputies arrested on 2 June itself are far from homogeneous. The most obvious distinction between them, and the only one which need be mentioned here, is that between those who were named individually in the Convention or by the Sections, and those who were members of the Commission of Twelve. This Commission was appointed to investigate reports of conspiracy against the Convention at the very time when the insurrection of 31 May–2 June was being prepared with at least the tacit approval of Robespierre. It naturally became anti-Jacobin, but its members included men of several shades of opinion. Two of them, Boyer-Fonfrède and St. Martin, were

---

[1] AUDREIN: *Tuetey*, ix, p. lxxxvii, and Hémon, *Audrein, Yves-Marie, député du Morbihan*. PAINE: *Moniteur*, xvi, 683, and xix, 54, 101, and Conway, *The Life of Thomas Paine*, i, 350 ff., ii, 1–100, particularly p. 53. Conway suggests that Paine's arrest was the result of an intrigue by Gouverneur Morris (p. 77 ff.), and Robespierre's note that Paine should be indicted 'for American as much as for French interests' is relevant: see *Rapport fait . . . par E. B. Courtois* (Paris, 1794).

specifically exempted from proscription on 2 June. Gommaire and Viger were also exonerated and released by the Committee of General Security in August, and Gommaire was not further disturbed. Viger was less fortunate: his name was added to Amar's list on 3 October on the proposal of Levasseur, and he was condemned with the others. Apparently his real crime was a single rash speech made on 30 April, a bare three days after his arrival at the Convention, when he urged the assembly to cut its way to Versailles if disturbances made orderly debate impossible in Paris. Gardien was equally unlucky: after resigning from the Commission on 30 May, he was placed under provisional arrest for having had counter-revolutionary connections three years before. Although the charge may not have been baseless, it was probably primarily designed to discredit the Commission, and Gardien was exonerated by the Committee of General Security next day. The order for his release, however, was never effected, and he too was executed as one of the conspirators.[1]

The story of Bertrand LaHosdinière points to the same conclusion that the arrest of these individual deputies was an incidental consequence of an attempt to put the Commission out of action. Bertrand was arrested as one of the Twelve, but he was recalled to the Convention by Saint Just on 9 July and praised as one who had boldly opposed the activities of his colleagues. This fact would suggest that he was sympathetic to the Mountain, but in a pamphlet which he published while he was under arrest he asserted that a 'monstrous authority'—presumably the Commune—had successfully plotted to usurp the authority of the Convention, and had made the Committee of Public Safety its puppet.[2] The most probable explanation of this

---

[1] GOMMAIRE: *Suis-je assez puni? Ai-je mérité de l'être?* (Paris, 1793), B.M., F.R.63.9; *Proscription*, p. 297; Kuscinski. VIGER: *Moniteur*, xvi, 272, 467, 471, and xviii, 38. At his interrogation Viger claimed that he did not even know Brissot by sight until he met him in the Convention, and the examining magistrate eventually asked him why he had been arrested: A.N., w.292.204, Part 5, No. 16. GARDIEN: *Jean François Gardien . . . à ses concitoyens* (Paris, 1793), B.M., F.1015.4; *Moniteur*, xvi, 517, 519–20, 538. At his interrogation, Gardien asserted that he met Brissot for the first time in prison: A.N., w.292.204, Part 5, No. 20.

[2] BERTRAND LAHOSDINIÈRE: *Moniteur*, xvi, 569, 741, and xvii, 77; *Le citoyen Bertrand LaHosdinière . . . au Président de la Convention* (Paris, 1793, mis-dated 9 May), B.M., F.993.9. A letter written to the Committee of General Security (A.N., w.292.205, Part 2, No. 67) is similar in tone. According to Kuscinski and to Guiffrey, *Les Conventionnels*, he resigned on 27 July 1793.

apparent contradiction is that Bertrand was, as he said, an independent deputy whose opposition to the somewhat arbitrary activities of the Commission was quite consistent with his hatred of the seizure of power by an armed minority.

Discussion of the position of such men as Brissot himself and of Barbaroux, Buzot, Gensonné, Guadet, Lanjuinais, Lasource, Louvet, Pétion, Salle and Vergniaud—to name the best known of the nineteen deputies arrested by name on 2 June—would be inappropriate at this stage. The Sections and the Montagnards may be assumed to have known at least their most obvious opponents. Even so, it may be said here that this first proscription list is something of an amalgam of names. When it was first presented by the Sections on 15 April Lasource poured scorn upon it, pointing out that eight of those named had voted for the death of the King—the supreme test of revolutionary purity—and that particular charges were advanced against only four men.[1] Shortly afterwards, Doulcet alleged that the majority of those named were virtually unknown to the Sections, the true purpose of the attack being to strike down six men whose patriotism made them the equivalent of a vigilance committee in the Convention.[2] Similarly many of those who were accused on 2 June later maintained that their proscription was so obviously haphazard that their conspiracy could safely be regarded as a myth.[3] Pétion, for example, insisted that the mass arrest must have developed from personal antagonisms since in the absence of specific charges deputies had been accused quite indiscriminately, the list varying from one moment to the next according to the personal prejudices of one accuser or another.[4]

Writing in 1810, Paganel compared Vergniaud, one of those arrested on 2 June and possibly potentially the greatest statesman in the Convention, to a man caught in a circle of others, and driven hither and thither regardless of his own will; his

---

[1] *Moniteur*, xvi, 167.

[2] *Gustave Doulcet . . . sur la pétition présentée contre vingt-deux Représentans du Peuple* (Paris, 1793), B.M., F.1026.9.

[3] Some idea of the atmosphere may be gained from Lanjuinais's account of Chabot's remark to Legendre: 'Why is Lanjuinais on the list? He is a good b . . .': Fragment by Lanjuinais, 1823, in Barrière, *Bibliothèque des mémoires*, xxx, p. 7.

[4] *Opinion de J. Pétion* (1793), B.M., F.666.4.

social contacts, he asserted, made him seem to be one of a party 'whose hopes and opinions he shared only very slightly'.[1] It is perhaps not surprising that few, if any, of the many biographers of the arrested deputies should be prepared to agree that the subject of their own particular study was truly a member of the supposed party, but that contemporary writers should often express similar views is significant. Cloots, no friend of Brissot's, once said of him that he knew no one who was less of a Brissotin than he,[2] and an anonymous pamphleteer, in a bitter attack upon Pétion, described him as the leader, the spokesman and the friend of the villains of the Plain,[3] that is, of the mass of undistinguished deputies in the Convention. Such expressions do not seem compatible with the existence of even a hard core of party politicians. Rather do they support the contention advanced by a biographer of Buzot, J. N. Davy—who describes Buzot, incidentally, as 'a Montagnard strayed into the midst of the Girondins'—that understanding of the men can only be achieved by the abandonment of such terms as 'Girondin opinion' and 'Girondin party' as overworked and meaningless.[4]

In fact in 1793 the opponents of the Mountain were known by a wide variety of names, the term 'Girondin' usually being used only to refer to the deputies from the Gironde Department.[5] Thus Camille Desmoulins gave his political pamphlet the title *The History of the Brissotins*, Marat habitually called his opponents 'the statesmen', and Vergniaud, on 13 March, deprecated attacks on 'the brissotins, the girondins and the rolandins'.[6] Those who were arrested on or after 2 June were simply referred to as the 'arrested deputies', and later the term 'federalist deputies' became common. Even at their trial the accused were called by such general names as 'the faction', 'the conspirators', or 'the intriguers'. The proscribed themselves, who insisted that all such terms were deliberately designed to ensure their

---

[1] Paganel, *Essai historique*, ii, 117–26.
[2] *Ni Marat ni Roland: Opinion d'Anacharsis Cloots* (Paris, 1792), B.M., F.776.5.
[3] *Histoire de deux célèbres législateurs du dix-huitième siècle: Vie politique de Jérôme Pétion* (n.d.), B.M., F.1291.1.
[4] Davy, *Les Conventionnels de l'Eure*, pp. 29, 66–7.
[5] The name Girondin does not occur in the Index to the *Moniteur*, where reference must be made to the heading 'federalist deputies'.
[6] *Moniteur*, xv, 704.

collective discredit, spoke of their associates as 'men of good-will', as 'true Jacobins', as 'philosophers', as 'republicans', and, more simply, as 'our friends'.

The name Girondin was indeed sometimes used in 1793 in a way which suggests that it was beginning to acquire generic significance. Paganel,[1] for example, quotes Ducos, a deputy for the Gironde, as saying 'I am neither a federalist nor a Girondin in the sense in which these words are being used', and Fauchet,[2] in an appeal to the Revolutionary Tribunal, denied any part in conspiracy by Brissot or by 'those whom they call Girondins'. Similarly, Madame Roland[3] was asked at her interrogation about her associations with Vergniaud, Guadet 'and others known by the name of Brissotins, Girondins, etc.', and Desfieux[4] gave his evidence against 'the faction known as the Gironde'.[5] This usage, a not unnatural consequence of the reputation which the deputies of the Gironde had gained both at the Bordeaux bar and in the Legislative Assembly, was not, however, general until after the Revolution.[6] Names like 'brissotins' or 'rolandins', derived directly from personalities, were much more usual. Others, like 'Buzot's party' or 'the Guadet-Brissot faction' occur frequently, and sometimes multiplication is met, as when Madame Roland heard a newsvendor outside her cell in the Conciergerie crying the discovery of a great conspiracy by 'the Rolandistes, Buzotins, Pétionistes, Girondins, with the Vendéan rebels and the agents of England'.[7]

---

[1] Paganel, *Essai historique*, iii, 60.

[2] *Claude Fauchet au Tribunal révolutionnaire et au Public* (Paris, n.d.), B.M., F.246.14.

[3] *Madame Roland*, ii, 440.   [4] *Moniteur*, xviii, 262.

[5] Lacaze's call to Ducos on 12 April, 'Be silent, Ducos, you are a Girondin', might be read in this sense, but both men came from the same Department, the Gironde. *Moniteur*, xvi, 134.

[6] The name Girondin was not even in general use after Thermidor. Although, as stated in Chapter II above, Lebreton in an undated pamphlet then found it necessary to state that none could be recognized as a deputy of the Gironde 'save those who really belonged to that constituency', the popularity of the name dates from Lamartine's *Histoire des Girondins*. See Lebreton, *Réponse à quatre pages d'impression* (Paris, n.d.), B.M., F.R.63.25, and cp. *Moniteur*, xxii, 699 ff.

[7] An extreme example of this multiplication occurs in Guiffroy's journal, *Rougiff*, No. 7: 'the Buzotins-Pétionistes, the Lesages-Barbarouxistes, the Louvetino-Rolandistes, the Lanjuinais-Fernandistes, the Salles-Fauchetistes, the Gensonno-Chambonistes, the Guadeto-Gorsalistes, the Brissotino-Vergniaudistes, and all the virtuous frogs of the marshland.' Cited by Guadet, *Mémoires de Buzot*, appendices, p. 355.

This multiplicity of names suggests that the Montagnards found it difficult to define their opponents. They themselves appear to have been seeking some collective term for their more obvious enemies, amongst whom no single person, or group of persons, may have been really predominant.

The type of terminology employed also shows that in the Convention people and personal relationships were at least as important as principles.[1] Nor is this unlikely. Even in the contemporary English Parliament political life was dominated by the family 'connection' of the great proprietors. In revolutionary France, an unstable society in which the bourgeoisie had but recently acquired political power, neither the land nor the family could provide the nucleus of an 'interest', and it is possible that personal friendships may have begun to do so. The extent to which any such 'connection' existed among or around the deputies who were arrested in June 1793 becomes apparent if the friendships formed by such men as Brissot and Roland are examined.

III

Brissot's political career began well before the Revolution, and he seems from the first to have sought to establish as wide a circle of friendships as he could. In 1782, when he was no more than the thirteenth son of a Chartres pastry-cook and one who had reached his late twenties without achieving more than a measure of notoriety as a radical pamphleteer, he had set out on a journey to Switzerland. His object, he explained in the memoirs he subsequently wrote in prison shortly before his execution, was to meet friends who would share his ideas and to open up as many contacts as possible. Beyond this lay the plan to which he later gave the rather grandiose title of the 'London School', that of 'weakening despotism by propagating the principles of liberty from beyond the borders of France'. The plan was not a success, though its soaring scope and the restless energy which drove its author across Europe are revealing. The visit to Switzerland is however of interest since Brissot

---

[1] Terms like 'fédéralistes' and 'appelants' suggest political distinctions. The one, however, was not used generally until after 2 June, and the other, which originally referred to those who supported a referendum to decide upon the King's sentence, rapidly became indiscriminate.

F

was there introduced to various reformers, including Clavière, who became, as he says, his life-long friend and who was eventually to become Minister of Finance in Roland's administration in 1792.[1]

Both Brissot and Clavière were soon known to Condorcet, the renowned mathematician and philosopher. In 1784 Brissot was imprisoned in the Bastille, and according to his own account his plight attracted the sympathetic interest of 'a great many people who were then practically strangers to me, such as Condorcet, with whom I have since been so honourably associated'. Although the association was probably somewhat reserved on Condorcet's part, other evidence indicates that all three men co-operated in support of the demand for reform on at least one occasion before 1789.[2]

After Brissot had gained his freedom—which he appears to have done principally through the influence of Madame de Sillery-Genlis,[3] the employer of Felicité Dupont, the future Madame Brissot—he renewed his political activities. In 1786 and 1787 he was associated with Bergasse, whose scientific circle was a cover for the distribution of political propaganda, and since Carra and Gorsas, two men of good education who had held various minor administrative and professional posts before drifting into journalism, were also writing under the patronage of Bergasse at this time it is likely that Brissot met them there.[4] Then, in 1788, Brissot founded the Club called *Les Amis des Noirs*. The twelve original members of this famous

---

[1] *Brissot*, i, 238, 244; Ellery, *Brissot de Warville*, 3, 21–2. The two men co-operated in a work on the *caisse d'escompte* published under Mirabeau's name in 1784–5, and they may have joined Condorcet in an appeal for a national assembly in 1788: see Ellery, *op. cit.*, p. 34, and Hatin, *Bibliographie historique et critique de la presse périodique française*, p. 92. Clavière acknowledged association with Brissot, Pétion, Condorcet, Guadet, Gensonné, Grangeneuve when he was interrogated (A.N., w.300.308. *bis*).

[2] *Brissot*, ii, 10, and Hatin as above. See also Cahen, *Condorcet et la Révolution française*, p. 250.

[3] *Brissot*, ii, 9–14; *J. P. Brissot sur la dénonciation de Robespierre* (Paris, 1793), B.M., F.675.9. Sillery, the associate of Orleans, was the friend of Saladin (*Saladin sur le décret de 21 août* (Paris, 1793), B.M., F.1031.2), and some acquaintance with him was admitted by Gensonné (*Interrogation*, A.N., w.292.204, Part 5, No. 7), by Pétion (*Réponse très succincte* (Paris, 1793), B.M., F.66.5) and by Carra (*Précis de la défense de Carra* (Paris, 1793), B.M., F.1022.4).

[4] *Brissot*, ii, 53–6, and P. Montarlot, 'Les députés de Saône et Loire', *Mém. Soc. Eduenne*, xxiii (1904), pp. 226–7.

society for the promotion of negro emancipation included Clavière and Carra, as well as Valady, a young aristocrat who had quarrelled with his family and who had become friendly with Brissot. Condorcet joined soon afterwards, as did Mercier, a satirical writer then enjoying some short-lived fame, whom Brissot had met in Switzerland. Brissot also introduced Lanthénas, a doctor closely attached to the Rolands, to the Club. When the National Assembly met in 1789 many of the new deputies, including the radical *abbé* Grégoire, the lawyer Pétion, and Doulcet de Pontécoulant, then a Lieutenant-Colonel, became members, and Brissot and Condorcet were then elected to a committee appointed to watch all legislation likely to affect the welfare of the negro. Pétion, the future Mayor of Paris, came, like Brissot, from Chartres, the two men having been friends from boyhood. It may have been he who introduced Brissot to his fellow-deputy, Buzot, another man of the law. Madame Roland says on several occasions that these three were close friends at the time of the National Assembly, and Pétion and Buzot remained intimate until they died together in the Gironde in 1794.[1]

In these early days of the Revolution Brissot was also meeting his friends regularly at his house, Lanthénas and his lawyer friends Bancal des Issarts and Creuzé-Latouche often being present. He was a member of the Paris Commune, where it is likely that he met another minor literary man, Manuel, Pétion's future colleague and Brissot's own 'courageous and worthy friend'. His newly established paper, the *Patriote français*, was popular, and was receiving contributions from a wide circle of correspondents, including Madame Roland herself.[2] Some consideration of the contemporary development of her circle of friends is therefore appropriate.

Madame Roland, who was in her middle thirties when the Revolution began, had been married at the age of twenty-six to an inspector of manufactured goods considerably her senior. Roland was at that time employed by the Paris Municipality,

---

[1] *Brissot*, ii, 70–4; Brissot, *Correspondance et Papiers*, pp. 171, 174–5; Ellery, *Brissot de Warville*, pp. 106–9; Combes, *Des Gardes françaises à la Convention*, pp. 30–5; *Madame Roland*, i, 65, 140; and *Lettres de Madame Roland*, Appendices P and R.

[2] Brissot, *Correspondance et Papiers*, pp. lii–liv, and *Réponse de J. P. Brissot* (Paris, 1791), B.M., F.674.1.

but he later moved first to Amiens and then to Lyons, and the volume of Madame Roland's correspondence may be taken as some measure of her dissatisfaction with the life of a provincial civil servant under the unreformed monarchy. One of the earliest friendships which she and Roland formed was that with Lanthénas, whom they had met in Italy some twelve years before the Revolution. This friendship was certainly an intimate one: Madame Roland says in her memoirs that she regarded Lanthénas as a brother, and another friend, Champagneux, confirms this in an early biographical study. The connection is important, for Lanthénas later introduced the Rolands to many other notable revolutionaries, and was described by Barbaroux as their confidential secretary.[1] Another early friendship was that with Bosc, whom both the Rolands and Lanthénas knew in 1780 and who corresponded with Madame Roland almost every day after 1782. He probably introduced the Rolands to his old friend Creuzé-Latouche, who was later to care for their daughter Eudora after their proscription. The Rolands also knew Champagneux in 1785.[2] Neither he nor Bosc were to become deputies, but they both helped to form the connection between the Rolands and Brissot.

The development of this link has been traced in detail by Perroud. In 1787 Brissot sent Roland a copy of a volume entitled *De la France et des Etats-Unis*, which he and Clavière had just published and which contained references to some of Roland's writings. Madame Roland explains that the inter-mittent correspondence which followed was extended by the intervention of a friend who spoke highly of Brissot in his letters, and Perroud has identified this friend as Lanthénas, who was by this time a close friend of both parties. Moreover, Bosc, who was employed in the postal service, later revealed that he used to send Lanthénas all the letters that reached him from Madame Roland, and that these were given by Lanthénas to Brissot for use in the *Patriote français*. That Madame Roland, her husband

---

[1] *Lettres de Madame Roland*, Appendix L; *Madame Roland*, ii, 253–4; Champagneux, *Discours préliminaire*, p. xxxii; *Mémoires de Barbaroux*, p. 117; and C. Perroud, 'Souvenirs inédits de Sophie Grandchamps', *La Révolution française*, xxxvii (1889), pp. 85–6.

[2] *Madame Roland*, i, 49–50; *Lettres de Madame Roland*, Appendix K; and Champagneux, *op. cit.*, p. xvii.

and her friends contributed much of the material published in the *Patriote français* is clear both from Perroud's detailed analysis of the paper and from Madame Roland's explicit statement that 'the letters I wrote with such ardour pleased Brissot greatly, and he often used extracts from them in articles in his paper'. She adds that 'as this correspondence became more frequent it came to form a bond of friendship between us'.[1] The connection was further strengthened in 1790 by the collaboration of the Rolands with Brissot, Lanthénas and Bancal des Issarts—whom Lanthénas had introduced to the Rolands in July of that year—in an attempt to purchase land for the development of what they fondly hoped would become a model rural society.[2]

So far the relationship between Brissot and the Rolands was limited to correspondence or indirect contacts. In 1791, however, Roland came to Paris on financial business for the municipality of Lyons, and Madame Roland explains that Brissot then called upon them, and introduced them to his friends who were deputies in the National Assembly. She names both Buzot, later the dearest and most loyal of her admirers, and Pétion. Some acquaintance with Grégoire and with Servan, the future Minister of War, was also established at this time.[3]

By 1791, therefore, two of the important elements in the future opposition to the Mountain had become closely connected. Brissot and Madame Roland were both profoundly dissatisfied with the state of society in France before the Revolution, and both, through their correspondence and publications, had formed many associations with people of similar views. Their common discontent had led to correspondence, to the formation of common friendships, to collaboration in idealistic plans of philanthropy, and eventually to personal association. Their groups of friends and acquaintances overlap so much that they can scarcely be distinguished, and they include two

---

[1] *Lettres de Madame Roland*, Appendix P; C. Perroud, 'Brissot et les Rolands', *La Révolution française*, xxxiv (1898); Dauban, *Etude sur Madame Roland*, p. lxvi–lxvii; Ellery, *Brissot de Warville*, pp. 38–9.

[2] *Lettres de Madame Roland*, Appendix Q; Brissot, *Correspondance et Papiers*, p. lvii; Mège, *Le Conventionnel Bancal des Issarts*, p. 21; C. Perroud, 'Un projet de Brissot pour une association agricole', *La Révolution française*, xlii (1902), p. 260.

[3] *Madame Roland*, i, 54, 60–5; *Lettres de Madame Roland*, Appendix P; Herissay, *Un Girondin, François Buzot*, p. 104, asserts that Pétion introduced Buzot to the Rolands.

men who were to become Ministers with Roland and at least thirteen men who were to become deputies to the Convention and to share, in greater or lesser degree, in Brissot's proscription in 1793.[1]

IV

According to Madame Roland, the dissolution of the National Assembly at the end of September 1791, caused some dispersal of her acquaintances. As only four of the men mentioned so far were deputies in that assembly, she may have been unduly influenced by her own brief return to Lyons on 15 September, and by the absence of Buzot from Paris. In fact, the meeting of the Legislative Assembly brought new deputies to Paris and extended the number of Brissot's and Roland's acquaintances.

Among the newcomers were the deputies from the Gironde— Ducos, Gensonné, Grangeneuve, Guadet and Vergniaud. All these men had been lawyers at Bordeaux, and Gensonné, Guadet and Vergniaud had been particularly prominent there. All were founder members of their local Jacobin Society, and all were personally acquainted, Ducos and Vergniaud being particular friends. Exactly how or when they became friendly with Brissot is not certain, although Brissot's own explanation, that they were attracted together by a common interest in the cause of negro emancipation, is not improbable.[2] Certainly considerable intimacy had been reached by the beginning of 1792, when Guadet and Gensonné were meeting Brissot regularly at the apartment which Vergniaud shared with Ducos. Guadet seems to have become more intimate with Brissot than did his colleagues. It was he who secured accommodation for him and his wife at Saint Cloud, and he later publicly avowed his friendship for both Brissot and Pétion. Grangeneuve and Ducos, on the other hand, seem to have remained on the fringe of the circle of acquaintances.[3]

---

[1] Too much should not be made of the coincidence of the appearance of individual names at this time and in 1793, since many who were united at first differed later. The figure thirteen, of course, disregards future Montagnards, notably Robespierre himself.

[2] See, e.g., *Vergniaud*, pp. 36–44, Guadet, *Les Girondins*, pp. 30, 83–93, *J. P. Brissot . . . à tous les républicains* (Paris, 1792), B.M., F.673.6, and *Moniteur*, xvi, 130, 132, and xviii, 250.

[3] Ducos, *Notes pour ma défense*, A.N., w.292.204, Part 3, No. 29.

The deputies of the Gironde were probably less closely connected with the Rolands than with Brissot. Guadet and Gensonné were probably the more attached to them. In the speech referred to above,[1] Guadet also admitted his esteem for Roland, saying that he had met him for the first time at Pétion's, on the day after Roland became Minister of the Interior (i.e., 25 March 1792). He also said that his association with Brissot brought him into contact with Clavière, and that he knew Servan during the first Roland ministry. Gensonné and Vergniaud, when they were interrogated, admitted to some slight relationship with Roland, but by July 1792 Madame Roland had a positive dislike for Vergniaud, who was not as industrious, nor perhaps so serious-minded, as she would have wished.[2] Thus the relationship between the Rolands and these deputies may have been somewhat indirect. Brissot and perhaps Guadet may have been connecting links, and Perroud has shown that Lanthénas acted as an intermediary between the salons of Vergniaud and of Madame Roland.

A further connection may have been provided by Louvet de Couvrai, a book-seller's clerk and successful radical pamphleteer. From December 1791 he worked with Brissot and his associates, Lanthénas and Bosc, on the correspondence committee of the Jacobin Society, and on 17 January 1792, after he had made a speech to the Society, he was embraced by Guadet, who was acting as President. According to Louvet's own account,[3] this proved the beginning of a life-long friendship. In March 1792 Louvet also became acquainted with the Rolands, for Lanthénas took him to meet them and arrange the publication of a new journal, the *Sentinelle*. An active and ubiquitous man, he probably knew many deputies, and Madame Roland's statement that he later became the particular friend of Buzot and Barbaroux suggests that he may have had some part in introducing his new friends to Barbaroux and other men from Marseilles.[4]

However it occurred, this last association is interesting in that the friends of Brissot, of the Rolands and of the deputies of

[1] i.e. Guadet's reply to Robespierre on 12 April 1793, *Moniteur*, xvi, 130–2.
[2] A.N., w.292.204, Part 5, Nos. 7 and 14, and *Madame Roland*, i, p. 156.
[3] *Mémoires de Louvet de Couvrai*, i, 36, 45–6.
[4] *Ibid.*, i, 50, 76–7, 83, 90, 93, and *Madame Roland*, i, 83, 161.

the Gironde were all brought separately into direct relationships with the newcomers. This was not the result of chance.
On 11 February 1792, the handsome and impetuous Barbaroux,
then aged twenty-five, arrived in Paris as the leader of a delegation which Marseilles had sent to denounce its deputy,
Martin, as a reactionary and to plead the cause of the city
against that of the royalists at Arles. It was therefore Barbaroux's task to gain as much support as possible in the Legislative Assembly, and with this end in view he approached those
whom he considered to be influential radicals. His first meeting
with Roland took place on 24 March, the day of his appointment as minister. It was unsuccessful, and there was some cool-
ness. Barbaroux next cultivated Pétion, who was then mayor of
Paris and whom he regarded as an intimate friend of the
ministers. A second approach to Roland, by way of Lanthénas,
was then more successful than the first. Their meeting on
31 May began a friendship which Madame Roland says became
stronger after the fall of the administration, when a chance
meeting led to discussion of a plan to defend France from
beyond the Loire if Paris should fall to the allied armies.
Barbaroux was even offered a secretaryship when Roland
returned to power on 10 August 1792.[1]

Barbaroux's relationship with Brissot seems a little more
indirect, although acquaintance through Pétion, and perhaps
through Grangeneuve and Gorsas seems probable at this time.
Apparently the young delegate felt that the orators from the
Gironde would be more useful to his cause. He himself speaks
particularly of Grangeneuve, saying that it was he and his
friends who succeeded in obtaining the decree by which
Rebecquy, a leader of the patriots at Marseilles, was summoned
to the bar of the Assembly instead of being condemned un-
heard as the Feuillants, those of royalist sympathies, desired.
He also praises Vergniaud, Guadet and Lasource for their part
in securing an amnesty for those concerned in the troubles in
Avignon in 1791, and a later reference by Gensonné shows that
by 1793 Barbaroux was deeply attached to him also.[2]

For his own part, Barbaroux had his own circle of friends, and

---

[1] *Mémoires de Barbaroux*, pp. 117–19, 123, 126, 157, and *Madame Roland*, i, 60.
[2] *Mémoires de Barbaroux*, pp. 111, 113, 116, 153–4.

was deeply involved in the provincial antagonisms of Marseilles. Lauze-Deperret, a liberal gentleman from the Bouches du Rhône whom Barbaroux is said to have loved as a father, was already a member of the Assembly, and later he admitted that he was more intimate with Barbaroux than with any other member of the Convention.[1] Another friendship was that between Barbaroux and Rebecquy, who lodged together after Rebecquy arrived in Paris on 5 June 1792, to justify himself before the Legislative Assembly. Rebecquy apparently drew Barbaroux closer to Roland, for, stirred by a letter of admonition and warning which Roland sent to the King on 10 June, he declared that he would be for ever Roland's friend, an incident which Barbaroux said was 'the beginning of our own friendship and of our association with Roland'. Another future deputy to the Convention, Jean Duprat, a silk merchant, had come to Paris with Rebecquy, and he later said that while he disapproved of much that Barbaroux did, he had remained a life-long admirer of Rebecquy.[2]

Some other associations which could have led to friendships during the period of the Legislative Assembly may also be noticed here. The elderly deputy Dusaulx, who was later to be dismissed by Marat as 'too old a dotard to be a party leader', had been a member of the Commune of Paris at the same time as Brissot and Manuel. Manuel himself and Pétion were now respectively *procureur* and mayor of Paris. Kersaint, a naval officer frustrated in his efforts for reform in his service, had become a deputy in April 1792, after contributing with Brissot, Clavière and Mercier to Condorcet's paper, the *Chronique du Mois*. A more certain friendship, and a more important one, was that of Gensonné for General Dumouriez,[3] with whom he had been sent to investigate conditions in the Vendée in 1791.

---

[1] *Interrogation* of *Lauze-Deperret*, A.N., w.292.204, Part 5, No. 10, and Kuscinski. Cp. *Interrogation* of Fauchet, A.N., w.292.204, Part 5, No. 25.

[2] *Mémoires de Barbaroux*, pp. 116–17, and the pamphlets exchanged between the brothers Duprat, B.M., F.340.25 and F.1012.16. (See p. 55, n. 1 above.)

[3] *Correspondance de Dumouriez avec Gensonné*, B.N.., MSS., *Nouv. acq. françaises* 3534, No. 36 ff., and *Mémoires du Général Dumouriez*, i, p. 147. Cp. R. M. Brace, 'General Dumouriez and the Girondins, 1792–1793', *American Historical Review*, lvi, No. 3 (1951), p. 493 ff.; A. Sorel, 'Dumouriez: un général diplomate au temps de la Révolution', *Revue des deux mondes*, lxiv (1884), p. 308 ff.; and Michon, *Robespierre et la guerre révolutionnaire*, p. 63.

Clearly, the circle of friends widened considerably during the period of the Legislative Assembly. The associates of Brissot and Roland formed friendships with the deputies of the Gironde and with the delegation which Barbaroux brought from Marseilles. If all the associations which have been mentioned may be provisionally assumed to have continued as friendships, the group of friends and acquaintances would now include twenty-six future deputies to the Convention, as well as the Ministers Roland, Clavière, and Servan, and General Dumouriez.[1]

V

The transition from the Legislative Assembly to the Convention was not disruptive. As deputies from both the Legislative and the National Assemblies were eligible for re-election, a few old associations, like that between the Rolands and Buzot, were renewed, and some fresh friendships were formed with newcomers. Pache, an old acquaintance of the Rolands, became Minister of War with their help, and was for a short time allied with them.[2] But with certain exceptions the newcomers were men of comparative unimportance, and no notable increase in the number of associations is apparent.

Amongst the new deputies were Dufriche-Valazé, whom Professor Lefebvre has described as an unsuccessful bourgeois living on a shrinking patrimony, and Boyer-Fonfrède, a merchant who was a new deputy for the Gironde. Valazé, who had been an army officer until commissions were withdrawn from those not of noble birth, proclaimed in his first speech, on 29 September 1793, that 'Roland and Servan are names very near to my heart'. There is no evidence that he was acquainted with any well-known deputies before he reached Paris, but by January 1793, he was able to write of Buzot, Barbaroux, Salle and Grangeneuve as his friends.[3] Boyer-Fonfrède, who was

---

[1] There were several other deputies in the Legislative Assembly who were later to be proscribed in 1793, such as Isnard, Fauchet and Lasource, but no evidence of friendship with those mentioned here is available.

[2] *Madame Roland*, i, 143, 146, and Champagneux, *Discours préliminaire*, p. xxxi.

[3] *Valazé*, introduction by Lefebvre and 85–7, 95; *Moniteur*, xiv, 78. Cp. *Interrogation* of Valazé, A.N., w.292.204, Part 5, No. 17, his *Défense*, B.M., f.1023.17, and *Vergniaud*, p. 70.

brother-in-law to Ducos, joined him in admiration for Vergniaud. The three men shared lodgings in Paris, and Boyer later attributed his arrest to his loyalty to his friends.[1]

Another new deputy from the Gironde, the surgeon Bergoeing, shared accommodation with Buzot, who now became intimate with Barbaroux and Louvet.[2] Two other lawyer-deputies from Buzot's constituency, Savary and Vallée, also lived with him in 1793,[3] and both these men were associated with others whose names have already been noticed. Vallée seems to have acted as a link between the deputies who remained in Paris after 2 June 1793 and some of those who fled to the provinces. His name occurs in the correspondence of both Valady and Barbaroux—who, in the time of crisis, named him, as well as Chiappe, Duprat, Noël and Bresson, as friends.[4] Savary, when questioned by the Committee of General Security in July 1793, agreed that he had renewed his friendship with Buzot after some temporary disagreement during the elections to the Convention.[5]

Two other probable friendships may also be mentioned. Mollevaut, another lawyer, is said by his biographer to have been friendly with Vergniaud, and Duprat, one of the deputies referred to by Barbaroux, lived at Versailles with Minvielle, a silk merchant like himself and an old associate in the revolutionary struggles at Marseilles.[6] Minvielle became a deputy for the Bouches du Rhône when Barbaroux's friend Rebecquy resigned, and some association with Barbaroux seems likely in spite of Minvielle's subsequent denials.

Beyond this point good evidence of any further extension of the circle is lacking. If, as before, no account is taken of friendships which may have been broken, or of distinctions between close and casual associations, the group of friends and acquaintances includes thirty-six deputies to the Convention, as well as

---

[1] *Interrogation* and notes of Ducos, A.N., w.292.204, Part 5, No. 13, and Part 3, Nos. 18, 27, 29 and 32.
[2] Tuetey, ix, p. lxxxvi; *Madame Roland*, i, 161, and the *Almanach national* for 1793.
[3] A.N., F⁷.4443, plaque 4, 210 and 239.
[4] A.N., F⁷.4443, plaque 10, 700, and Mortimer-Ternaux, vii, 467, 471.
[5] Kuscinski, citing A.N., AA.47.
[6] Claude, *Etienne Mollevaut et la vie politique en Lorraine, 1744–1816*, p. 182, and A.N., F⁷.4443, plaque 5, 354 and 352.

four Ministers.[1] In all probability, however, the number of those who were really intimate is considerably smaller than this.

VI

Thus a group of friends, interested in politics before the Revolution, continued and extended their association in active political life during the days of the National Assembly. In the Legislative Assembly, they formed new friendships and acquired influence, some of their number becoming ministers and others being leaders of debate. In the Convention, many of them were among the principal opponents of Robespierre and the Mountain. Since almost half of those arrested on 2 June were of their number, a 'connection' can be said to have existed among the deputies who were purged on that occasion.

This, however, does not necessarily imply that the group formed a considerable body of united opinion, or that it was in any way unusual. Even if some allowance is made for omissions —and the names of some men who are often spoken of as prominent 'Girondins', such as Isnard, Lanjuinais and Lasource, have not occurred at all in this review—the number of those concerned is small in comparison with the two hundred names derived from the proscription lists. Amongst these deputies, differing degrees of intimacy and varying periods of association certainly existed, and no common policy towards any specific political problem has yet emerged.[2]

Moreover, the essential unity of the group even in terms of personal relationships is debatable. Where Dulaure, writing in January 1793, considered that the names 'girondins', 'brissotins' and 'rolandins' referred to the same group of deputies, Paganel's historical essay of 1810 distinguished the

---

[1] i.e.: *Deputies:* Brissot, Bancal des Issarts, Barbaroux, Bergoeing, Boyer-Fonfrède, Bresson, Buzot, Carra, Chiappe, Condorcet, Creuzé, Deperret, Doulcet, Ducos, Dufriche-Valazé, Duprat, Dusaulx, Gensonné, Gorasas, Grangeneuve, Grégoire, Guadet, Kersaint, Lanthénas, Louvet, Manuel, Mercier, Minvielle, Mollevaut, Noël, Pétion, Rebecquy, Savary, Valady, Vallée and Vergniaud. *Ministers:* Roland, Clavière, Pache, Servan.

[2] cp. Roland's reply to the allegation that he had plotted with the Brissotins: 'I have no belief in this supposed faction. I know and esteem Brissot, but his opinions are not always mine' (13 September 1792, *Moniteur*, xiii, 670).

'Girondins' from the 'Rolandins', and Ellery, a recent biographer of Brissot, separates those whom he regards as
'Brissotins' from a more active and impetuous group whom he
calls the 'Buzotins'.[1] The evidence which has been considered
here seems to show that the mesh of associations between
Brissot, Roland, the deputies from the Gironde and those from
Marseilles, was so close-woven that no clear distinction can be
made between the friends and acquaintances of any of these
men, although these four separate nuclei are clearly apparent
in the development of the connection.

A further comment, from incidental evidence, is also relevant:
even among the two hundred deputies to whom this inquiry has
been restricted there were many other small circles of friends.
Several deputies, some of whom have appeared as friends of
Brissot or his associates, shared living accommodation with
others from the same Departmental delegation as themselves,
and in these circumstances there is a strong presumption that
common interests and friendships would have united these
deputies closely. The existence of other and more important
groups is also apparent. One of these probably centred on
Grégoire. He was admired by Cazeneuve, by Audrein and by
La Revellière-Lépaux, to name no others.[2] A second group,
possibly composed more of admirers than of friends, is apparent
around Condorcet. In addition to his relationships with Brissot
and Clavière, he was closely associated with Jean Debry and
Tom Paine, and probably with Fauchet and Rabaut St.
Etienne as well, apart from possible connections with the
Montagnards.[3]

The fact that at least one deputy in each of these separate
groups was friendly with one or more of Brissot's friends suggests a way in which Brissot could have built up a considerable

---

[1] Dulaure, *Physionomie de la Convention nationale* (Paris, 1793), B.M., f.r.61.28;
Paganel, *Essai historique*, ii, 344, and iii, 37–8; Ellery, *Brissot de Warville*, p. 420.

[2] T. Lemas, 'Ignaze de Cazeneuve', *La Révolution française*, xviii (1890), p. 332;
Hémon, *Audrein, Yves-Marie*, introduction; La Revellière-Lépaux, *Mémoires*, i,
p. 157; Bougler, *Mouvement provincial en 1789 et biographies des députés de l'Anjou*,
p. 177 and *passim*.

[3] Pingaud, *Jean de Bry*, p. 9; Conway, *Life of Thomas Paine*, ii, p. 48; J. Charrier,
Claude Fauchet, i, p. 149; Mirabaud, *Rabaut St. Etienne*, pp. 63, 211; Alengry,
Condorcet, guide de la Révolution française, pp. 174–5, 198–203; Cahen, *Condorcet et la
Révolution française*, pp. 457 and 381.

connection. No evidence has as yet appeared, however, to show that these various groups can be considered as one, or that any-one of importance ever essayed to weld them into a coherent whole. Brissot himself, who said on one occasion that he always loved to introduce his friends one to another, yet said later—but before his fall—that he scarcely knew forty members of the Convention and was only intimate with three or four truly enlightened friends.[1] The only legitimate conclusion from the evidence is that, in the absence of organized parties, personal friendships were a common and natural form of political asso-ciation. What may perhaps best be described as the groups of the Brissotin connection were by no means an isolated pheno-menon. It remains to be seen whether they should be regarded as groups of friends in only a personal or the vaguest political sense, or whether they ever endeavoured to formulate and effect any particular policies. An answer to this question may first be sought in an investigation of the 'secret meetings' for which they became notorious.

---

[1] *Brissot*, i, 176, and *J. P. Brissot . . . sur la dénonciation de Robespierre* (Paris, 1793), B.M., F.675.9.

CHAPTER IV

Government by Salons

THE private meetings held by some of Brissot's associates were accepted by the Montagnards as sufficient proof of conspiracy, and some historians have also regarded them as strong indications of the existence of an organized party.[1] Unfortunately there is little positive evidence either to support or to refute these contentions. Conspirators naturally take some care to conceal their activities, while innocent men do not normally trouble to record the details of discussions at private dinner-parties or social gatherings. The evidence is either casual, blatantly hostile, or strictly non-committal.

The general unreliability of Montagnard allegations may be illustrated by some brief reference to the controversy over the alleged meetings at Saint Cloud. According to Saint Just, Saint Cloud was a centre of conspiracy; there, lodging in the royal palace, Madame Brissot received most of the deputies who planned and prepared the provincial risings of 1793. This accusation Madame Roland treated with contempt, drawing a satirical picture of the supposed cell of conspiracy in which Madame Brissot, seated in a small and shabby apartment, patiently sewed her husband's shirts. The truth seems to be that after the birth of her third child, in 1791, Madame Brissot sought accommodation outside Paris in order that the boy might benefit from a healthier air. Through the good offices of Guadet's brother-in-law, Robert Bouquey, who was caretaker of the château of Saint Cloud, she obtained two rooms in a disused lodge. There she remained until mid-April 1793, when the accusations brought against her compelled her to move to other rooms in a workman's cottage, lest she should compromise her husband's political position. Both she and Brissot denied

---

[1] e.g., Lamartine, *Histoire des Girondins*, iii, p. 128; and, less dogmatically, Aulard, *Orateurs*, i, p. 155 and Lefebvre, *La Convention*, i, 8.

that she had ever met any deputy except Guadet at Saint Cloud, and that he and Brissot should occasionally have gone there together, as Brissot said, seems quite natural. The Montagnards' accusations rest upon a single denunciation, and that certainly untrustworthy.[1]

There is yet a good *prima facie* case for the existence of clubs and salons frequented by those who opposed Robespierre. Such meeting places were an integral part of French society in the eighteenth century. *Sociétés de pensée* flourished alongside the salons of such great ladies as Madame de Deffand or Madame de Tencin, and if the discussion was literary and intellectual rather than of a political nature, this may be ascribed to the rationalism of the period and to the sterility of political life in an autocracy. The disintegration of the *ancien régime* after 1787, and the political emancipation brought by the Revolution, were however accompanied by the rapid development of clubs and salons for political purposes. The salons of Madame Necker and Madame de Genlis, the Club of 1789 and *Les Amis des Noirs* may be cited as Parisian examples, while the Club Breton, better known by its later name of the Jacobin Society, was to dominate France through the affiliation of innumerable local societies, which had often been created to gratify the universal hunger for news of events in the capital. In this respect, the Revolution adopted and adapted the social pattern of the *ancien régime*.

It is not therefore surprising that clubs and salons should have played an important part in the development of the group or groups associated with Brissot, Roland and the deputies of the Gironde. These men were all intimately involved in politics, and political life necessarily involves some private discussion. But in the Revolution, public opinion became increasingly hostile to all such 'secret meetings'. Led by Robespierre, the Jacobins interpreted the doctrine of popular sovereignty literally, at least so far as the people of Paris were concerned. They regarded themselves not as members of a private club but as representative citizens, meeting for the public discussion of

---

[1] *Moniteur*, xvii, 155; *Madame Roland*, i, 302; *Brissot*, ii, 259–60; *Interrogation* of Madame Brissot, A.N., F7.4443, plaque 4, No. 198; denunciation of Madame Brissot, A.N., BB372, dossier 10, No. 1; and Brissot, *Correspondance et Papiers*, p. lvii.

PIERRE VICTURNIEN VERGNIAUD

CHARLES JEAN MARIE BARBAROUX

public events, and after 14 October 1791 their meetings were held before crowded and vociferous public galleries. To this attitude much of their power was due. Other meetings, being more exclusive, were regarded as reactionary and malevolent. When the Jacobin deputies seized power in June 1793, the salons and clubs, other than the Jacobin Club itself, disappeared, only reappearing in the more congenial atmosphere which followed Thermidor. This conflict between the political convenience of private discussions and the uncompromising publicity demanded by the doctrine of popular sovereignty is in fact a reflection of the conflict between the habits of the *ancien régime* and the exigencies of an absolutist democracy.

Four meeting places—the Reunion Club and the salons of Madame Roland, Madame Dodun, and Valazé—are often alleged to have been of particular importance in the development of the opposition to the Mountain. Some knowledge of when each of these was important, of the names of those who were present, and of the nature of their activities, is therefore relevant, and the salon of Madame Dodun, which is particularly associated with the deputies from the Gironde, will be considered first.

The Salon of Madame Dodun and Vergniaud[1]

In his evidence at the trial of Brissot, Chabot alleged that 'a few weeks after his presidency at the Jacobin Society' Brissot had invited him to attend meetings held by deputies of the Gironde. This, if true, would indicate that these meetings were being held shortly after 17 October 1791, when Brissot's presidency of the Jacobin Society ended. Chabot's reputation, and his obvious hostility to the accused, do not encourage a belief in the general trustworthiness of his evidence, but Brissot's reply shows that the invitation was in fact given, and that regular meetings had been arranged with the deputies of the Gironde when they became friendly with him soon after the beginning of the

---

[1] This section is based upon evidence in the trial of Brissot, *Moniteur*, xviii, 241, 250–3, and upon *Madame Roland*, i, 66–8, 229; Dumont, *Souvenirs sur Mirabeau*, particularly pp. 201–3; C. Perroud, 'Souvenirs inédits de Sophie Grandchamps', *La Révolution française*, xxxvii (1899), p. 85; *Vergniaud*, pp. 71–88; E. Lintilhac, 'Le salon de Madame Dodun', *La Révolution française*, lxxi (1918), p. 6 ff.; Laurent's edition of *Le Défenseur de la Constitution*; and the particular references which follow.

G

Legislative Assembly in October 1791. One of Vergniaud's biographers, Eugène Lintilhac, has identified the regular meeting place as No. 5, Place Vendôme, where Vergniaud and Ducos shared lodgings after the middle of January 1792. The salon is associated with Vergniaud, but the evidence of Ducos shows that the owner of the house, Madame Dodun, was really the hostess. In the words of Madame Roland, she was 'a respectable and wealthy woman who could without any inconvenience put at their disposal a spacious room, which they were free to use even in her absence'.[1]

Some idea of the names of those who met there can also be gained from Chabot. According to him, Brissot's invitation had been accompanied by a boastful reference to the presence of Vergniaud, Guadet, Gensonné, Condorcet, 'and other well-intentioned deputies', but despite this both he and Grange-neuve, who was also invited on the same occasion, had refused to attend. In their replies, Brissot and Gensonné admitted that they had been present at these meetings, which Brissot said occurred three times a week, before the opening of the Legislative Assembly's sittings. He added that Gensonné's attendance was irregular, since he lived at a distance. The presence of the others named by Chabot is confirmed by other evidence. Etienne Dumont, in his *Souvenirs sur Mirabeau*, claimed that he was himself present at some of these meetings, which he says were usually attended by Brissot, Clavière, Roederer, Gensonné, Guadet, Vergniaud, Ducos and Condorcet, 'etc.'. Moreover, in the reply referred to above, Brissot spoke explicitly of the deputation of the Gironde, which then included Gensonné, Guadet, Vergniaud and Ducos. The presence of Ducos, indeed, seems almost certain, since he was Vergniaud's friend and fellow-lodger. One further piece of evidence is available. Madame Roland says that her husband was invited to be present, but seldom went as the distance was too great. She adds, however, that one of her friends was a frequent visitor, and Perroud has shown that this friend was Lanthénas. A small but intimate group is therefore apparent at the Place Vendôme, of which—apart from those not later to be in the Convention—Brissot,

---

[1] Notes for his defence by Ducos, A.N., w.292.204, Part 3, No. 27; *Madame Roland*, i, 229.

Condorcet, Ducos, Gensonné, Guadet, Vergniaud and Lan-thénas were among the more important members.

There is no doubt that the meetings of this group were political in purpose. Both Brissot and Gensonné admitted that the forthcoming business of the Legislative Assembly was discussed, while Dumont, a hostile witness, said that deputies met at the Place Vendôme to await the opening of the Assembly and to agree upon their policy in it. According to him, the members of the group were determined to steal a march upon the Robespierrist Jacobins by leading an attack upon the so-called 'Austrian Committee', a general name for the Court and its supporters at home and abroad. This allegation is not without foundation, for the five deputies Brissot, Condorcet, Gensonné, Guadet and Vergniaud were prominent advocates of the policy of war with Austria, were foremost in the denunciation of the 'Austrian Committee' in the spring of 1792, and were attacked by Robespierre in the first numbers of his journal, *Le Défenseur de la Constitution*. Dumont also alleged that these men were united in their ambition to obtain control of the administration, an allegation which may be compared with Madame Roland's own statement that Roland's appointment to the Ministry of the Interior was first proposed at the Place Vendôme, Roland hearing of it from Brissot. It seems probable, too, that Gensonné's friendship with Dumouriez was a contributory cause of the General's appointment to the Ministry of Foreign Affairs in March 1792,[1] although Ducos, Gensonné and Vergniaud all strenuously denied this at their trial. Thus the development out of the meetings of this 'little committee', as Madame Roland called it, of a parliamentary group aiming at the overthrow and replacement of the Delessart Ministry in the spring of 1792 is not at all improbable.

On the other hand, the influence and importance of the salon in the Assembly should not be exaggerated. No reliable evidence has appeared to show that the deputies concerned really co-ordinated their actions or accepted any limitation of their personal independence. Dumont did not have any high opinion of their organizing abilities, and his account suggests an atmosphere of political gossip and tittle-tattle rather than one of decision

---

[1] See above, p. 69, n. 3.

and action. Brissot alone seems to have impressed him, and that by his activity, not his ability. Moreover, only a limited number of deputies appear to have taken part in the discussions, and the only indication of anything approaching an attempt to extend their circle is Chabot's tale of Brissot's invitation to him, a story which refers to a single, and perhaps impulsive, gesture.

The duration of the salon cannot now be established with any certainty. It may have continued after the meeting of the Convention in September 1792, or even until Vergniaud's removal to the Rue de Clichy in March 1793,[1] but the latest known references to it appear in a letter from Madame Roland to Bancal des Issarts dated 7 July 1792, and in a note which she received from her husband in the following September. Since she refers in her memoirs only to the deputies of the Legislative Assembly in this connection, and since all the available evidence relates to events in the first half of 1792, the probability is that these meetings, beginning in mid-autumn 1791, continued intermittently until the Legislative Assembly was dissolved in September 1792.

THE REUNION CLUB[2]

Even an approximate chronology is difficult to achieve for the obscure Reunion Club. Little is known about it, and the evidence is often obviously distorted by political prejudice. A brief appreciation of the general political situation in the middle of 1792 is indeed necessary before any conclusions can be reached.

In spite of their quarrel with Robespierre over the war with Austria, Brissot and his friends remained influential in the Jacobin Society during the early months of 1792. The coincidence of the sittings of the Society with those of the Legislative Assembly, however, often compelled these deputies to be absent from the important evening meetings of the Society, and their influence there declined. Vergniaud, who was President of the Jacobin Society from 2 to 16 April, took the chair on only three

---

[1] A.N., F[7].4443, plaque 3, No. 176.

[2] This section is based upon evidence in the trial of Brissot, *Moniteur*, xviii, 238, 245, 255–6; *Jacobins*, iii, 655, 670, and iv, 50–8, 165, 319, 323–8, 352, 354, 360, 366, 380, 385, 394 and 466, according to the appropriate dates; Mathiez, *Girondins et Montagnards*, pp. 71–80; *Mémoires de Choudieu, 1761–1838*, pp. 124–6; and the particular references which follow. Cp. Michelet, *Histoire de la Révolution*, v, 57–62.

occasions. Lasource's Presidency from 16 April to 2 May was the last time that the chair was held by anyone who was subsequently to be condemned as a member of the faction, and its close was marked by Pétion's failure on 29 April to secure a reconciliation between conflicting groups in the Society. By the beginning of May the quarrel had reached such a pitch that orderly debate had become almost impossible.[1] This conflict, however, was soon overshadowed by the increasing danger of a major counter-stroke by the supporters of the Court. This danger was first apparent on 18 to 20 May, when a magistrate ordered the arrest of three well-known radical deputies, Chabot, Basire and Merlin de Thionville. It continued at least until the insurrection in Paris on 10 August, and possibly until the general in charge of the Army of the North, Lafayette, deserted to the Austrian lines ten days later. In these circumstances a brief reconciliation was effected between the friends of Brissot and those of Robespierre in the Jacobin Society on 28 June.

The Society itself, as one of the principal centres of radical opinion in Paris, was naturally in danger during this period, and it appears that at least two distinct attempts were made to bring about its closure. On the first occasion an effort was made to obtain ownership of the hall in which the Society met, and this threat was averted through the generosity of a member of the Society, Guiraut, who undertook to put up the greater part of the necessary purchase money personally—a promise he had some difficulty in fulfilling. The same man was probably instrumental in assisting the Society on the second occasion also. His later statement was that 'at a time when very sharp dissension' had prevented members from using their hall he had 'made facilities available for some deputies to meet in an adjacent one'. This probably refers to the events of 29 June, when Lafayette attempted to lead a march against the Society. If, as seems likely, these meetings of deputies developed into the Reunion Club, the name might well refer to the reconciliation between the factions in the Jacobins made on the previous day, 28 June. This chronology is supported by later Jacobin statements. On 1 October 1792 Thuriot said that the association

---

[1] See also Walter, *Histoire des Jacobins*, p. 249 ff., and Michon, *Robespierre et la guerre révolutionnaire, 1791–1792*, pp. 109–10.

called the Reunion had been formed during the stormy time when the aristocracy was strong in the Legislative Assembly. A fortnight later Chabot, speaking of the Reunion, said that it had been necessary 'to muster the whole weight of the Brissotins and the patriots of the right against the centre and lower benches of the Assembly'.[1]

The other possibility is that the club was established at some earlier date by a secession from the Jacobin Society of a body of deputies which included Brissot and other opponents of Robespierre. In this case Guiraut's reference to 'a time of very sharp dissension' would refer to the period of conflict in the Jacobin Society which preceded Lafayette's bid to control Paris. There is some evidence to support this interpretation of the situation, but it is ambiguous and obviously coloured by prejudice, particularly that of the later Jacobin desire to discredit the Reunion as a rival association. In his evidence at the trial of Brissot, the witness Chaumette made the damaging accusation that Brissot had formed the Reunion 'in order to neutralize the Jacobin Society'. This allegation had however aroused protests in the Jacobin Society itself when it was made there. In mid-October 1792 a Jacobin circular, drafted immediately after the expulsion of Brissot from the Society, alleged that he and his followers had become irregular in their attendance at the Society and had formed a new club, the Reunion, which had promoted the 'partial' and unsuccessful insurrection of 20 June, an event described as a consequence of Brissot's fury at the dismissal of Roland and his colleagues on 13 June, and as one of which the Jacobin Society had disapproved. This version of the facts was challenged at once. This was the occasion on which Chabot referred to the need there had been to rally 'the patriots of the right', and he demanded the erasure of the passage about the Reunion as reflecting upon what he called 'the Montagnard

---

[1] In the Legislative Assembly the terms 'left' and 'right' were used to refer to the position of deputies as seen from the table of the President. Chabot's 'patriots of the right' thus refers to the more radical members of the assembly. The same arrangements were kept in the Convention, where the high tiers of the 'Mountain' were to the right of the President. The Montagnards sometimes referred to their opponents as the 'right' either because the table had once stood on the opposite side of the hall or because they, as deputies, were facing the President. See Dulaure, *Physionomie de la Convention nationale* (Paris, 1793), B.M., F.R.61.28, and, e.g., *Moniteur*, xv, 705–6.

members of the Legislative Assembly'. Eventually he and
Collot d'Herbois were asked to amend the circular, which they
did in such a way that the responsibility for the events of
20 June was shifted from the Reunion to Brissot personally. The
greater probability therefore seems to be that the Reunion
began, as its name may imply, at the time of the reconciliation
at the end of June 1792.[1]

This is not to say that the Reunion did not subsequently
become a centre of what the Jacobins called 'moderation'. All
the references to it, including its own prospectus, dated 21
September 1792, and published by Mathiez,[2] show that it was
composed wholly of deputies, and it would indeed be remarkable if such an association did not represent a less radical attitude than that of the more popular Jacobin Society, to which
Robespierre was confined until he was elected to the Convention in September. Moreover, in the course of July the truce
between the supporters of Robespierre and those of Brissot in
the Jacobin Society, if truce it can be called, broke down. The
Robespierrist Jacobins came to suspect that Brissot's delay in
launching a demand in the Legislative Assembly for the dismissal and impeachment of Lafayette concealed an attempt on
his part to effect a compromise with the Court, and on 1 August
it was proposed that he should be excluded from their Society.
This proposal coincided with a series of attacks upon the
Reunion Club. Desfieux and Merlin de Thionville alleged, on
hearsay evidence, that Brissot and Isnard had there demanded
the official indictment of Robespierre.[3] Other speakers accused
the Club of favouring 'partial' measures, particularly the suspension rather than the deposition of the King and the inauguration of a period of government by a commission of deputies.

---

[1] This view is in accordance with that of Lefebvre, *La Chute du Roi*, p. 197. In
describing *Le Journal des Amis de la Paix* as 'the organ of the Reunion Club',
Challamel (*Les Clubs contre-révolutionnaires*) presumably refers to an earlier association of the same name: see B.N., 8.Lc?646, a royalist sheet dated 1791.

[2] Mathiez, *Girondins et Montagnards*, p. 71, citing A.N., F⁷.4439·3.

[3] *Jacobins*, iv, 165. The identity of two deputies from whom the Jacobins derived
this story is obscure, but it is clear that Aulard is incorrect in supposing the indictment of Lafayette to have been in question, as his footnote suggests. At the trial of
Brissot an effort was made to shift these events to the more compromising date of
8 August (*Moniteur*, xviii, 255). See also: *Fr. Chabot à Jean Pierre Brissot* (Paris, n.d.),
B.M., F.674.5.

Since measures very similar to these were actually adopted by the Legislative Assembly on 10 August, and since the writers of the Club prospectus later claimed credit for the Club for what they called 'the excellent decrees passed by the Assembly since 10 August', it is likely that at this time its members tried with some success to promote a settlement of the situation more cautious than that favoured by Robespierre. Indeed, Mathiez's interpretation of the prospectus as an indication that the Club constituted the first parliamentary group in French history would seem to be supported by this reading of the evidence.

Unfortunately only a very few of those who were members of the Club can now be identified. Ducos admitted to a dozen visits, and Fauchet published in January 1793, a speech he claimed to have delivered to the Reunion.[1] Brissot and Isnard were named as members by Desfieux and Merlin de Thionville at the Jacobin Society on 1 August. Lasource's presence was alleged by Chabot at the Jacobins on 7 November 1792, and before the Revolutionary Tribunal in the following October. At the trial another witness, Montaut, spoke of Brissot, Isnard and Lasource as members, and Choudieu in his memoirs mentioned Isnard, Grangeneuve and Gensonné. Neither Brissot nor Lasource denied their membership when they were on trial, although they put another colour on their conduct at the Club. In all, seven names of men who were later to be proscribed occur, of which the first two stand on personal written admissions. They are: Ducos, Fauchet, Brissot, Gensonné, Grangeneuve, Isnard and Lasource.

The significance of the presence of these men is however almost completely obscured by the fact that the membership of the Club was clearly considerable, and its composition varied. Its size is indicated by the reiterated complaints at the Jacobin Society about the absence of deputies who were believed to be attending the Reunion, and by Thuriot's anxiety on 1 October lest the Jacobins should 'deprive themselves of 200 enlightened members' by insisting on the expulsion of all who attended the Reunion. Moreover, the evidence indicates that Robespierre's sympathizers continued to participate in the Club's activities.

[1] Ducos, notes, A.N., w.292.204, Part 3, No. 27; Fauchet, *Journal des Amis* for 19 January 1793, B.M., F.1579.1.

Choudieu, for example, wrote of its members as Montagnards, and Ducos, in the speech he prepared as his defence at his trial, claimed that he had co-operated at the Reunion 'with a great many Montagnard members'. As we have seen, too, the Jacobins were reluctant to accept any sweeping condemnation of the Club in the autumn of 1792. Men like Chabot and Guiraut praised it for its work, and Thuriot said that it had saved France from great misfortunes. As late as 7 November, indeed, Chabot spoke of it as 'sympathetic to Brissot, but not dominated by him'.[1] Although all this is vague in terms of time, and is coloured by the interest of all concerned to claim some share of whatever credit was due to the work of the Reunion, or to avoid antagonizing some of those who belonged to it, it indicates that for much of its duration the Club drew its support from deputies of all shades of radical opinion. This, indeed, is what the circumstances of its formation would lead us to expect.

Although nothing is known of its activities after the insurrection of 10 August, there seems much likelihood that it continued to be of considerable importance, particularly during the month of September. The fact that the prospectus is dated 21 September, the day of the first sitting of the Convention, suggests that it may have been designed to attract new deputies to the Club, and to keep them from the Jacobin Society.[2] Its summary of the purpose of its members as 'to expose and thwart the criminal plans of all enemies of the public good, and to disrupt all unpatriotic associations' could bear this interpretation. Moreover, it was on the same day that Guiraut, in the Jacobin Society, appealed to all patriots to assemble there, and to put an end to private meetings and private intrigues, words which were echoed two days later by Deperret, Collot d'Herbois, Chabot and Bourdon, as well as by Réal on 30 September. They were accompanied by allegations that the events of 10 August had been grossly misrepresented in the press, that part of the Convention was being abused as disruptive and anarchical, and that an effort was being made to keep the new deputies from the

---

[1] 'Un peu brissotin, je ne dis pas brissotière.' *Jacobins*, iv, 466.

[2] cp. Roland's announcement on 20 September of the availability of a room for the first meeting of the Convention: 'an announcement the more necessary since a notice by certain deputies of Paris invites their colleagues to meet this morning at the Jacobin Society'. *Moniteur*, xiii, 746.

Jacobin Society. These protests, and the proposal to exclude from the Society anyone who attended 'partial and exclusive societies such as the Reunion', culminated in Calon's announcement on 1 October that the members of the Reunion had resolved 'to return *en bloc* to the Jacobin Society and to amalgamate with it completely from henceforward'.

In sum, therefore, it seems likely that the policy of the Reunion was at first to resist an attempt at reaction, and that it later showed signs of hostility towards Robespierre and endeavoured to control and modify, if not to prevent, the insurrection which took place on 10 August. Later still, when the Convention first assembled, an attempt was probably made to make the Club a centre of attraction for the new deputies, and to prejudice them against Robespierre and the Jacobin Society. But to identify the Reunion with any specific party or faction remains difficult, and the paucity of the evidence precludes the making of any clear conclusions on this point.

It would however be inaccurate to leave the Reunion at Calon's bold announcement of its extinction. Although Thuriot had spoken on 1 October of the danger of the loss of two hundred members, Pétion, on 5 October, could report the return to the Jacobins of only 113 deputies, and renewed appeals to patriots to assemble only at the Jacobins culminated on 14 October in the final exclusion of all who had proved obdurate. This however is not proof that the Reunion continued to exist as a separate association, and although Mathiez refers to a statement by Sieyès as an indication that it may have survived even after the proscription of Brissot in June 1793,[1] the general absence of evidence suggests that it ceased to be of importance after what was clearly the Jacobin victory of October 1792.

MADAME ROLAND'S SALON[2]

The salon of Madame Roland is the best known of the private assemblies associated with the opposition to Robespierre, and a major count in the indictment against her at her trial was that

---

[1] Mathiez, *Girondins et Montagnards*, p. 80, and C. Perroud, 'Notice sur la vie de Sieyès', *La Révolution française*, xxii (1892), p. 269.

[2] Since the allegations of the Montagnards amount to little more than accusations of conspiracy and petticoat government, this section is based principally upon *Madame Roland*, i, *passim*, and ii, 314, 321-4, 440, 445. See also C. Perroud,

she had 'provided the leaders of the conspiracy with every facility for holding their secret councils, meetings of which she was herself the inspiration'. In the account which she wrote while in prison, Madame Roland explains that when Brissot visited her soon after her arrival in Paris, it was agreed that 'patriots' might meet regularly at her apartment, which was conveniently situated. This understanding was presumably reached soon after 20 February 1791, when the Rolands reached Paris from Lyons, the apartment in question being on the first floor of the Hotel Britannique, Rue Guenegaud. Although Madame Roland explains that few deputies visited her during the period of reaction which followed the King's flight to Varennes, the meetings apparently continued until Roland's work in Paris was completed and he and his wife returned to Lyons on 15 September 1791, a fortnight before the first meeting of the Legislative Assembly.

The Rolands returned to Paris on 15 December of the same year, but if Madame Roland's account is correct the salon was not immediately resumed. She explains that their friends of the Constituent Assembly had dispersed, and that even Brissot's visits were infrequent. The appointment of Roland as Minister of the Interior is the occasion of her next reference to her receptions, and it may well have been the occasion for their resumption—at the *Hôtel de l'Intérieur*. In all probability they continued until the dismissal of the ministry on 13 June 1792, and were again held during the second ministry, which began on 10 August 1792. The question whether the salon continued during the interval between the two ministries can only be answered tentatively, for Madame Roland herself writes principally of the times when her husband was in office. It is often alleged that Roland and his friends made great efforts to regain power during these three months, and, as we have seen,[1] it was then that Barbaroux's visits became frequent and that the possibility of withdrawing the seat of government beyond the Loire was discussed. On the other hand, Madame Roland

'Recherches sur le salon de Madame Roland en 1791' and 'Le premier ministère de Roland', *La Révolution française*, xxxvi (1899), p. 326 and xlii (1902), p. 511; Dauban, *Etude sur Madame Roland*; Champagneux, *Discours préliminaire*; and the references which follow.

[1] Above, Chapter III, p. 68.

subsequently denied that she had had any knowledge of the preparations for the insurrection of 10 August, a denial which Perroud accepts. Since some diminution of influence presumably followed the loss of the Ministry, it is likely that even if the Rolands continued to meet their friends their salon was no longer of the first importance during this period.

Madame Roland's own references to her first salon, as the meetings held at the time of the Constituent Assembly may be called, show that her friends assembled four times a week between the hours of the sittings of the Assembly and of the Jacobin Society, and that Pétion, Buzot, Brissot and Clavière formed the nucleus of a group united, as she says, by friendship and by common opinions.[1] She also explains that during the period of Roland's first ministry, in the early summer of 1792, her guests assembled twice a week. She then received the ministers on the Friday of each week, in accordance with an arrangement they had made amongst themselves to dine together on the days when the Executive Council met. On a second day, identified by Perroud as Monday, a wider variety of guests assembled, which included deputies. Women were not invited on either occasion. Madame Roland adds that meetings usually lasted from five o'clock until nine o'clock, and that the number of guests was usually fifteen, sometimes eighteen, and on one occasion twenty. What happened during the period of the second ministry is not specifically explained in the Memoirs, but presumably a similar course was followed.

In the Memoirs, which were written in prison, Madame Roland is naturally reticent about names, and on each of the two occasions when she was interrogated she insisted that only personal friends, and men with whom Roland had official business relations, were invited to her receptions. Her caution gives added authority to the few specific names she mentions, and her statement that Brissot, Pétion, Buzot, Barbaroux, Louvet, Guadet and Gensonné were regular visitors, Buzot coming particularly frequently, can be accepted without further question.

[1] Robespierre also visited her salon at this time, and Madame Roland's correspondence shows that she still regarded him as a friend when she left Paris in September 1791, but that the friendship died soon after her return to the capital in December 1791: *Madame Roland*, i, 62, 196; *Lettres de Madame Roland*, ii, 384, 413, 418; Thompson, *Robespierre*, i, 175, 223.

The evidence of her domestic staff, who were interrogated about her activities, is slightly less trustworthy. One of these servants, Fleury, the cook, flatly denied all knowledge of such matters. Lecocq, the porter, named Brissot, Buzot, Gensonné, Gorsas, Guadet and Louvet as the most frequent visitors. His position, and his refusal to speak ill of any of these men, enhance the value of his statement. Another employee, M'selle Mignet, tutor to Madame Roland's daughter, alleged that Brissot, Buzot, Gensonné, Gorsas and Louvet came most regularly, and that amongst others Barbaroux, Chasset, Condorcet, Deperret, Duprat, Guadet, Pétion and Vergniaud were also often present. This witness was obviously hostile to her mistress, but her evidence cannot be disregarded. For example, a statement by Madame Roland that Deperret, one of those named by M'selle Mignet, did not visit her after Roland's final fall from office implies that he had done so before then. On the other hand the well-known antipathy between Madame Roland and Vergniaud makes it improbable that he came often, as the tutor alleged.

Some additional evidence about Madame Roland's guests is also available from other sources. Dufriche-Valazé, for example, admitted when he was interrogated that he had dined twice with the Rolands in January 1793.[1] The attack made upon the salon by Anacharsis Cloots in the pamphlet *Ni Marat ni Roland*, and the replies which it evoked,[2] are also informative. Cloots alleged that he was introduced to Roland on 5 September 1792, and was invited to dine at the *Hôtel de l'Intérieur* by Lanthénas on behalf of Madame Roland. According to his account, Buzot, Bancal des Issarts, Barbaroux and Rebecquy were amongst those he met as guests. A reply published by Bancal confirms his presence on this particular occasion, and another written by Guadet shows that he too was familiar with the salon and with visits to it by Gensonné.

Thus the evidence shows that Brissot, Buzot, Gensonné, Guadet, Louvet, Pétion, Barbaroux and perhaps Rebecquy[3] were probably regular visitors; that Gorsas, Bancal, Deperret

---

[1] A.N., w.292.204, Part 5, No. 17.
[2] *Ni Marat ni Roland: Opinion d'Anacharsis Cloots; Réponses au prussien Cloots par Roland, Kersaint, Guadet et Brissot; Un mot d'Anacharsis Cloots sur les conférences secrètes;* and *Henri Bancal . . . à Anacharsis Cloots son collègue* (Paris, 1792), B.M., f.775.3, f.776.5 and 6, and f.777.2.   [3] *Correspondance de Barbaroux*, letter cxxvii.

and Lanthénas were probably present frequently; and that Duprat, Chasset, Condorcet, Valazé and Vergniaud were also probably there on occasion. If the ministers and a few occasional callers are added to the seven or eight who seem most likely to have been present regularly, Madame Roland's figure of about fifteen guests seems reasonably accurate.

Unfortunately our knowledge of this otherwise comparatively well-documented salon does not extend to any certainty about what happened there, beyond the fact that the receptions were obviously concerned with politics. Madame Roland herself admitted that from the time of her first arrival in Paris, in February 1791, deputies came to her apartment to discuss public affairs, and there is no reason to suppose that this ceased to be so in 1792. Beyond this, however, she said very little about what occurred. She claimed that occasionally some specific proposals were made, which were subsequently put forward and accepted in the National Assembly in 1791, but in general she tended to disparage her visitors in her memoirs, remarking that for all their discussion they could never agree upon any definite policy. Certainly there is no evidence that any particular measures originated at her receptions in 1792: there are only allegations and denials. It was commonly alleged, particularly by Cloots, that the salon favoured some sort of federalist solution to the difficulties of France, but beyond the admission that Buzot once spoke of the difficulty of applying republican government to so large a country, and the fact that, as has been said, the possibility of withdrawing the government from Paris was once discussed with Barbaroux, there is nothing to support the allegation. The pamphlets which were written in reply to Cloots suggest that the discussion on the particular evening to which he referred had been more academic than practical, and Madame Roland herself dismissed his accusation as the vindictive outpourings of a man injured in his self-esteem by the intellectual superiority of his fellow-guests. She consistently maintained that the talk at her table was concerned either with the administrative problems of her husband's Ministry, or with public affairs in general terms.

But even if the conversation was as abstract as she suggests, it is unlikely that the salon was without positive political influence. The recrimination which followed Cloots's visit at least shows that a certain conformity of opinion existed amongst those who were regular visitors, although whether Madame Roland was in any way personally responsible for this must remain uncertain. According to her own account, she knew what was expected of one of her sex, and so sat apart from her guests during their discussions, busying herself with her letters. She adds, however, that as she was able to concentrate on different subjects simultaneously she seldom missed a word that was spoken, and often had to bite her lips to avoid comment. Her husband's position naturally put her in the centre of affairs, and it seems likely that on at least two important occasions in 1792—in his letter of admonition to the King on 10 June, and in his condemnation of the massacres in September—he acted on her advice.[1] Thus although there is no direct proof that positive policies were prepared at her salon, the probability appears to be that her influence was considerable, and that her guests represented a political attitude in general conformity with her own views.

It does not however seem likely that the salon retained any influence after Roland's final resignation from the Ministry on 22 January 1793. On three occasions Madame Roland claimed that her relationship with the deputies ceased at that time, and Perroud has accepted this claim, pointing out that although the Rolands continued to receive their more intimate friends, many deputies avoided them when they became unpopular in Paris, while their own efforts were concentrated on pressing for some official recognition of Roland's financial probity, which they were determined to obtain before they left the capital.

THE COMITÉ VALAZÉ[2]

The growth of the assemblies held by Dufriche-Valazé and his wife is comparatively easy to trace. Arriving in Paris as a deputy

---

[1] Dauban, *Etude sur Madame Roland*, pp. cxi and cxxvii–cxxxiii.

[2] This section is based upon the trial of Brissot, *Moniteur*, xviii, 241, 256, 265; the *Interrogations* of the accused deputies, A.N., w.292.204, Part 5, Nos. 4, 6, 9, 15, 17 (Valazé), 23; *Madame Roland*, particularly ii, 303; *Mémoires de Meillan*, pp. 1–15 and 37; *Mémoires de Louvet*, i, 79; *Mémoires de R.D.G.* (Desgenettes), pp. 222–9; *Valazé, passim; Vergniaud*, p. 70; Vatel, *Charlotte de Corday et les Girondins*, i, p. lxxxix, and ii, pp. 339 and 402; and the references which follow.

for the Orne on 29 September 1792, he took a large apartment in the Rue d'Orléans St. Honoré, and there, according to his own statement in a letter to his constituents dated 26 January 1793, a considerable number of his colleagues began soon afterwards to meet. Other evidence shows that these meetings became politically significant at the time of Louis XVI's trial, which began on 26 December 1792. At his interrogation, Brissot said that Valazé's friends had been particularly concerned to secure the submission of the sentence passed on the King to a referendum—the famous 'appeal to the people', a proposal first made in the Convention on 28 December 1792. Further, in his biography of Valazé, Paul Nicolle has published a report of the commissioners of the Section Halle au Blé who were sent on 27 January 1793, to investigate rumours of illegal meetings in the Rue d'Orléans. This report[1] includes a statement by Valazé's concierge, citizeness Lescarlot, that the meetings had begun at the time of the trial. Nicolle's conclusion, that they had begun late in December, and had become known to the Jacobins late in January, after the inquiry by the Section and a possible interception of Valazé's letter of 26 January, corresponds with the known facts and may be accepted with the reservation that the meetings may have begun at an earlier date, as Valazé claimed.

Their form was again that of the salon, but interesting differences are apparent between these assemblies and those held by Madame Roland and by Vergniaud. One peculiarity lies in their frequency. At his interrogation Valazé said that they sometimes took place once a week, and sometimes three or four times, but both his concierge and his daughter spoke of them as daily occurrences, as indeed he himself did on another occasion. Moreover, definite efforts seem to have been made to bring together as many deputies as possible. When they were under examination, Brissot said that Valazé was responsible for the invitations, Boilleau alleged that Valazé had pressed him to attend, and Fauchet agreed that he had been invited many times, by Barbaroux and perhaps by Guadet. Indeed, most of the available evidence suggests that the salon was well attended. The highest figure is the estimate of between forty and fifty

[1] *Valazé*, p. 135, citing A.N., F.7.4775.37.

CHARLES ELÉONORE DUFRICHE-VALAZÉ

JEAN BAPTISTE LOUVET DE COUVRAI

given by the concierge Lescarlot to the commissioners of the local Section. She probably spoke of both sexes, for ladies were present,[1] and may have said what the commissioners hoped to hear, but both Saint Just and Madame Roland referred on other occasions to the attendance as forty members of the Convention, while Brissot put the number at between thirty and forty. Smaller figures were given by Meillan, who mentions 'twelve, fifteen, or sometimes more', and by Lehardy, who told the magistrates that he had seen seven or eight men and women at Valazé's. On balance, it would at least seem that the number of guests was usually considerably larger than that at the salons of either Madame Roland or of Vergniaud.

Useful evidence about the names of those present was given by Valazé himself, who referred to individuals on three occasions—in a letter to his constituents on 21 January 1793; at his interrogation; and at his trial. Those he named are: Barbaroux, Buzot and Salle (all named three times); Brissot, Chambon, Duprat, Gensonné, Guadet, Lacaze and Lidon (all named twice); and Bergoeing, Deperret, Grangeneuve, Hardy, Lehardy, Lesage and Mollevaut (all named in one instance only). Some of these deputies later admitted their visits: Brissot acknowledged two or three, Meillan, in his Memoirs, said that he was there every evening; he spoke also of the presence of Louvet (whose own Memoirs confirm this); Duprat admitted four or five visits, and Lehardy one. Duchâstel, too, agreed under examination that he had been to Valazé's two or three times in May 1793.

In addition to this first-hand evidence, there is that of other witnesses who seem reasonably reliable. Valazé's daughter told the historian Vatel of her memories of Barbaroux, Gensonné, Guadet, Louvet, Pétion and Gorsas, saying that the first four of these were frequent visitors. Only Pétion's presence is unconfirmed by other evidence. Again, Valazé's nephew, Desgenettes, wrote of the presence of Grangeneuve, Guadet, Buzot and Salle, as well as of Rabaut St. Etienne and Valazé's neighbour,

---

[1] Desgenettes speaks of his aunt and his cousin as well as of the wives of the deputies Ricord and Girard; Valazé's daughter told Vatel of Madame Louvet and of Madame Pétion and her daughter. *Mémoires de R.D.G.*, p. 222, and Vatel, *Charlotte de Corday*, ii, 402.

H

Girard. The Jacobin, Réal, who lived in the house as a lodger, named Barbaroux and Gorsas as guests, and, as has been said, Fauchet spoke of Barbaroux and Guadet.

This evidence makes it possible to compile a fairly reliable list of those who were among Valazé's visitors. By their own admissions, Brissot, Duchâstel, Duprat, Lehardy, Louvet and Meillan were sometimes present. In the other evidence, Barbaroux's name is mentioned six times, Guadet's five times, and those of Buzot and Salle four times each; Gensonné's name occurs three times, and those of Chambon, Gorsas, Grangeneuve, Lacaze and Lidon occur twice; Bergoeing, Deperret, Hardy, Lesage and Mollevaut were mentioned once by Valazé, and Girard, Pétion and Rabaut St. Etienne were named by one other witness. Including Valazé himself, this gives a total of twenty-five names, a figure corresponding reasonably well with the average of those given by both friendly and hostile witnesses and again suggesting that attendance at Valazé's salon was comparatively large.

Apparently meetings usually lasted from about nine o'clock until midnight, and the evidence of Valazé's daughter suggests that in the course of the evening the deputies separated from the ladies, who awaited the end of their discussions in an adjacent room. Both she and her cousin, Desgenettes, agreed that these discussions were political, and both Brissot and Valazé admitted that the object of the assemblies was the preparation of business for discussion at the Convention. Vatel, indeed, concluded that Valazé and his friends formed a preparatory committee for parliamentary business; but the size and frequency of their assemblies, as well as the apparent endeavour to recruit new friends, seem more suggestive of an attempt at wider organization. An effort to persuade deputies with common sympathies to act together with some measure of system certainly seems likely at this time, when Brissot and his friends were being bitterly attacked in the Convention by a dissident Montagnard minority. When pressed by the examining magistrate, Valazé indeed admitted that his guests had agreed to be punctual in their attendance at the Convention, and the note which he sent to thirty or forty deputies, denounced as a scandalous abuse on 23 May 1793, had that very purpose. If indeed this was an attempt to create a bloc of deputies who would concert their efforts to resist the Mountain, the *Comité Valazé* would appear to be more what Lefebvre has called it in his introduction to Nicolle's biography of Valazé, a party headquarters, than the preparatory committee seen by Vatel. Valazé's meetings first became important as a centre of the attempt to refer the sentence passed on Louis XVI to the people for ratification. Whether this attempt reflected a genuine sympathy for the monarchy or whether it was intended as a device to out-manœuvre Robespierre, the deputies who met in the Rue d'Orléans were certainly united by their opposition to the Montagnards. According to Meillan, a veritable state of war existed in the Convention after the King had been executed,[1] and the deputies who met at Valazé's did so to seek some means of ending the conflict or of avoiding the disasters it was expected to bring. Valazé himself went further than this: in his letter to his constituents on 26 January he claimed that his receptions should be given credit for any victories that the Convention had won over the ill-disposed, and on 25 May he told the Convention that the purpose of his meetings was to thwart the plots of 'malignant slanderers'. Later, at his interrogation, he endeavoured to distinguish between these slanderers and the Montagnards, but the distinction seems desperately equivocal. Fauchet, apparently less directly concerned with this particular charge, said in similar circumstances that he understood the object of the deputies who met at Valazé's was 'to oppose the plans of the deputies of the left, the Montagnards'.

There is little evidence to suggest that this opposition to the Mountain ever led to the adoption of any more positive policies. Louvet states that he was instructed by the *Comité Valazé* to denounce in the Convention the plot which he alleged to underlie the disorders in Paris on 10 March 1793, but when he did so he had little support. Nicolle, Valazé's biographer, has only an allegation by Marat on 23 May to support his belief that the group sponsored Guadet's proposal on 18 May to order the dissolution of the Commune of Paris and to summon an emergency parliament at Bourges, and he does not prove his assertion that it was a centre of federalist propaganda. On the other

---

[1] Not, in reality, immediately after the execution: cp. Chapter VII below.

hand, the house was undoubtedly a haven for those deputies who believed that plans had been prepared for the massacre of all but the most radical members of the Convention. Valazé told the magistrate who examined him that this plan had almost matured on the night of 10 March, and had been revived in the middle of May. Duchâstel and Meillan told similar stories. This rather hysterical credulity seems typical of this group of deputies, for there is no real evidence to support Vatel's designation of them as men of action. Both Meillan and Valazé said that each man's opinion differed from that of his neighbour, and Madame Roland, while praising their principles, said that motions, not measures, were the only results of their conferences. The note in which Valazé urged his friends to attend the next session of the Convention 'with arms in their hands'[1] again seems more compatible with panic than with any constructive policy. Fauchet's comment, that the members of this group were more remarkable for 'their excessive and self-opinionated conceit' than for any tendency towards conspiracy, seems nearer to the truth than does Vatel's encomium.

In general, the *Comité Valazé* appears as a political assembly different in kind from the smaller and more exclusive salons of Vergniaud and Madame Roland. These have the appearance of political groups, but the size of Valazé's group, the frequency of its meetings, its invitations, the preponderance of comparatively unimportant men and the apparent influence of hotheads, all suggest that it represented an attempt to organize, from among the rank and file of the Convention, something like a party of resistance to Robespierre. Any more positive policy appears improbable, for Saint Just's allegation that it planned a mass assassination of Montagnards is of little significance. The group's feverish opposition to the Mountain may have led some of these deputies to call for assistance from their Departments in the critical days of May 1793, but the evidence is against the probability that they ever acted as a united body. Their meetings, which were certainly continuing at the time of Valazé's

---

[1] 'In arms at the assembly at ten o'clock precisely. Only cowards will not come. Warn all our colleagues whom you can.' *Moniteur*, xvi, 459, and Mortimer-Ternaux, vii, 253. Cp. A.N., w.292.204, Part 3, No. 38, a page in Valazé's hand which asserts that only self-defence was envisaged on this occasion.

clash with Marat in the Convention on 23 May, clearly ended on 2 June, when Valazé himself was placed under guard, even though he still received many visitors while supervised by the police.

Contemporary records contain many references to other places where deputies hostile to the Mountain are said to have assembled. Mention is made of dinners given by Pétion, of meetings at the houses of Defermon, Doulcet, Couppé, Bernard de Saintes and Venua, and of assemblies in the salons of Madame Condorcet, Madame de Staël and Madame Talma. When the revolution of 2 June 1793 began, several of those who anticipated arrest awaited the outcome at Meillan's apartment near the Tuileries, and soon afterwards Pétion evaded his guards during a visit to a meeting of deputies in Masuyer's rooms. None of these assemblies seem of sufficient importance to the present study to warrant detailed examination, but their existence is significant. It indicates how fine was the distinction between normal social activities and political liaisons, and suggests that private political discussion was the natural corollary of an attempt at government by ill-organized and interminable debate. On the other hand the Montagnards' references to such gatherings show that they regarded them with considerable suspicion. Thus on 21 September 1792, Guiraut said that as the days of disunity were over, all patriots and friends of the people must be ceaselessly under the public eye. Nine days later Réal repeated this exhortation, saying that the true friends of the people were those who served them in public, and that private meetings were injurious to the public interest.[1] Whether it was to Brissot in 1791 that he spoke, as he alleged at the trial, or whether his words were addressed only to the Revolutionary Tribunal, Chabot struck at the Achilles heel of Brissot and his friends when he said: 'Since the people are on our side we are not afraid to act in the open.'

Of the four assemblies which have been examined here, three follow the form of the salon. The fourth, the Reunion Club, was different, being a political club, distinct from the Jacobin

---

[1] *Jacobins*, iv, 319, 352.

Society in its restriction of membership to deputies and in the privacy of its meetings. The evidence suggests that the salons and the club existed rather in succession than simultaneously. If their periods of probable maximum importance are considered, a series emerges fairly clearly, i.e., Madame Roland's first salon (February to September 1791), Vergniaud's salon (mid-autumn 1791 to September 1792), Madame Roland's second salon (March to June 1792), the Reunion Club (June to October 1792), Madame Roland's third salon (August 1792 to January 1793) and Valazé's salon (December 1792 to May 1793). Further, analysis of the names of those who can be shown to have been present at these meetings[1] shows that Brissot and Gensonné were present at all four of them, and that a limited but increasing number of deputies met together with these two fairly regularly over a period of about eighteen months. These conclusions are interesting supplementary evidence of the development of a 'connection' around Brissot and his closest friends.

The evidence about these 'secret meetings of the Girondins' does not, however, afford sufficient ground to show that the connection ever formulated or tried to effect any policy more specific than that of resistance to Robespierre and the Montagnards. This defensive attitude is apparent even in the alleged preparations by Vergniaud and his friends of their attacks upon the 'Austrian Committee', and thereafter it becomes ever more obvious. Further, all the evidence indicates that the men who attended these assemblies remained independent both in thought and in action. Perpetual indecision and persistent individualism appear to be the hall-marks of their private meetings.

---

[1] See Appendix B.

CHAPTER V

The Brissotins in the Legislative Assembly

THERE were in the Legislative Assembly thirty-eight deputies whom historians have classified as Girondins. Of these,
Brissot, Condorcet, Jean Debry, Ducos, Fauchet, Gensonné,
Grangeneuve, Guadet, Isnard, Lasource and Vergniaud are
probably the best known. Coustard, Dusaulx, Gamon, Henri-
Larivière, Kersaint, Masuyer, Rouyer and Saladin occasionally
intervened in debates, and the remaining deputies spoke seldom
or not at all.[1] The actions and attitudes during this period of
some other future members of the Convention, such as Pétion,
Manuel, Louvet, Gorsas and Carra, who were prominent in the
political life of Paris although they were not members of the
Assembly, may also be of interest.

As we have seen, a fairly close connection existed between
many of these deputies by 1792. Early in that year Brissot,
Condorcet, Ducos, Gensonné and Vergniaud were meeting in
private and in all probability discussing political problems.
After the appointment of Roland as Minister of the Interior,
similar meetings, to which Louvet and Pétion were probably
invited, took place at the Ministry, and later Isnard and
Lasource seem to have been associated with Brissot and the
deputies of the Gironde in the Reunion Club. Moreover, Bancal
des Issarts, Carra, Gorsas, Lanthénas and Manuel, to name no
others, had personal associations with some members of the
same group. But although private meetings and ties of personal
friendship are strongly suggestive of some similarity of opinion,

[1] Of the deputies named here, some took their seats at a late stage: Dusaulx,
Gamon and Kersaint entered the Assembly on 6 June, 15 March and 2 April 1792,
respectively. Olivier-Gerente came still later, on 27 August, and is not included in
the thirty-eight to whom reference is made. The 'remaining deputies' are: Andrei,
Belin, Bohan, Corbel, Descamps, Despinassy, Faye, Fiquet, Giroust, Laplaigne,
Lauze-Deperret, Lebreton, P. Louvet, Loysel, Moreau, Rivery, Salmon, Soubeyran
and Tocquet.

they do not necessarily imply continuous conformity in public conduct. Deductions about the formation of a political group remain dependent upon examination of these deputies' reactions to the principal problems of the time, and in the present and the following chapters this examination is essayed.

THE RADICAL LEADERS OF THE LEGISLATIVE ASSEMBLY

It seems very probable that it was the colonial question, one of the first problems to confront the deputies in the Legislative Assembly, which first drew Brissot, as he later said, towards the deputies of the Gironde.[1] He had long been an opponent of slavery and the slave-trade, and in the Constituent Assembly the members of the club he had founded, *Les Amis des Noirs*, had helped to secure the passing of the decree of 15 May 1791, which granted mulattos some share in the government of San Domingo. When subsequently news of a revolt in the colony was received in Paris, both Brissot and Guadet suggested that the reports were exaggerated, and opposed precipitate action. Brissot later endeavoured to ascribe all responsibility for the rising to a group of wealthy 'colonials' led in the Constituent Assembly by Barnave, claiming that it was their action in modifying the decree of 15 May which had excited the rebellion. Guadet, Gensonné, Vergniaud, Ducos and Lasource were amongst those who supported Brissot in his attempt to ensure that any troops sent to the island should protect the whites and the mulattos alike, and not be used only to consolidate the supremacy of the planters. In this matter these five deputies were the leading advocates of a policy more liberal than that favoured by the majority of speakers, though minor differences of opinion amongst them suggest that they were supporting the same principles without having reached any precise agreement together.[2] A similar attitude was also taken by Guadet,

---

[1] At his trial: *Moniteur*, xviii, 250. See also Ellery, *Brissot de Warville*, chapter viii.

[2] See the reports of debates in the *Moniteur*, x, 517–21, 534, 540–76 and xi, 512–19, 690–719. The lack of precise agreement is apparent, e.g., on 3 December 1791, when Guadet and Vergniaud urged simpler and quicker measures than those supported by Brissot (*ibid.*, x, 540).

Vergniaud, Lasource and Grangeneuve towards the proposal to grant a general amnesty to all those who had been concerned in the bloodshed which had occurred during the revolution in Avignon.[1] In both these matters, as well as in others under discussion at this time, Brissot and those who were probably becoming associated with him supported policies which were liberal or even radical.

Before any decision on any of these comparatively unimportant questions had been reached, the Assembly was distracted by the more pressing problem of counter-revolution. Many of the nobility, including the King's brothers, had left France, and were threatening the new *régime* from beyond the frontiers. This question of the *émigrés* led to a campaign for a declaration of war against Austria, their supposed protector, and this was to be a matter of considerable importance for Brissot and his friends. He and Carra, the editor of *Les Annales patriotiques*, had long deplored the weakness they found in French foreign policy. In his speech on 20 October 1791, Brissot urged the Assembly to strike resolutely at the headquarters of the *émigrés* at Coblentz, and to use force against any foreign power which dared to interfere. In his view, an open conflict would be less dangerous to France than the cold war[2] to which the foreign intrigues of counter-revolutionaries were subjecting her.[3] In the same month Vergniaud, in the Assembly, and Carra, in the Jacobin Society, spoke in favour of offensive action, while Isnard's fiery rhetoric stirred the passions of deputies and Jacobins alike.[4] In November, Lasource demanded rearmament. In December, the agitation for war increased, and amongst others Lasource, Condorcet, Manuel, Sillery, Gensonné, Guadet, Bancal and Louvet gave it their support. Jean Debry and Grangeneuve adopted the prevailing bellicose

---

[1] Sagnac, *La Révolution* (in Lavisse, *Histoire de France contemporaine*), i, 334, and *Moniteur*, x, 398, 647, 673–4.

[2] An appropriate modern equivalent. Brissot spoke of 'une guerre de plume', Vergniaud of 'une guerre de préparatifs' and 'une guerre cachée' (*Moniteur*, xi, 148, 157–8).

[3] Brissot, *Patriote français*, 28 July, 11 and 20 August, 6 and 8 October 1791, and *Moniteur*, x, 163. See also *ibid.*, x, 239, 753 and xi, 597, and *Journal*, 16 and 30 December 1791 and 20 January 1792.

[4] Vergniaud: *Moniteur*, x, 207, 261, 740; Carra: *Journal*, 9 and 24 October, 11 and 25 December 1791; Isnard: *Moniteur*, x, 268, 503, 728.

attitude in January 1792, when Fauchet also demanded an assault upon Austria.[1]

These demands may not have been altogether spontaneous. Brissot, Isnard, Condorcet and Clavière were already consorting at the salon of Madame de Staël with a group of royalists led by Narbonne, the Minister of War, who was seeking support for that short and successful war which he hoped would rally patriotic opinion to the throne and serve to consolidate royal authority.[2] Moreover, Etienne Dumont later alleged that Brissot and the deputies of the Gironde discussed at the Place Vendôme ways in which they could out-manœuvre Robespierre, and some developments in the Jacobin Society might be interpreted as indications of such collaboration. Thus Brissot and Isnard, who hardly appeared in the Jacobins in September and October, spoke there frequently after mid-November, when they became exponents of the war-policy, and the Jacobin Correspondence Committee, on which Brissot and several of his friends were influential, drafted and despatched bellicose circulars to the provincial clubs in spite of Robespierre's protests. Similarly, the clashes over the order of business at the Jacobin Society on 26 and 29 January 1792, and Gorsas's misrepresentation in the *Courrier* of 22 January of a supposed reconciliation between Robespierre and Brissot, are perhaps suggestive of some private agreement.[3]

This possibility of collaboration should not however be taken to mean that all those who were accused with Brissot were in full accord at this time. Some of them took no public part in the debates about the war, and Masuyer even openly opposed it. Differing opinions and variations of emphasis are apparent, too,

---

[1] *Moniteur*, x, 728 (Guadet, Louvet), 735 (Gensonné), 762 (Condorcet), and xi, 21 (Debry), 133–4 (Lasource, Debry and Grangeneuve), 177 (Fauchet); *Journal*, 25 November (Lasource), 18 December (Sillery), 27 December (Manuel and Bancal), 9 and 16 January 1792 (Louvet); and Condorcet, *Chronique de Paris*, e.g., 11 January 1792.

[2] See, e.g., Dumouriez, *Mémoires*, ii, 132; Lacretelle, *Précis historique de la Révolution française: Assemblée législative*, pp. 124–6, 141; and the letters of Pellenc to the comte de la Marck, cited and discussed by Lefebvre, *La Chute du Roi*, pp. 38, 56.

[3] For the activities of the Correspondence Committee, see *Jacobins*, iii, 323, 376, 410, 412, *Journal*, 145–51, and Michon, *Robespierre et la guerre révolutionnaire, 1791–1792*, p. 78. For the supposed reconciliation, see *Courrier*, 22 January 1792, *Patriote français*, 21 January 1792, Michon, *op. cit.*, p. 67, Walter, *Robespierre*, p. 258, and *Correspondance de Robespierre*, i, 135.

in the views expressed by the more prominent speakers. Guadet and Gensonné did not wholly commit themselves to support for war until the comparatively late date of January 1792. Lasource, like Jean Debry, was moderate in attitude, and hesitated even on 20 April, when war was finally declared. Fauchet's call, on 20 January, for a limited offensive, was in sharp contrast to Brissot's more ambitious projects, and Condorcet's first proposals were opposed by Brissot and Vergniaud in debate as well as in the press. Condorcet himself hesitated in January, and Vergniaud's speeches, carefully phrased and arriving at tentative conclusions, read very differently from those of such men as Brissot, Carra and Isnard.

The debates in general suggest that a small group of deputies, of whom the most prominent were Brissot and Isnard, made themselves the spokesmen of those who desired a declaration of war. This campaign was on the whole supported by Vergniaud, and was advocated also by Guadet and Gensonné, who had previously associated themselves with Brissot in the debates about San Domingo. Condorcet was sympathetic, and eventually Lasource, Fauchet, Jean Debry and Grangeneuve adopted a similar attitude. It has sometimes been suggested[1] that in urging France on to war these men were the spokesmen of mercantile interests, but this is a hypothesis which has never been adequately examined. The association of Brissot and his friends with such democratic exiles from other countries as Clavière is however demonstrable, and these exiles were undoubtedly pressing for a revolutionary crusade, which incidentally would put them into authority in their own countries. The danger from abroad, too, certainly appeared much greater then than it is now known to have been in reality. However, political ambition, the belief that the war would promote their own political interests without adversely affecting the mercantile interests of such great ports as Bordeaux, has generally been taken as their strongest incentive.

These deputies' radicalism in foreign affairs is reflected in a hostile attitude towards the King and his ministers—although the events which followed suggest that few of them were in reality as implacable as they would have had either the King or

[1] e.g., by Professor Lefebvre, *La Révolution française*, p. 225.

Robespierre believe. The first phase of their attack upon the Court naturally coincided with the demand for a declaration of war, for the King was strongly suspected of supporting the *émigrés*, and Brissot believed that open war would compel him to reveal his real attitude towards the Revolution. As he said in the Jacobin Club on 16 December 1791, 'the accepted leader of the nation will be forced to rule in accordance with the Constitution. If he does his duty, we will support him whole-heartedly. If he betrays us—the people will be ready.'[1] The group which in the Assembly or in the Jacobins threatened and abused the King and attacked his ministers for their alleged treachery and vacillation was therefore almost identical with that which had led the demand for war. Brissot, Isnard, Guadet, Gensonné, Vergniaud, Carra and Lasource were again the leaders of the attack, and they were supported from time to time by Condorcet, Grangeneuve, Fauchet, Bancal, Sillery, Gorsas, Manuel, Louvet and Jean Debry.[2]

Criticism of the Court, however, did not end with the out-break of war. It continued until the fall of the ministry led by Delessart and the appointment on 10 March 1792 of that in which the offices of Minister of the Interior and Minister of Justice were at first both held by Roland, the friend of Brissot and the deputies of the Gironde. Clavière, another of Brissot's friends, became Minister of Finance, and shortly afterwards Servan replaced de Grave as Minister of War, probably on Madame Roland's recommendation. According to Dumont, the overthrow of Delessart had been put forward by Brissot as an essential objective for the deputies who assembled at Verg-niaud's salon and had been described by him as 'a good party move'.[3] The matter was probably arranged in collaboration with Narbonne, whom Delessart had dismissed from office and whom Brissot and his associates defended in the Jacobin

---

[1] Buchez and Roux, *Histoire parlementaire*, xii, 409.

[2] See the speeches referred to above, p. 102, n. 1, and *Moniteur*, x, 163, 261, 268, 332, and xi, 15, 27, 117, for more particular expressions of hostility to the throne by Brissot, Vergniaud, Isnard, Guadet, and Gensonné respectively. Further evidence may be found in the published *Discours* of Carra, Lasource, Sillery, Manuel and Louvet (B.M., F.337.26, F.338.6, F.336.23, F.338.4 and F.336.28 respectively).

[3] For the appointment of the ministry, see Dumouriez, *Mémoires*, i, 424 ff., *Madame Roland*, i, 67 ff., and C. Perroud, 'Le premier ministère de Roland', *La Révolution française*, xlii (1902). For Dumont, *Souvenirs sur Mirabeau*, p. 203.

Society,[1] as well as with Dumouriez, Gensonné's associate, who as Minister of Foreign Affairs was the true head of the new administration. Certainly Brissot, Isnard, Guadet, Gensonné and Vergniaud were prominent in the attacks which were made upon Delessart in the Assembly and in the Jacobin Society; Condorcet, Fauchet, Grangeneuve, Carra and Sillery also participated in these, and Rouyer, Ducos, and Larivière spoke more cautiously in support.[2]

The appointment of Roland was followed by a quieter period, a fact which seems to confirm the accuracy of a comment to the King that 'the conduct of these gentlemen in committee is very different from the attitude they adopt in the Assembly'.[3] They had in reality little control of the Executive Council,[4] for Lacoste at the Ministry of Marine and Duranthon, called from the Gironde to take over the Ministry of Justice, were both nearer to Dumouriez and the Court than to Brissot, whose friends could now do little but procrastinate. On 15 May, however, Isnard cautioned the King against giving any encouragement to counter-revolution, and a new display of hostility towards the Court followed as Brissot, Vergniaud, Guadet and Gensonné attacked the 'Austrian Committee', the intriguers whom they alleged to be prejudicing the King against the Constitution, and as Lasource, Condorcet, Fauchet, Rouyer, Debry, Ducos, Kersaint, Masuyer and Saladin joined in condemnation and warning.[5]

---

[1] See above, p. 102, n. 2, and *Jacobins*, iii, 524 ff. For the earlier attitude towards Narbonne, see, e.g., *Moniteur*, x, 603, 636, and xii, 20, 73, and *Chronique de Paris*, 13 December 1791.

[2] e.g., *Moniteur*, xi, 594–7 (Brissot, Gensonné), 604 (Isnard, Vergniaud), 616 (Guadet), 631 (Guadet, Gensonné); *Journal*, 7 and 14 March 1792 (Carra, Sillery, Grangeneuve). See also Cahen, *Condorcet et la Révolution française*, pp. 296–300, Charrier, *Claude Fauchet*, i, 170–5, and for Ducos, Larivière and Rouyer, *Moniteur*, xi, 279, 604 and 544, 561 respectively.

[3] Report of Ruhl to the Convention on the letters found in the *armoire de fer*, 3 December 1792 (*Moniteur*, xiv, 640), continuing 'We have found them reasonable. They want an effective government.'

[4] Since the composition of the Council was so mixed, the common term 'Girondin Ministry' is misleading. For its convenient identification reference is sometimes made here to it as the 'Roland Ministry', but its character is better indicated by Professor Lefebvre's description, the 'Ministry of Dumouriez'. Lefebvre, *La Révolution française*, p. 233.

[5] *Moniteur*, xii, 392 (Isnard), 418 (Fauchet, Saladin), 431 (Vergniaud, Guadet, Gensonné, Lasource, Masuyer), 462–5 (Gensonné, Brissot), 468 (Rouyer, Kersaint,

These expressions of dissatisfaction, however, served only to aggravate the situation. On 13 June, after Roland had presented the King with a particularly blunt warning of the dangers to which his reluctance to sanction popular policies was exposing him,[1] he and his two colleagues, Clavière and Servan, were dismissed from their posts. The attacks upon the Court in the Assembly and the Jacobin Society were then renewed by Guadet, Brissot, Vergniaud, Gensonné and Isnard. Debry, Lasource and Condorcet gave strong support, and Ducos, Grangeneuve, Rouyer, Fauchet, Manuel, Kersaint, Dusaulx, Gamon and Pétion, now Mayor of Paris, spoke in sympathy.[2] Moreover, although the evidence remains obscure, it is possible that some of these men may have given some encouragement to those responsible for the invasion of the Tuileries on 20 June, a demonstration which seemed to favour the recall of Roland to the Ministry.

The general course of these developments therefore shows that Brissot, Guadet, Gensonné, Vergniaud and Isnard were leaders of the attack upon the Court. The regularity with which their names appear and the similarity of their views and conduct are suggestive of some co-operation between them. Lasource and Jean Debry, too, seem to have been fairly close to them, particularly in the later stages, while Condorcet supported their attitude in his journal and in his occasional speeches. All these men save Isnard and Debry had previously supported the cause of the mulattos in San Domingo, and all had advocated the declaration of war against Austria. The general conformity of their views and conduct, and the personal friendships which existed between several of them, provide considerable support for the supposition that they constituted something like a parliamentary group at least superficially radical in tendency.

Ducos), 525–8 (Guadet, Lasource, Debry, Vergniaud), and Condorcet, *Chronique de Paris*, 30–1 May 1792.

[1] Two decrees, one sanctioning the assembly of provincial troops near Paris and one imposing severe penalties upon recalcitrant priests, were awaiting the royal assent.

[2] e.g., *Moniteur*, xii, 656 (Guadet, Vergniaud, Debry, Lasource, Dusaulx), 719 (Isnard), and xiii, 25 (Masuyer), 92 (Gamon), 97 (Condorcet; see also Cahen, *op. cit.*, 394, 406), 122 (Rouyer), 155 (Manuel), 217 (Brissot, Gensonné, Ducos, Kersaint), 248 (Fauchet), 271 (Grangeneuve), and 324 (Pétion).

THE BREAK BETWEEN BRISSOT AND ROBESPIERRE

A proper appreciation of the position of these men nevertheless implies some consideration of the course of developments in the Jacobin Society, for in the Assembly all those with pretensions to radicalism stood together against the majority whose sympathies were with the King.[1] In the Jacobin Club, however, a distinction between the supporters of Brissot and those of Robespierre became apparent when the desirability of war against Austria was in question. Robespierre was from the first severely critical of the expediency of trusting the fortunes of the nation to the direction of ministers and generals whom he regarded as the secret enemies of the people, and he disliked the irresponsibility of deputies who could deliberately contemplate placing the people in a position in which their safety might depend upon the doubtful outcome of an armed insurrection. Where Brissot maintained that counter-revolution could best be defeated by an immediate attack upon Austria, its foreign fountain-head, Robespierre believed that a successful campaign could only be undertaken by a united nation, and that it was therefore essential to consolidate the revolution in France before embarking upon foreign adventures.[2] Moreover Robespierre was suspicious of Brissot's sincerity, believing that his relations with the royalist war-group led by Narbonne implied some ulterior motive for his policy. The dismissal of first Narbonne and then Delessart, and the subsequent appointment of Roland and his friends, naturally enhanced his suspicions. The reservations of his original welcome to the 'patriot ministry' soon gave place to references to those who sought only personal profit from the people's revolution, and when the Roland ministry was in turn dismissed, Desmoulins, Robespierre's supporter, suggested that from its beginning it had been the dupe of the royalists.[3]

---

[1] Their practically unanimous voting on seven occasions between 1 February and 8 August is recorded in the *Tableau comparatif* (Paris, 1792), B.M., F.826.2.

[2] Buchez and Roux, *Histoire parlementaire*, xiii, 129, 133; *Jacobins*, iii, 518, 546; Michon, *Robespierre et la guerre révolutionnaire, 1791–1792*, pp. 40–3, 51–8; and Walter, *Robespierre*, p. 240.

[3] *Jacobins*, iv, 8.

The development of opposing factions in the Jacobin Club was nevertheless a gradual process. The discussion about the expediency of attacking counter-revolution abroad before curbing it at home remained a friendly one until 30 December 1791, when Danton and Robespierre rose in protest against Brissot's innuendo that those who opposed him were creating dissension amongst patriots and so dishonouring the Revolution.[1] Thereafter all attempts to effect a reconciliation failed, and members of the Society began to be drawn to one side or the other, a process which continued at least until Brissot's failure to secure the impeachment of Lafayette ended all hope of unity and precipitated the insurrection of 10 August. During this period debates were frequently tumultuous. The attendance of the Legislative Assembly of those members who were also deputies provided Robespierre with opportunities to assert his leadership in the Society, and the presence of the public in the galleries favoured his ascendency. Even so, it may be doubted whether either side could rely upon the support of a large number of members before the middle of May 1792. At the end of April many Jacobins remained neutral, and a reference to a Brissotin faction on 30 April was qualified by the words 'if one is being formed'.[2]

At that time several of those who were later to be regarded as Brissotins had broken with Robespierre and his supporters. Louvet's breach with them may be dated from his scolding speech of 18 January, if not before, and that of Lasource from his open conflicts with Robespierre on both 1 and 26 January. Guadet's antagonism only became evident later, when on 26 March he became involved in a dispute with Robespierre about the part played by Providence in the Revolution. The patriotism of Isnard was questioned on 2 April by Chabot, who at the end of the month attacked Fauchet also, accusing him of protecting the royalist Narbonne. The hostility which Gorsas

---

[1] *Ibid.*, iii, 303. See also pp. 541, 585, for the failure of attempts at reconciliation. I have rejected the more sudden formation of opposing factions suggested by Walter, *Robespierre*, p. 250.

[2] *Jacobins*, iii, 547. On this development in general, see also pp. 552, 561, 573, 614, 639, and Walter, *Histoire des Jacobins*, 246–9. I would suggest 27 May 1792 as a likely date for the beginning of the ascendancy of Robespierre's supporters in the Club, where Walter (*Robespierre*, p. 291) suggests the end of April.

JEAN MARIE ROLAND

had shown to Robespierre in the *Courrier* on 22 January was made more obvious by his suggestion on 28 March that Robespierre's policy could only benefit the monarchists, and by his failure to publish Robespierre's letter of protest on 4 April. Madame Roland's letter to Robespierre on 25 April, reproaching him for his rejection of her offers of reconciliation, might be regarded as marking the completion of the break between her friends and his.[1]

The cleavage, however, was not so extensive as it was later to become. The Jacobin attitude towards Condorcet and Vergniaud, for example, was still reserved, and Chabot excepted Vergniaud from his criticisms of Brissot and his friends on 27 April. Several other men who were later to be proscribed with Brissot were either neutral, like Dusaulx and Rouyer, or were in sympathy with Robespierre. Carra, an extravagant striker of attitudes, had supported Brissot on the Correspondence Committee in February, but he, like Ducos and Grangeneuve, remained popular in the Club. Deperret, Manuel, Pétion and Saladin also remained in favour, as did Sillery despite one difference of opinion with Robespierre.[2]

THE FAILURE OF THE RAPPROCHEMENT

The dismissal of Roland on 13 June, and the subsequent revival of his friends' attacks upon the Court, provided an opportunity for the reconciliation of differences in the Jacobin Club. During June and July the danger of counter-revolution appeared increasingly imminent, and Brissot and the deputies of the Gironde had plenty of occasions to redeem their reputation as revolutionary leaders. But although Brissot's war-speeches in the previous December had foreshadowed an appeal to the people if the Court should prove disloyal to the Constitution, he and his associates did not adopt this course when the occasion

---

[1] Louvet, *Mémoires*, i, 36; *Jacobins*, iii, 307, 345 (Lasource), 451 (Guadet), 458 (Isnard), 522, 525 (Fauchet); Gorsas, *Courrier*, 22 January, 28 March and 4 April 1792, and *Correspondance de Robespierre*, i, 135, 140; *Lettres de Madame Roland*, ii, 418; and Walter, *Robespierre*, pp. 254, 258, 271, 284–5.

[2] *Jacobins*, iii, 538, 596–7 (Condorcet, Vergniaud), 506 (Carra; see also *Moniteur*, xii, 287, and Walter, *Robespierre*, p. 266), 476 (Ducos), 359, 703 (Grangeneuve), 585, 648 (Manuel), 432, 442 (Pétion) and iv, 9 (Sillery, Deperret) and 63 (Saladin).

I

arose. Some of them, indeed, publicly repudiated the rising republican agitation. Acting as spokesman for the Commission of Twenty-one—a commission of the Assembly which was reorganized immediately after the fall of Roland, and which then seems to have been dominated by Vergniaud, Condorcet, Guadet and Jean Debry—Vergniaud, supported by Lasource and Rouyer, condemned a republican petition presented by the Section Mauconseil on 4 August.[1] Condorcet similarly censured another such petition presented by the authorities of Paris on the eve of the insurrection of 10 August, and on other occasions Brissot threatened republicans with the penalties of the law, and Vergniaud, Guadet and Isnard all deplored excessive disorders. Lasource even tried to secure the removal from Paris of the provincial troops who soon afterwards took a prominent part in the insurrection, saying that they might be used to excite a tumult 'which could serve no useful purpose'.[2]

The principal purpose of these deputies was certainly to win the reinstatement of a ministry headed by Roland. Vergniaud urged this on the Assembly on 21 July, and Isnard eventually secured it on 10 August, the day of the insurrection.[3] The two letters written to the King in July, one signed by Guadet, Vergniaud and Gensonné—the probable author—and one written by Vergniaud alone, both advised him that the monarchy could be saved only if their programme were accepted— and this included the immediate appointment of a patriotic and trustworthy ministry. Moreover, Joly, at that time the Feuillant Minister of Justice, was in touch with these three deputies of the Gironde through their friend Roederer, and he claimed to have had the approval of Vergniaud in urging the King to accept their recommendations.[4]

---

[1] *Moniteur*, xiii, 328, 333.

[2] *Moniteur*, xiii, 218, 241, 372, 375, and for Lasource, *Jacobins*, iv, 153–5. On the conduct of Vergniaud and his closest associates, see Vatel, *Vergniaud*, ii, 128–30, and for Condorcet see Alengry, *Condorcet, guide de la Révolution française*, pp. 150–6, and Cahen, *Condorcet et la Révolution française*, pp. 406, 419.

[3] *Moniteur*, xiii, 206, 211, 382, and Vatel, *loc. cit.*

[4] A. Mathiez, 'Les Girondins et la cour à la veille du 10 août', *Annales historiques de la Révolution française* (1931), p. 193 ff.; Lefebvre, *La Chute du Roi*, p. 202; Vatel, *Vergniaud*, ii, 121—where the second letter is mistaken for the first—and Vermorel, *Œuvres de Vergniaud*, pp. 311–16; see also *Vergniaud*, p. 80, and *Gensonné à ses collègues* (Paris, 1793), B.M., F.1021.11.

Louis's failure to respond to these overtures left the deputies concerned irresolute. The Commission of Twenty-one, which had been instructed by Brissot's motion on 26 July to examine the question of deposing the King, did not report to the Assembly until 9 August, when its spokesman could say no more than that the members of the Commission would give their separate opinions individually. Pellenc's letter to Lamarck on 5 August also suggests that feeling in the Commission was wavering from one session to the next. He asserts that only Guadet favoured the Mauconseil republican petition, and that Vergniaud had recommended delaying deposition until the forces of Austria had advanced far enough into France to excuse the measure—'and in the meanwhile we should see if we can get by threats the benefits which might follow deposition'.[1]

In the event, the Assembly accepted the provisional suspension of the King which Vergniaud belatedly proposed on 10 August, a measure which seemed to the Robespierrist Jacobins to be designed to facilitate the survival of the monarchy.[2] It is at least possible that Brissot, Condorcet, Vergniaud, Guadet, Gensonné, Isnard and Lasource would willingly have agreed to this if the King had been prepared to accept as ministers those who were their friends. On the other hand Jean Debry, who had aided these men in their attacks upon the Court, accepted the popular movement and so retained the friendship of the Jacobins. Others who were later proscribed actively encouraged the insurrection at this time. Carra, Gorsas and Grégoire were members of a secret revolutionary committee. Barbaroux was a popular leader. Manuel warned the Assembly on 29 July that the people would act if their ills were not remedied within a week, and Dulaure hastened on 11 August to inform the newly formed Commune of Paris of the existence of a royalist plot. The position of Pétion was more ambiguous: his irresolution was later held against him, but he

---

[1] *Moniteur*, xiii, 253, 278–81, 375; Glagau, *Die französische Legislative und der Ursprung der Revolutionskriege*, pp. 366–8. Cp. the *Défense de Vergniaud*, A.N., w.292.204, Part 3, No. 24, for the claim that Vergniaud was anxious to prevent a Regency.

[2] *Moniteur*, xiii, 380, 382; Lefebvre, *La Première Terreur*, p. 8; F. A. Aulard, 'Le Détrônement de Louis XVI, 1792', *La Révolution française*, xxxvi (1899), p. 67.

eventually sanctioned the distribution of cartridges to the insurgents, and his relations with Robespierre, although strained, were not yet broken.[1]

The gradual recognition of the hesitancy of Brissot and his friends in the Assembly had however ended all hope of an abiding reunion in the Jacobin Society. A reunion had taken place there after the dismissal of Roland, but it was conditional, brief and barren. There was first a series of appeals for reconciliation and unity, from Lasource on one side and from Merlin and Fabre on the other. Even Robespierre, who hastened to warn the Society that the safety of France was of greater importance than the fall of a ministry, called upon the members to support the Assembly. The attack upon the Tuileries on 20 June was hailed in a circular as 'momentous and praiseworthy', Guadet and Vergniaud were praised, Fauchet was complimented upon his 'conversion', and Brissot, Guadet and Condorcet were called upon to prove their patriotism by returning to the Society. After some delay Brissot appeared on 28 June, exhorted his audience to forget their differences, and undertook to prove to the Assembly that General Lafayette was a traitor. Robespierre approved, in guarded language.[2]

This *rapprochement* was nevertheless clearly conditional upon the impeachment of Lafayette, and suspicion soon disrupted the new-found harmony. Doubts of Brissot's sincerity appeared soon after the incident known as the 'Kiss of Lamourette' on 7 July, when deputies of royalist and radical opinion in the Assembly embraced each other in a moment of common emotion. Next day Robespierre spoke in the Jacobins, recalling the Assembly to its duty of striking down Lafayette, and adding that 'if no one will defend the rights of the people, the immutable rights of all mankind, the people themselves must take action'. On 16 and 20 July he again censured the Assembly's lethargy, saying significantly that: 'If Lafayette is immune from

---

[1] Pinguad, *Jean De Bry, 1760–1835*, pp. 14–17; Lefebvre, *La Chute du Roi*, p. 224, and P. Montarlot, 'Les députés de Saône et Loire', *Mém. Soc. Eduenne, Nouv. Série*, xxxiii (1905), p. 239 for the secret committee; for Barbaroux, *Mémoires*, pp. 132–4, 155, 159; for Dulaure, Lefebvre, *La Première Terreur*, p. 75; for Manuel, *Jacobins*, iv, 155; and for Pétion, *Correspondance de Robespierre*, pp. 147–8, 152, Thompson, *Robespierre*, i, 214, 231, 262, and Lefebvre, *La Chute du Roi*, pp. 220–6.

[2] *Jacobins*, iii, 692, 698, and iv, 3–7, 11, 16, 32, 40, 52, 54.

punishment, we have no constitution.'[1] But it was left to a more obscure member, Baumier, to condemn the inactivity of Brissot and Vergniaud outright: 'It looks as if the result of all this is going to be a deal to put certain Ministers back in office on the understanding that the Lafayette question is dropped.'[2]

As the days went by and the General remained secure, this hostility was intensified. On 29 July Lasource's demand for the withdrawal of provincial troops from Paris was drowned in uproar. On 1 August the alleged activities of Brissot, Isnard and Lasource at the Reunion Club were deplored, and an anonymous member proposed the exclusion of Brissot from the Society on the grounds that certain people in the Assembly were opposing the deposition of the King and seeking to solve the situation by such partial measures as his suspension and the control of government by the Commission of Twenty-one. Albitte supported this proposal, denouncing Brissot as a man who wishes 'to pull the wool over our eyes until we believe that the recall of the Ministers . . . will suffice to end all dangers and to save the country'. Even Réal, a staunch supporter of Brissot earlier in the year, turned against his hesitations on 6 August, and the general attitude of the Society was expressed by Goupilleau on 8 August: on hearing the news of the failure of the long-awaited attack on Lafayette, he said that it would be madness to continue to hope that the majority of the Assembly could be trusted to act wisely. 'The people', he added, 'must be told that the Assembly cannot save them, and that only a general insurrection can.'[3]

Goupilleau's complete loss of faith in the constitutional government of France is significant, for it illustrates the important fact that the Revolution of 10 August was directed not only against the King but also against the Legislative Assembly, a body which, as the Commune soon made plain, was to be allowed to exist only by the tolerance of the people of Paris.

THE BRISSOTINS AND THE COMMUNE

The storming of the Tuileries on 10 August provided no permanent solution to the problems which beset France. The

---

[1] *Jacobins*, iv, 82, 84, 109, 124. Cp. Walter, *Robespierre*, pp. 306–8.
[2] *Jacobins*, iv, 117.   [3] *Jacobins*, iv, 165–6, 185–6.

Austro-Prussian army crossed the frontier on 19 August and a royalist rising appeared more imminent than ever. The removal of the untrustworthy King had ended one impasse only to create another, for it left a vacuum at the centre of affairs which no single group was then strong enough to fill. In an atmosphere still electric with suspicion compromise proved impossible. A conflict for power inevitably developed.

At first the position of Brissot and his friends seemed to be a strong one. Vergniaud had secured the suspension of the King until a Convention should meet to decide upon a new Constitution,[1] and in the meantime the group profited from the insurrection it had hesitated to lead. After Brissot had proposed the dismissal of the old Ministry, Isnard's motion for the recall of Roland, Clavière and Servan was passed unanimously.[2] Monge and Lebrun, both of whom were friends of the Rolands, were also appointed. Only Danton came from outside their circle, to protect them, as Condorcet put it, from popular distrust.[3] Their control of the Commission of Twenty-one was also increased by the election to it of Brissot, Gensonné and Lasource,[4] and their influence in the Assembly was certainly enhanced by the absence of many of those who had hitherto supported the Court.

In practice, however, this parliamentary strength was illusory, for the Assembly itself was weak. Since it had been content to wait upon events before the insurrection, it had lost the confidence of Paris. Even its claim to represent the sovereign people was usurped in the capital by a new authority, the Commune, which still retained the prestige and power it had acquired on 10 August. More important still, the Commune could count in an emergency upon the support of the armed Sections of Paris, while the Assembly had no force at its disposal to compel obedience to its decisions. Thus Brissot and his friends were for a second time burdened by responsibility without effective power in Paris, where they were by now profoundly distrusted by the more militant revolutionaries. Doubts had been bred by their neglect of the Jacobin Society in favour of their salons; and their preference for the company of men of

[1] *Moniteur*, xiii, 380.
[2] *Moniteur*, xiii, 380, 382.
[3] Cahen, *Condorcet et la Révolution française*, p. 424.
[4] *Moniteur*, xiii, 466.

rank and substance had cost them their contact with popular feeling. As the shadow of counter-revolution and invasion had deepened over the capital, suspicion of them had flourished. Their apparent concentration upon the pursuit of office and their readiness to compromise with the Court had caused men to question their motives; and their failure to react vigorously to the appearance in high places of disloyalty to the Revolution suggested that they were themselves disloyal. What was regarded as their protection of the King on 10 August seemed conclusive evidence of their unreliability, and just as Brissot had earlier conducted a press campaign against the moderates, so Marat and Hébert now campaigned against him and his friends. The continuation of their influence after the insurrection thus contributed considerably to the increasing restiveness of the *sans-culottes* during the next six months. On the other hand, the superficial weakness of the small group of deputies who favoured Robespierre concealed a position of considerable potential strength. They were free to criticize and question the provisional Government and to dominate the important *Comité de Surveillance*[1] which soon began to challenge the authority of the Commission of Twenty-one.[2]

The last six weeks of the Legislative Assembly were therefore a period of confused conflict for power, the principal competitors being the Brissotins in the Assembly, and the Commune, led by Robespierre. The apparent menace of counter-revolution, and the reluctance of even the Jacobin deputies to underwrite the threats of the Commune, delayed the appearance of sharp distinctions in the Assembly itself, but the inconclusive struggle nevertheless embittered relationships, particularly when it had its natural consequence in a temporary outbreak of anarchy in Paris.

The primary task of the Assembly after 10 August was to consolidate the popular victory by ensuring the maintenance of internal security and by providing for the efficient prosecution of the war. On 10 August Gensonné supported a proposal to send commissioners to the armies, and carried an amendment

---

[1] First constituted in November 1791 and reconstructed on 12 August 1792 as the Committee of General Security.

[2] Lefebvre, *La Première Terreur*, p. 30, and Delville, *La Commune de l'An II*, p. 13.

which empowered them to dismiss and arrest both civil and military officials. Two days later he proposed the first important decree of state security, vesting in local administrators wide powers of investigation and arrest wherever treasonable activities were suspected. Vergniaud and Lasource also obtained decrees providing for a measure of conscription, for a check upon the indiscriminate distribution of rifles, and for the delegation of the widest emergency powers to the commanders of besieged towns.[1] The efficacy of such measures, however, depended upon the creation of a strong and unified central government, competent to enlist and direct the full strength of the nation, and this was hindered by the clash which arose between the Assembly and the Commune over this same question of internal security.

On the day of the insurrection the leader of a deputation from the Commune had warned the Assembly that the people for whom he spoke 'can never recognize as competent to sanction emergency legislation any authority except the primary electoral assemblies,[2] in whom all sovereignty resides'.[3] The Assembly had at first yielded to this pressure, consenting for example to Manuel's demand for the imprisonment of the King in the Temple. But when Robespierre came in person to demand that all suspected conspirators should be tried in a court of final jurisdiction composed only of representatives of the Sections of Paris, Brissot spoke of the undesirability of despotic government. Two days later the 'Tribunal of 17 August' was created as proposed by the Commission of Twenty-one, with both judges and jury duly elected by the Sections from men acquainted with the law.[4] The Commune, fearful lest royalists be protected, remained distrustful and dissatisfied.

Its suspicions seemed to be confirmed on 25 August, when Gensonné prevented the dissolution of the High Court at Orléans, which dealt with the more important cases of *lèse-nation*, saying that to attribute its powers to a tribunal in Paris would be to deprive the provinces of their due part in the

---

[1] *Moniteur*, xiii, 382, 397, 548, 550, 645.
[2] i.e., in Paris, the Section or District assemblies, now in permanent emergency session.
[3] *Jacobins*, iv, 196 and Lefebvre, *La Première Terreur*, p. 7.
[4] *Moniteur*, xiii, 430, 432, 444, 467.

exercise of sovereignty. Later, after the Court had acquitted the royalist Montmorin, Roland and the Commission of Twenty-one vainly endeavoured to prevent the National Guard of Paris from seizing other prisoners and bringing them to the capital—a journey which culminated in their massacre at Versailles.[1] Then, on 30 August, the Assembly attempted a decisive step. Twice Roland complained of violations of the law by commissioners of the Commune. A letter was read from Girey-Dupré, co-editor with Brissot of the *Patriote français*, in which he protested that he was being held under arrest at the Hôtel de Ville, and Gensonné reported that the Ministry of War was being besieged by an angry crowd. With the support of Grange-neuve, Larivière and Kersaint, Guadet obtained a decree ordering the immediate dissolution of the Commune.[2]

Although within three days sheer necessity compelled the Assembly to restore the civic authority it had thus endeavoured to destroy, irreparable harm had been done. Public feeling in Paris, already fanned to fever heat by panic and suspicion, was stimulated still further on 2 September by a premature proclamation that the enemy was at the gates and by Danton's thunderous defiance of the invader.[3] Terrible events ensued: within three hours of Danton's speech, suspected persons in the prisons of Paris were being murdered by the mob.

It is still perhaps an open question how far the prolonged butchery which followed was simply a spontaneous result of popular passion or how far there was some measure of deliberate organization behind it.[4] Whatever the truth, the Massacres of September had the effect of terrorizing moderation into silence during the critical period of the elections to the Convention[5]—and Brissot and his friends therefore believed, or affected to believe, that the Jacobins had encouraged them. They had other reasons also for this belief. Just before the Massacres began, Robespierre had denounced his opponents, obtaining warrants from the Commune for the arrest of Brissot and Roland, if not of others also. There is no evidence that he then

---

[1] *Moniteur*, xiii, 532, 602, 680.   [2] *Moniteur*, xiii, 571–8.
[3] *Moniteur*, xiii, 590, 599, 601.   [4] See Caron, *Les Massacres de septembre*.
[5] Compare Vergniaud's statement in the Assembly on 16 September: 'Respectable people are remaining indoors' (*Moniteur*, xiii, 719).

foresaw what was about to happen, but even his apologists have found it hard to isolate his action from its sinister aftermath.[1] Whatever the intention, the consequence is clear enough: both Brissot and Roland, who stood for a time in deadly peril of their lives, had good reason to think that Robespierre would have had them murdered if he could.[2] Mortal hatred henceforward dominated their attitude towards him.

The effect of the massacres upon the erstwhile radical leaders of the Legislative Assembly is, however, even greater than this personal antagonism. Few of them had experienced the similar outbreaks in Paris in 1789, and most of them had already shown a tendency to shrink from the implications of anything approaching direct action. The deliberate slaughter of scores of defenceless people was in all probability a severe shock to their philosophical faith in progress and in the natural goodness of the people, to their dreams of the sober and virtuous republicanism of ancient Rome. This fearful proof of the collapse of public order in Paris seems, not unnaturally, to have awakened in them an enhanced respect for the law and an abiding dislike of the capital and its Commune, of its Jacobin deputies and its disorderly populace.[3]

This reading of their attitude is not nullified by the fact that they expressed much more horror later, when they tried to saddle the Jacobins with responsibility for the atrocities, than they did at the beginning of September. The limited evidence that is available certainly suggests that their first reaction was one of acquiescence or even approval. On 3 September, Roland, in a famous phrase, advised the Assembly to draw a veil over what had happened, since the people tempered its vengeance with a kind of rough justice, and Condorcet reserved his judgement in almost identical terms.[4] But even in these expressions, made when it was thought that only traitors were being slain,

[1] See Mathiez, *La Révolution française*, ii, 29 and, Thompson, *Robespierre*, i, 275–7.

[2] e.g., *Madame Roland*, i, 31, 104; *Patriote français*, 15 September 1792; *Moniteur*, xiii, 621, 727, and xiv, 41, 49.

[3] e.g., *Madame Roland*, i, 110, or Bancal's letter to his constituents on 18 September (Mège, *Le Conventionnel Bancal des Issarts*, p. 237).

[4] *Moniteur*, xiii, 611, and *Chronique de Paris*, 4 September 1792. For the use of similar expressions by Gorsas, Brissot, Vergniaud and Pétion, see *Courrier*, 2 September, Brissot, *A tous les républicains de France* (Paris, 1792), B.M., F.673.6, and *Moniteur*, xiii, 635, and xiv, 49.

an undertone of revulsion is apparent, and this the continuity and extent of the massacres, and the discovery that many innocent people had perished, certainly enhanced. In his speech on 3 September Roland called upon the newly reconstituted municipal authorities to prevent further excesses, and ten days later he made his attitude still clearer: 'I did not hastily condemn the terrible initial upheaval . . . I did believe that its continuation had to be avoided.[1] The massacres placed in the hands of all who opposed the Commune and, at a later date, the Mountain, a powerful weapon with which to attack their adversaries. They used it to the full, but their exaggerations are quite compatible with a fundamental sincerity. Fear, ignorance and the consciousness of their own impotence combined to make acquiescence expedient during the disorders, but the lapse of time and the prestige of a new parliament gave men confidence to condemn.

Contemporary opinion may perhaps be gauged by the conduct of Pétion and Manuel, both of whom turned from Robespierre and his supporters at this time. Pétion had remained friendly with Robespierre until mid-August, although his idealism and his irresolution suggest that his character was always more akin to that of Roland. After 10 August, he was overshadowed by Robespierre and was robbed by the Commune of much of his rightful authority as mayor of Paris. Worried by the irregular conduct of affairs and perplexed by his own ambiguous position, he interviewed Robespierre on 17 August and rebuked him for his inflammatory speeches, to be bluntly told that he was himself the dupe of the Brissotin faction.[2] Injured vanity no doubt accounts for much of the bitterness of his later attacks upon Robespierre, but he seems to have regarded Robespierre's dissemination of suspicion amongst the people of Paris as a contributory cause of the massacres, and his personal experiences of these had left, as he said, an indelible impression on his mind.[3] Similar motives, with the influence of Pétion,

---

[1] *Moniteur*, xiii, 674.

[2] *Correspondance de Robespierre*, i, 152, and *Discours de Jérôme Pétion sur l'accusation intentée contre M. Robespierre* (Paris, 1792), B.M., F.665.9.

[3] According to his English friend Miss Helen Williams (*Souvenirs de la Révolution française*, p. 19) Pétion regretted that he had not perished with those for whose deaths he felt some responsibility.

probably affected his colleague Manuel, the *procureur* of the old municipality. He had acted as the leader of several delegations from the Commune to the Assembly, but after the massacres he wrote proposing the creation of a tribunal 'to maintain order in Paris, to track down the guilty and to do justice swiftly'. Later, at the Jacobin Society, he made an open avowal of what amounted to heresy, saying that the sight of the dead had awakened an awful doubt in his mind: 'Is it better to dream of Liberty than to possess it?'[1]

Vergniaud, who also condemned the Commune for its illegal and indiscriminate delegation of its authority, demanded that in future its members should be made to answer with their heads for the safety of all prisoners.[2] In practice such a proposal was as futile as Roland's warnings of impending anarchy had been on 3 September, and in the last days of the Legislative Assembly a move was made to establish an armed force for the effective protection of the new parliament and for the preservation of order in Paris. Roland pleaded for such a force on 17 September, and next day Gensonné embodied the suggestion in a formal proposal.[3] His decree was accepted, but had but little effect.[4] The idea behind it was to dominate the thought of the opposition to the Mountain in the Convention.

It is arguable whether the men whose conduct has been considered here were ever sufficiently united even to be called a faction. Individually, they expressed points of view and supported policies which were broadly similar, and they may therefore be described as a '*parti*' in the French sense, as men being of a certain persuasion, maintaining, consciously or by chance, a common political position. If the factor of personal friendship is added to this definition, seven deputies in the Legislative Assembly—Brissot himself, Condorcet, Gensonné, Guadet, Isnard, Lasource and Vergniaud—can confidently be called Brissotins. The political conduct of Isnard and Lasource conforms so closely to that of the others that some personal association may be presumed in spite of a shortage of more positive

---

[1] *Jacobins*, iv, 460.   [2] *Moniteur*, xiii, 728.   [3] *Moniteur*, xiii, 722, 736, and xiv, 11.
[4] A force for this purpose appears to have been recruited in Paris, but to have been disbanded in mid-October 1792. See Chapter VI below.

evidence, but the name of Jean Debry has to be omitted since no proof has appeared that he was personally intimate with Brissot, with whom his political association seems to have been brief. Other men of less prominence, particularly Bancal, Dusaulx, Fauchet, Gamon, Kersaint, Lanthénas, Larivière, Louvet, Manuel, Masuyer and Pétion, may be regarded as being or becoming sympathetic to the principal speakers, and others again—Barbaroux, Carra, Deperret, Ducos, Gorsas, Grange-neuve, Grégoire, Rouyer, Saladin and Sillery—remained on more or less friendly terms with Robespierre and the Jacobins.

During the first weeks of the Legislative Assembly Brissot, Gensonné, Guadet and Vergniaud were prominent in the debates about San Domingo, and Guadet, Vergniaud and Lasource were influential in those about Avignon. With Condorcet and Isnard these men became leaders of the agitation for war against Austria, and all were active opponents of the Court and its so-called 'Austrian Committee'. Whatever justification there may have been for this policy, its advocates cannot be acquitted of irresponsibility in the pursuit of an end which brought them popularity and some measure of power. After their friends had been appointed as Ministers their conduct become more restrained, so that they came to occupy a half-way position between the royalist majority in the Assembly and the radical supporters of Robespierre in the Jacobin Society, having a place in both but effective political power in neither. At this period they produced no idea more constructive than the preservation of what influence they had, and when that declined they renewed their attacks upon the King without any other aim than to compel him to accept the re-creation of a situation that had already proved impracticable and perilous. Yet all seven men baulked at the prospect of using force to depose the King whom they belittled and abused.

To Robespierre and his supporters, who had come to believe that either the Royalists or the Revolution must perish, this ambiguous conduct could bear but one interpretation. The Brissotins' co-operation with the nobility during the agitation for war, their conservative tendency as soon as they had gained some spurious success, and above all their failure to react with vigour to the threat of counter-revolution, seemed to prove them to be self-seeking intriguers, indistinguishable from the enemies of the people. Their reputation was therefore very seriously compromised in Paris by mid-August—Chabot was later to say that the expression '*parti Brissot*' meant those who had opposed the insurrection of 10 August[1]—and after that date they again showed themselves irresolute and unwise in the exercise of their renewed, if still restricted, authority. Creditable in itself, their reluctance to sanction revolutionary methods even to save Paris from attack or betrayal seemed to confirm existing suspicions of their loyalty, and the ill-timed effort to dissolve the Commune appeared as a final proof of their outright treachery.

On the other hand, the September Massacres seem to have left the Brissotins with a clearer perception of the desirability of the rule of law, a profound distrust of Paris, and an abiding hatred for Robespierre. Thus when the Assembly was dissolved an unbridgeable abyss separated them from Robespierre and his supporters, for neither side could even credit the good intentions or patriotism of the other. The Convention could only provide an arena for an inevitable conflict.

---

[1] *Jacobins*, iv, 465 (7 November 1792).

CHAPTER VI

The Struggle for Control of the Convention

AFTER an inaugural meeting in the Tuileries Palace[1] the Convention assembled in the Manège on 21 September 1792, the day after the battle of Valmy. Great things were expected of it. Bound by no constitution, untrammelled by the traditional authority of the Crown, its theoretical power was limited only by the ultimate sovereignty of the people. Yet it was from the beginning bedevilled by the bequests of its discredited predecessor. It inherited not only 187 of the old deputies, but even the wretched building which had already been the scene of three years of controversy and which illustrates the profound influence physical conditions may exercise upon parliamentary affairs. The Manège, the home of the first revolutionary assemblies of France, was an enclosed riding school that had been hastily converted into a debating chamber. Its accommodation was cramped, its accoustics poor and its air unhealthy. A long and narrow amphitheatre, with high tiers at either side, it naturally fostered faction. On 13 August 1792 Vergniaud condemned it as a place in which noise, disorder and irritability were inevitable, and advised his colleagues to authorize the erection of a more spacious hall in the Madeleine to prevent the reappearance of partisan divisions. An alternative proposal to use the theatre in the Tuileries was sponsored by Brissot and eventually accepted, but the work of conversion took so long that this new accommodation did not become available until 13 May 1793.[2] In the meanwhile, the Convention was compelled to exist in conditions which probably did much to aggravate acrimony and to transform personal antagonisms into political divisions. In an interesting account of this matter Dulaure explains that the deputies avoided the benches on

---

[1] *Moniteur*, xiii, 746, and xiv, 5.
[2] *Moniteur*, xiii, 405–7, 654, 670, 704; Lefebvre, *La Convention*, i, 1–5.

which the Feuillants had sat, until lack of space forced them to fill the room. Then, the Convention began to divide as men moved away from those whom they disliked, drifting towards either end and leaving the long central benches to those most tolerant of their fellows' failings.[1]

In the first few days of the Convention unity seemed a possibility, as immediate needs and common ideals transcended lesser considerations. Together the deputies guaranteed the security of person and property, and ratified the authority of existing laws and institutions. Together they proclaimed the right of the people to approve the constitution they were to draft, and, amid scenes of great enthusiasm, they announced the abolition of the ancient monarchy of France.[2] Even after this initial unity of purpose had spent itself, men could still hope that concord would prevail, for Brissot and his friends seemed to be in a position of commanding strength. Brissot, Condorcet, Lasource, Isnard, Vergniaud, Guadet and Gensonné had all secured seats, as had such men as Fauchet, Kersaint, Masuyer and Henri Larivière, who had supported them fairly consistently in the Legislative Assembly; and several new deputies, like Buzot, Barbaroux, Bancal, Lanthénas, Louvet and Pétion, were also friendly with them. These men, who had already acquired a considerable reputation throughout France, were in many respects representative of the great majority of the Convention. The new deputies, for the most part provincial lawyers and local officials who had benefited by the system of indirect election, were as shocked as they by the September Massacres and shared their distrust of Paris. They showed their sympathies by electing Pétion as their first president, by choosing Brissot, Condorcet, Vergniaud and Lasource as their secretaries, and by confirming the powers of the Commission of 21 and of the ministry of Roland.[3]

But in the Convention, as at the close of the Legislative Assembly, the more radical deputies or 'Montagnards' were again in a much stronger position than the smallness of their

[1] Dulaure, *Physionomie de la Convention nationale* (Paris, 1793), B.M., F.R.61.28. Cp. Bancal's letter to his constituents, 25 September 1792: Mège, *Le Conventionnel Bancal des Issarts*, p. 238.
[2] *Moniteur*, xiv, 6, 8.
[3] *Moniteur*, xiv, 5; Mathiez, *La Révolution française*, ii, 44–5, 58.

numbers implied. They still controlled the Committee of General Security, and they were now led by Robespierre, whose formidable qualities had been proved at the Jacobin Society and at the Commune. More important still, they represented Paris. As we have seen, the elections in the capital had taken place during the 'First Terror', when few moderates dared to show their sympathies. Consequently the Parisian delegation was almost wholly Jacobin in the Robespierrist sense, and it was intimately associated with the Commune, which controlled the only organized forces in the city. Except in the event of a sharp division between the capital and its deputies, the Montagnards could in the last resort rely upon the support of the Sections of Paris, against which the Convention had no effective defence.

In these circumstances the leaders of the Convention might profitably have sought reconciliation with Robespierre and his friends. Some evidence suggests that Danton tried to effect such a *rapprochement*, but the surviving stories indicate little more than the bitterness and suspicions which made the attempt a vain one. We hear how Madame Roland walked out of the Opéra rather than share the ministerial box with Danton, whom she detested and despised as an instigator of the September Massacres. Again, according to Durand de Maillane, Barbaroux refused to attend a meeting arranged by Danton with the words 'Honest men can have no truck with criminals'.[1] Whatever the truth of these stories, there is every reason to suppose that the events of the past year had aroused antagonisms which no one in Brissot's circle was magnanimous or far-sighted enough to overcome.

Open controversy began on 24 September when, in an attempt to solve the problems presented by a disorderly Paris and its refractory Commune, Kersaint proposed that the Convention should appoint four commissioners to examine the state of the country and the capital. This proposal, supported by Lanjuinais and Vergniaud, was then elaborated by Buzot into a more comprehensive decree ordering the appointment of six commissioners to report upon the domestic situation, to propose a law against incitement to assassination, and to draft

[1] Lefebvre, *La Convention*, i, 56.

K

a scheme for the recruitment in the provinces of an armed force for the protection of the Convention.[1] These proposals, which were accepted almost unanimously, amounted to a statement of policy for the Convention, and it was one to which its leading orators were to adhere until they were overthrown by insurrection. As a policy the proposals suffered from a fatal defect: the sound sense which inspired them was inextricably entangled with a motive derived from personal animosity—the desire to crush Robespierre. His name was not mentioned, but the attack upon him was none the less implicit in the situation. Montagnard criticism of the proposals soon evoked from Buzot the irate interjection, 'What! Do you suppose we are to be enslaved by certain deputies of Paris?'[2]

When the debate was reopened on 25 September the vindictive element in the policy became even more obvious. Now the unsullied reputation of the Montagnards as the men of 10 August,[3] the begetters of the new republican revolution, was to be destroyed by the allegation that they had encouraged the massacres of September, and so all the provincial deputies' latent distrust of the capital would be focussed upon them. After Lasource had repeated the tale of the attempted murder of the leaders of the Legislative, Brissot and Vergniaud openly accused the Montagnards, including Robespierre, of complicity.[4] Another allegation, initiated by Lasource and supported by Boilleau, Barbaroux and Vergniaud, was that certain intriguers were endeavouring to use the emergency powers still exercised by the Commune to gain control of the whole of France. Yet a third line of attack, also opened up by Lasource, was the assertion that the disorders in Paris were part of a conspiracy to establish a dictatorship, and to this charge, easily acceptable to an audience steeped in classical history, Barbaroux and Rebecquy added a direct denunciation of Robespierre. The intention to tarnish all the Montagnards with the evil reputation of Marat, an acknowledged exponent of bloodshed and

[1] *Moniteur*, xiv, 36, 39–40.
[2] *Moniteur*, xiv, 36.
[3] '. . . for it is not possible to speak of the events of 10 August except to applaud the conduct and courage of the people of Paris.' (Kersaint, 30 August 1792, *Moniteur*, xiii, 577.)
[4] *Moniteur*, xiv, 40–1, 47, 49.

dictatorship, is evident. Nevertheless the debate ended in a Montagnard victory. They in their turn suggested that the proposal to create a departmental guard was in reality a subtle move towards the inauguration of a federal system. The Convention ignored the alleged conspiracy, but passed a resolution proclaiming the Republic to be one and indivisible.[1]

This failure has no simple explanation. It may have been due in part to Robespierre's insistence upon reviewing his long record of uncorrupted patriotism, and to Marat's bold announcement that he stood alone in his belief in dictatorship. Moreover, the references to federalism, particularly damaging since the invasion made national unity imperative, certainly forced the leaders of the attack upon the Mountain back on to the defensive.[2] But the debate as a whole suggests that the fundamental cause of the failure was the ordinary deputy's dislike of a political dog-fight in an Assembly which should have been wholly concerned with the welfare of the nation. Vergniaud referred to the debate as deplorable, and the affair ended on the Montagnard Tallien's demand that the business of the day should put an end to scandal: 'Let us concern ourselves with the safety of the state, and leave individuals alone.'[3] At the same time the consequences were serious. Robespierre's enemies had incurred the odium of reopening a personal squabble without gaining any real advantage, and their attempt to saddle the Montagnards with responsibility for all the sins of Paris probably helped to harden the formidable alliance between the capital and its representatives in the Convention.

Events in October served to consolidate this same alliance still further. Initially, the authorities of Paris were divided amongst themselves: the General-Council of the Commune was at loggerheads with its own *comité de surveillance*, and several Sections, irritated by the delay in the arrangement of new municipal elections, came to the Convention to condemn civic tyranny and to assure the deputies that they need have no fear

[1] *Moniteur*, xiv, 46–7, 51–2. Cp. Bourdon at the Jacobin Society: 'Marat does us much harm at the Convention' (*Jacobins*, iv, 613—for 23 December 1792).

[2] *Moniteur*, xiv, 42, 44, 49.

[3] *Moniteur*, xiv, 49, 52. See also Mège, *Le Conventionnel Bancal des Issarts*, p. 238, and Soubeyran's letter to his fiancée on 21 November 1792, given in Soubeyran de Saint Prix, *Saint Prix*, p. 21.

of Paris. The office of Mayor was even again offered to Pétion.[1] The Convention, however, foolishly launched a series of indiscriminate attacks upon the city, estranging every potential ally of any consequence and benefiting none but its own Montagnard minority.

The municipal *comité de surveillance* was the first to be attacked. At the instigation of Kersaint, Louvet and Barbaroux, a new committee of twenty-four deputies was appointed on 1 October[2] to investigate its assertion that it had in its possession proofs of corruption among deputies who had belonged to the Legislative Assembly.[3] The committee of investigation appointed Barbaroux as its president and Valazé as its reporter. It took no effective action regarding the alleged corruption, but directed its energy towards attacking the *comité de surveillance*, which was accused by Barbaroux, Birotteau and Lehardy on 4 October of deliberately slandering the Legislative. Marat, who suggested that all this was an attempt by the Brissotins to conceal the truth about the activities of the King at that time, was then attacked by Buzot, Lasource, Guadet and Lidon, and a resolution was passed ordering the *comité* to point out the most incriminating documents in its voluminous records.[4] But unlike the General Council of the Commune, which had attempted to rally the Sections against the *comité*, the Convention made no effort to placate one opponent before it antagonized another. A demand by the Sections to be allowed to vote orally in the municipal elections was brusquely refused, and when the Théâtre Français Section announced its intention of ignoring the law, Guadet, Buzot and Lanjuinais condemned this as dangerous rebellion.[5] Requests for financial help were similarly rebuffed.

At the same time, such men as Barbaroux, Lanjuinais, Buzot, Lasource, Kersaint and Roland continued to speak of Paris in terms which roused general resentment, and to press for the

---

[1] Delville, *La Commune de l'An II*, Ch. iii; Mathiez, *La Révolution française*, ii, 113–16; Lefebvre, *La Convention*, i, 64–7.

[2] By-passing the Committee of General Security, ostensibly to ensure a completely disinterested examination of the allegations, but probably also because that Committee was in sympathy with the Commune.

[3] *Moniteur*, xiv, 96–8.

[4] *Moniteur*, xiv, 121, 128, 130–1.   [5] *Moniteur*, xiv, 183.

creation of a departmental guard.[1] This last campaign was temporarily dropped after the Convention adjourned consideration of Buzot's detailed proposals on 8 October, and a fortnight later Buzot and Barbaroux even asked that more pressing business should be considered first. A *fait accompli* may well have been in preparation, for on 20 October, just as the second detachment of federal troops which Barbaroux had summoned from Marseilles reached the capital, Lidon secured a decree disbanding the Parisian force set up by order of the Legislative. The manœuvre ultimately failed, for so many of the newcomers were attracted to the Jacobins that their presence became embarrassing to the Convention itself. The more immediate effect, however, was to unite the Sections and the Commune, and on 19 October these united authorities protested jointly against the illegality of what was happening.[2]

Danton,[3] too, was forced towards the Mountain. His quarrel with Roland became a public one on 29 September, when, wearying of an increasingly sycophantic discussion about the propriety of inviting Roland to remain in office as Minister of the Interior, he suddenly suggested that the invitation should be extended to Madame Roland as well—and revealed that Roland had contemplated leaving Paris when the Prussians were advancing. Roland's friends replied by demanding that Danton should follow Roland's example, and give a full account of his use of public money. On 18 October, Roland, Rebecquy and Larivière suggested that Danton dared not do this, and on 26 October Lidon's remarks on the same subject led to such an outcry that Danton could not make himself heard in reply.[4] The heat of debate might excuse the original innuendo, but not its systematic prosecution. Thus the leaders of the Convention united their opponents and produced the trend of opinion indicated by the narrowness of Guadet's election to the Presidency on 18 October and by Fabre d'Eglantine's claim in the Jacobins that the first general hostility towards the Paris delegation was being replaced by something like equilibrium. Probably

[1] *Moniteur*, xiv, 135, 138, 143, 153, 247.

[2] *Moniteur*, xiv, 153, 247, 253, 259. See also *Jacobins*, iv, 381, Mathiez, *La Révolution française*, ii, 117, and Lefebvre, *La Convention*, i, 68.

[3] Danton had resigned from the Executive Council in order to take his seat as a deputy in the Convention.   [4] *Moniteur*, xiv, 67, 243–4, 308.

many deputies shared the view of the speaker who on 25 October demanded that 'the Assembly should cease tearing itself to pieces for the sake of Don Quixotes like Barbaroux and Marat'.[1]

This swing of opinion may account for the renewal of the attempt to crush Robespierre. On 29 October Roland presented a report upon the state of Paris, producing papers which he said would show that the assassination of seven of his friends was contemplated and that Robespierre was still attempting to establish a dictatorship.[2] Guadet, as President, attempted to curtail Robespierre's reply, and Rebecquy, Barbaroux and Louvet all rose to denounce him. The attempt miscarried. Just as Buzot was about to seize the chance to present proposals for the capital punishment of sedition, Louvet obtained the rostrum and pronounced a long diatribe against Robespierre, Danton and Marat, ending by demanding that Buzot's proposals should be accepted without discussion, that Roland should call in regular troops to control Paris, and that Robespierre should be impeached. The Convention ignored the demands, and gave Robespierre a week in which to prepare his reply.[3] On the next day, 30 October, a similar situation recurred. A new denunciation of the Commune by Roland, and further far-reaching demands by Barbaroux, again diverted attention from Buzot's proposals.[4] On both occasions the men particularly hostile to Robespierre and to Paris manifested their disunity in action, and their individual and divergent attempts to rush stringent legislation, not untainted by personal vindictiveness, through a cautious assembly prevented the passage of the essential measures of security acceptable to the majority of deputies.

Indeed, by the beginning of November the swing of opinion appears to have led to the appearance of a moderate group, anxious to prevent the recurrence of personal recrimination. Camille Desmoulins referred directly to the existence of such a

---

[1] *Moniteur*, xiv, 245, 294, and Mathiez, *La Révolution française*, ii, 121. Cp. *Jacobins*, iv, 443.

[2] The seven being named as Brissot, Buzot, Barbaroux, Vergniaud, Lasource, Guadet and Roland: *Moniteur*, xiv, 337, 431.

[3] *Moniteur*, xiv, 338, 340. See also *Opinion de J. P. Birotteau* and *Discours de Jérôme Pétion* as supporting pamphlets against Robespierre (Paris, 1792, B.M., F.852.12 and F.665.9).

[4] *Moniteur*, xiv, 348, 350–3.

group in his journal *La Tribune des Patriotes*, calling it the *Phlegmatics* and naming Pétion, Barère, Rabaud St. Etienne, Condorcet and 'even' Lacroix and Vergniaud as its probable leaders.[1] This development was apparent on 5 November when Robespierre replied to Louvet's accusations, and Barbaroux and Louvet made themselves appear ridiculous by persistent efforts to renew their charges. Some deputies supported them, others opposed, and a third section, including Pétion, supported Barère's call for concentration on matters of public importance, so that after much disorder the Convention ultimately passed 'almost unanimously' to the business of the day.[2] The Presidency, too, was now bestowed upon less controversial figures: Guadet was succeeded on 2 November by Hérault de Séchelles, and the honour then went to Grégoire on 16 November and to Barère on 2 December.[3]

At the same time, however, an increase in the pressure of the Montagnards' opposition to the majority became apparent. On 6 November, for example, the Committee of General Security presented a report upon the state of Paris which suggested that minor disorders by misguided provincial recruits had been deliberately exaggerated by those who wished to discredit the capital and encourage federalism. St. André then called for the publication of this report, implying that only enemies of national unity would object. In their efforts to reply to this insinuation Buzot and Lasource were repeatedly interrupted. Dubois-Crancé attempted to invoke the support of the public galleries, and the voting was contested with cries for an *appel nominal*. Disorder continued until the President had actually quitted the hall.[4] In the Jacobin Club, too, a more doctrinaire attitude was increasingly adopted, and responsibility for the September Massacres, now acclaimed as the result of revolutionary zeal, was openly accepted and even made a cardinal point of the Jacobin faith.[5] Such aggressive confidence made more intransigent such men as Buzot, who on 6 November publicly identified himself with the principle with which Barbaroux is said to

---

[1] *La Tribune des patriotes*, No. 25, cited by Mathiez, *La Révolution française*, ii, 121.
[2] *Moniteur*, xiv, 389–96.   [3] *Moniteur*, xiv, 369, 501, 628.   [4] *Moniteur*, xiv, 406–10.
[5] 'Without those days the Revolution would never have been achieved'—Collot d'Herbois, 5 November 1792 (*Jacobins*, iv, 460).

have rebuffed Robespierre in September: 'Between virtue and vice there can be no compromise.' Thus the embryonic centre group was disregarded by both the Montagnards and their principal opponents. Its further emergence was prevented by the passionate pressure of the Mountain in ensuing debates about the position of Paris and the fate of the deposed King, pressure which ended the possibility that a division would appear between the friends of Brissot and the majority of the Convention.

Throughout the autumn conflict continued between the Convention and the Commune of Paris, and became increasingly embittered. Valazé and Pétion, for example, voiced the feelings of an outraged assembly when the Commune, over-zealous in guarding its royal prisoners, openly defied its authority. The Montagnard deputies upheld the cause of their municipality, and so great was the uproar over an attempt to end the permanence of the electoral assemblies of the Sections of Paris that the President actually broke his handbell in his attempts to secure some measure of silence.[1] In particular, the presence in Paris of some twelve thousand volunteers summoned by deputies from the provinces caused much disturbance. In November a Montagnard proposal to send them to fight the Austrians led to savage recriminations: Buzot suggested that the proposal came from the very men who had roused Parisian hostility to these volunteers, and who continually represented the rabble of Paris to be the sovereign people of France; and Barbaroux, calling the proposal part of an evil intrigue by the men of September, renewed his demand for a provincial guard for the Convention.[2] In December, the arrival of a fresh contingent of provincial troops from Finistère was marked by an address in which they undertook to crush anarchy in Paris. Their arrival focused Marat's attention on Kervélegan and the other deputies from Brittany—until significant references to the influence upon the newcomers of Pache, the Montagnard Minister of War, ended the episode.[3]

---

[1] *Moniteur*, xiv, 747, 754, and xv, 72–4.
[2] *Moniteur*, xiv, 447–9; *Jacobins*, iv, 418; Wallon, *La Révolution du 31 Mai*, i, 77–81.
[3] *Moniteur*, xiv, 831–3 and xv, 6.

By December, in fact, both the Montagnards and their opponents had good reason to complain of each other's attempts to exert illicit influence upon the assembly. Although they certainly exaggerated the amount of propaganda circulated by Roland's information service, the *Bureau d'Esprit Publique*, the Montagnards had some grounds for protesting about the tendency of their opponents to give highly coloured accounts of proceedings in Paris to their provincial constituents. These caused such an influx of addresses of protest from the Departments that the time allocated to their reception had to be doubled, and there were several stormy scenes in which the Montagnards alleged that an attempt was being made to stir up a civil war.[1] The Montagnards were also active in the Jacobin Club, and even in the Convention itself, before the formal session began. The public galleries were regularly filled with their supporters, and Manuel's attempt to restrict admission to ticket-holders met with a storm of Montagnard disapproval.[2]

In these circumstances the campaign for effective police protection of the Convention was renewed. On 11 January 1793, in a famous phrase, Buzot told the assembly that only if it had a guard drawn from the provinces could it be free enough to legalize the creation of such a force. As the trial of the King approached its climax the growing tension inclined the assembly to favour the plan, which was actually agreed to on 13 January. It might even have been enforced had not Boyer-Fonfrède, a deputy of the Gironde whose restraint gave him much influence in the Convention, cast doubts upon its expediency[3]—a notable illustration of the absence of anything approaching party discipline amongst those 'bound together by the bonds of friendship'.

Meanwhile the trial of the King proceeded. In this, the lofty legal issues first propounded were steadily superseded by the purely political considerations of what soon became another aspect of the struggle for control of the Convention and of

---

[1] *Moniteur*, xv, 21, 69–70. Expenditure on the bureau is analysed by Lefebvre, *La Convention*, i, 81–3. See also *Jacobins*, iv, 653, and *Valazé*, 119–21.

[2] *Moniteur*, xiv, 656, 738–9, and xv, 236; *Jacobins*, iv, 409, 509.

[3] *Moniteur*, xv, 112–14, 180.

France. From the beginning initiative in this contest lay with the Montagnards, who were in an advantageous position as critics of the existing situation. On paper, returning royalist *émigrés* were still severely penalized, but in practice much of the legislation was ineffective, a fact for which Roland, as Minister of the Interior, must bear some share of responsibility. Apparently some prominent deputies favoured an even more liberal *régime*. In October Vergniaud had pressed for the release of all persons irregularly arrested, and Lanjuinais on 8 November spoke disparagingly of the Tribunal of 17 August, which Buzot later condemned as a revolutionary instrument that had outlived its purpose.[1] Such leniency naturally enhanced the suspicions of the Montagnards, who recalled the ambiguous attitude the Brissotins had taken towards the Revolution of 10 August and the cautious provisional settlement they had made immediately afterwards. The argument that the suspension of the King and the summoning of the Convention showed only commendable willingness to await the decision of the nation as a whole carried little weight in the republican atmosphere prevailing in Paris four months later, appearing artificial and even equivocal. Thus the friends of Brissot were exposed to accusations of royalism even before the trial began, and the hesitations and evasions which they and a great many more deputies showed in the course of the ensuing debates provided endless opportunities for the reiteration of the charge.

Amongst other historians, Mathiez may be particularly mentioned as one who has accepted the truth of the Montagnard accusation. His arguments, however, do not seem convincing. For example, he regards the report which was presented to the Convention by Valazé on 6 November as inadequate and misdirected, comparing it unfavourably to that presented by Mailhe next day.[2] Valazé in fact spoke for the Commission of Twenty-four, which had been appointed to seek for proof of the alleged corruption in the Legislative Assembly. His report was negative, and was as much an indictment of the Montagnard

---

[1] *Moniteur*, xiv, 151, 424, 493. Mathiez, *La Révolution française*, ii, 114, regards the relaxation of the 'first Terror' as a deliberate attempt to win over the Feuillants: cp. Lefebvre, *La Première Terreur*, pp. 288–300.

[2] Mathiez, *op. cit.*, ii, chapter iv, particularly pp. 124–6, and *Moniteur*, xiv, 399, 414.

Committee of General Security as of the King. Mailhe, however, spoke for the Legislative Committee of the Convention, which had been considering the specific question of the legality of putting the King on trial. His conclusion, that the King could be judged by the Convention, was indeed, as Mathiez says, a substantial step forward, but it was not one that Valazé should have taken in advance.

Discussion of Mailhe's recommendation, which began on 13 November, was at first concerned with methods of procedure and the legal responsibility of the King. Although the Mountain at once began to press for quick decisions and to imply that reluctance to take them was an indication of royalist sympathies, the preliminary debates were conducted with great solemnity. Pétion's appeal[1] that even 'the silly dogma of royal inviolability' should be decided as a separate issue in order to establish the absolute legality of all subsequent proceedings, is typical of the cautious and rational approach generally adopted. On 20 November, however, Roland's account of his discovery of secret papers in a cupboard in the Tuileries—the notorious *armoire de fer*—revived the conflict of personalities. His foolishness in opening the cache without first summoning official witnesses exposed him to the charge immediately made by the Mountain that he had abstracted documents likely to implicate his own friends, particularly as the papers included letters from royalists advising the King to appoint Kersaint and others as ministers and stating that sixteen members of the Legislative were prepared to sell their services to the Court. Kersaint, Guadet and Rouyer, who were most directly concerned, succeeded in convincing the Convention of their innocence only after grave harm had been done to their prestige.[2]

As this matter was being investigated, discussion about the trial continued, becoming ever more embittered by prejudice and suspicion. Only the Montagnards' attitude was clear and uncompromising, for they steadily asserted that the very existence of the King was an implicit condemnation of the Revolution. In their view, developed by Robespierre on 3 December after a preliminary speech by Saint Just on 13 November, the people had already condemned Louis by rising in revolt against

[1] *Moniteur*, xiv, 464.   [2] *Moniteur*, xiv, 530, 639, 645, 652, and *Jacobins*, iv, 498.

him on 10 August, and any further attempt to bring him to trial could only call this verdict, and hence the Revolution itself, into question. They therefore proclaimed it the obvious duty of the Convention to condemn the King without further delay.[1] Although the majority of deputies were not at first ready to accept such stern realism, the Montagnard argument was ultimately irresistible, for none could oppose it without appearing to countenance counter-revolution. This was the terrible logic which eventually sent Louis to the guillotine and enabled the Mountain to brand as self-confessed enemies of the people all those who failed to record an unqualified vote for the penalty of death.

In these circumstances the position of the friends of Brissot and Roland was particularly invidious,[2] for if they ceased to oppose the Mountain they lost their last pretensions to leadership of the Convention. They were repeatedly accused of royalism, a charge given some semblance of substance as various documents written in the difficult days of July and August came to light, and to avoid both this stigma and a tame acquiescence in Montagnard leadership they were compelled to seek some middle course which would combine republicanism with a victory over Robespierre. This would appear to be the real explanation of their evasions and of the different proposals they put forward in the course of debates which ever became less academic and more marked by Montagnard turbulence and personal vituperation.

On the day following Robespierre's blunt pronouncement of principle, Buzot demanded that, as it had been suggested that the Convention contained royalist sympathizers, any attempt to re-establish the monarchy should be proclaimed a capital offence. Amid general applause Montagnard opposition became apparent, whereupon Buzot added 'under whatever name it appears'—a phrase implying that the Montagnards were in reality agitating on behalf of their colleague Philippe-Egalité, the Duke of Orleans. After considerable disorder the decree was accepted, no Montagnard daring to oppose it, but the campaign for a swift decision was at once renewed as Robespierre

[1] *Moniteur*, xiv, 446, 466.
[2] 'So long as Roland lives, all aristocrats are attracted to him.' *Jacobins*, iv, 574 (16 December 1792).

reiterated his demand that Louis should be condemned at once 'by virtue of the insurrection'. To this Buzot could only reply by insinuating that the Mountain had good reasons for wishing to silence the King.[1]

Two days later Marat directly attacked Roland and his 'royalist faction', and demanded that Louis's fate be decided by an *appel nominal* 'so that the traitors in this assembly shall be known'.[2] On the next day, 7 December, the Montagnards attempted to substantiate their innuendos through the Committee of General Security, which produced evidence relating to the relationship which had once existed between Fauchet, the Rolands and Narbonne.[3] Guadet's proposal on 9 December that the electoral assemblies should be empowered to recall all deputies whose loyalty they doubted was probably an attempt to recapture the initiative, but it was so obviously inexpedient that the Mountain easily defeated it as an appeal to the aristocracy.[4]

On 10 December Louis was formally indicted, and next day he had to appear before the Convention for questioning, an occasion which enabled Valazé to treat him with studied arrogance. The King's counsel were then allowed to prepare his defence, but even the interval which followed was interrupted. On 16 December the Montagnard Thuriot successfully moved a snap decree making any form of federalism a capital crime, and Buzot immediately counter-attacked by proposing that all the Orleanist family should be exiled from France. Violent controversy broke out, in which Louvet and Lanjuinais supported Buzot, and Kersaint defended Roland against diversionary attacks. Buzot's proposal was finally accepted in a mutilated form, only to be suspended three days later, after the Mountain had made it abundantly clear that they would not accept the decision of the majority.[5]

Hardly had Louis's counsel presented the defence on 26 December than controversy was resumed as the Mountain again demanded an immediate vote. On this occasion Lanjuinais

---

[1] *Moniteur*, xiv, 655–6.   [2] *Moniteur*, xiv, 673.
[3] The occasion of Madame Roland's dramatic appearance at the bar of the Convention (*Moniteur*, xiv, 684–92).
[4] *Moniteur*, xiv, 701.   [5] *Moniteur*, xiv, 723, 762, 767, 797.

boldly condemned the 'scandalous ferocity' shown by certain deputies, which he considered to be turning the whole trial into a farce. He and his friends, he said, 'would rather die than illegally condemn even the worst of tyrants', and he therefore asked the Convention to abandon the trial in favour of a simple declaration, to be openly passed as a measure of national security. The Mountain, however, was not to be diverted: the plea was represented as a device to save Louis's life, and much was made of Lanjuinais's ill-advised reference to 'the conspiracy of 10 August'.[1]

On 27 December the debate took another turn when Salle proposed that whatever decision was reached in the Convention should be referred to the people for their final approval. This, move is often represented as a desperate bid to save the King, for it seems certain that if a referendum had taken place the conservative countryside would have rejected the death penalty.[2] No such ulterior motive need be sought, however, for the idea of the appeal to the people afforded its advocates every prospect of success in the attempt to resist and discredit the Mountain. By supporting it, they could prove their ardour for the Revolution by their willingness to accept the decision of the sovereign people, and their patriotism by claiming that national unity would follow a national verdict. Above all, they could if necessary condemn the King without bowing down to Robespierre, who would be embarrassed in his turn if he tried to oppose so democratic a proposal.

Unfortunately for the *appelants*, as they came to be called, Robespierre remained obdurate, secure in the simplicity of his argument and confident of the support of Paris. Easily evading the trap, he repeated that the people had already spontaneously and decisively demonstrated their will on 10 August, and he seized upon the fundamental weakness of the new proposal— its inexpediency. A referendum, in his view, was not only superfluous but even positively dangerous, since at best royalist propaganda would be rampant and, at worst, civil war would break out in the already disordered countryside. Only partisans

[1] *Moniteur*, xiv, 848.
[2] *Moniteur*, xiv, 859. See also *Valazé*, p. 104, and Mathiez, *La Révolution française*, ii, 133.

of despotism, he thought, could seriously propose such folly.[1]
To add point to this argument, a deputation of the citizens of
Paris appeared before the Convention on 30 December, complete with representatives of those wounded or bereaved on
10 August, and when deputies persisted in desultory discussion,
even appearing to favour the idea of the referendum, the
Mountain suddenly revealed[2] their knowledge of the letters
written by Vergniaud to Louis just before the insurrection, in
the days when 'the Montagnards alone were guided by
instinctive patriotism'.

On 14 January 1793, after the debate had been adjourned
for a week in order to allow deputies to print and circulate their
personal opinions, the final stages in the conflict over the King
began. The *appelants* obtained priority of decision for their proposal, an arrangement which ought to have gained them the
initiative in the final vote upon punishment. But in the event
the referendum was rejected, and Lanjuinais's effort to subject
the decisive vote upon the penalty to an unusually large majority
was also a failure.[3] Leadership remained with Robespierre, and
his opponents were compelled to accept a public vote in which
they must either follow in his train or else appear to abjure the
Revolution itself.

This long struggle over the Trial should therefore be regarded,
not as a contest between royalists and republicans,[4] but as a
continuation of the conflict for leadership of the Convention.
This interpretation of the struggle as a series of political
manœuvres implies that some of the deputies were insincere in
their arguments, particularly perhaps those who pleaded for a
referendum. But sincerity is a hard commodity to measure. In
an assembly largely composed of lawyers, there were many men
who, like Fauchet, Lehardi or Pétion, had reasonable doubts
about the legality of the trial, or who, like Valady, distrusted
the appearance of retrospective law. Others, like Lanjuinais,

---

[1] *Moniteur*, xiv, 876.

[2] By his own account, Gasparin, who exposed the story of the letters written by
Vergniaud and his friends to Louis, had known of them and had told of his knowledge in the previous August. *Moniteur*, xv, 6, 41.

[3] *Moniteur*, xv, 144, 149–52, 183.

[4] See F. A. Aulard, 'L'opinion républicaine et l'opinion royaliste sous la Première
République avant le 9 Thermidor', *La Révolution française*, xxxvi (1899), p. 491.

Kersaint or Manuel, were horrified by the passions that prejudiced the debates. A great many deputies, too, doubted the expediency of so irrevocable an act as the execution of the King, with all its unforeseeable consequences at home and abroad.[1] Almost every man had his own opinion, and to study in the Croker Collection[2] those which were printed is to be convinced that proceedings were confused by a multiplicity of separate issues of conscience. To assume, as some have done, that all these arguments were counterfeit is to return to the fallacy that the Mountain sought to propagate, that all who opposed them were united in conspiracy and deception.

More interesting is the comment of the British Ambassador on 17 December that 'Roland and Brissot's party are certainly struggling to save the King in order to humble Robespierre'.[3] The Mountain was the minority throughout the debates which preceded the final voting, but its power bore little relation to its numerical strength. It became, in fact, intolerably vociferous and aggressive. Disorder was commonplace, and on two consecutive days, while the voice of the President was drowned in uproar, deputies streamed across the hall behind such tempestuous leaders as Barbaroux and Louvet in an effort to compel the Montagnards to be silent. Responsibility for incidents of this kind was no doubt divided, but the fundamental evil sometimes appeared clearly, as when Vergniaud protested that 'the majority of this assembly cannot remain for ever under the domination of a seditious minority', and when Tureau, a Montagnard, declared 'we are here under an oppressive majority'.[4] A noisy minority, determined to dominate, was making representative government impossible, and the majority, whose prejudices were a contributory cause of the trouble, was often forced to yield to the dictation of disorder.

The majority, moreover, was distinct only in its hostility

[1] e.g., *Moniteur*, xiv, 470–1, 650, 724, 736, 849, 851, and xv, 183, 187, 198, 206, 214.

[2] Amongst other material, I have consulted those pamphlets which record the opinions of many of those deputies who have since been called Girondins: B.M., F.914–19, 921, in the series 'Procès de Louis XVI'. For fuller particulars of some of the more significant of these pamphlets, see Bibliography, p. 233 below.

[3] Cited by Thompson, *Robespierre*, i, 303.

[4] *Moniteur*, xiv, 854 and 865 for 26 and 27 December 1792, and 767 and 866 for the comments of Vergniaud and Tureau.

towards the Mountain. At all stages of the debate about the King its disunity was manifest. As we have seen, some deputies felt that Louis could not legally be tried at all. Buzot secured the rejection of Pétion's proposed method of procedure. Rabaut St. Etienne criticized Pétion's acceptance of the competence of the Convention, and was himself criticized by Buzot. Even on the clear issue of whether or not voting on the appeal to the people should precede that on punishment Carra and Lanjuinais favoured the view of the Montagnards. When the vote on punishment was taken, Barbaroux voted for death, declaring that he did so freely, whereas Lanjuinais had deplored the taking of the vote 'under threat of the knives and guns of the factious'. Again, where Brissot, Louvet and Valazé demanded that execution should be delayed until domestic and foreign dangers had passed, Gensonné opposed any reprieve lest he should appear to question the decision of the majority.[1] Such disunity almost wholly accounts for the victory won by Robespierre's positive leadership of his purposeful phalanx of turbulent Montagnards.

The trial culminated in four separate votes, in each of which deputies had to pronounce their opinions publicly. These were to determine whether the King was guilty, whether there should be a referendum, what punishment was to be inflicted, and whether a reprieve should be granted. Every effort was made to ensure that all deputies voted, even the sick being brought to the hall, and the results were fully recorded[2]—indeed, many a man's future was decided by his decisions on these occasions, persecution from republicans and from royalists coming in the course of time. As there are only two other similar records of the way in which deputies voted in the period here considered, and those ones in which attendance was not nearly so complete, the information here available is most germane to any attempt to assess the unity and strength, or even the distinctiveness, of the so-called Girondin party. It is therefore necessary temporarily to revert to consideration of the list of 200 supposed Girondins, compiled by historians, as we have seen, from the Montagnard proscription lists of 1793.

[1] *Moniteur*, xiv, 483, 873, 875, and xv, 184, 151, 152, 214, 243.
[2] *Appels nominaux sur le jugement de Louis XVI* (Paris, 1793), B.M., F.1276.1.

L

On the first question, that of Louis's guilt, the Convention was not seriously divided. Of the 720 deputies who voted, 683 pronounced the King to be guilty, and of the 200 supposed Girondins 183 voted with the majority.[1] The first distinction which appears between the 200 and the majority of their colleagues appears in the voting on the second occasion, concerning the referendum, which the Convention rejected by 425 votes to 286, with nine abstentions. Of the 200, only fifty voted for this rejection, whereas 136 voted for the proposal.[2] This difference between the majority of the 200 and the majority of the Convention appeared in the other two divisions also. The Convention decided that the King should die by 387 votes to 334, but only thirty-six of the 200 were prepared to vote unconditionally for the death penalty.[3] Similarly, the Convention rejected the reprieve by 380 votes to 310, but only forty-four of the 200 did so.[4] The significance of these figures is seen if they are expressed as percentages, failures to vote and ambiguous voting being ignored. It thus appears that of the 200, 71 per cent favoured the appeal to the people, 74 per cent opposed the execution of the King, and 73 per cent voted for a reprieve. There is clearly here substantial majority support for more moderate courses than those favoured by the extreme element which dominated the Convention on this occasion.

The percentages, however, are not equivalent to proof of party unity, for they do not show to what extent the moderate majority was composed of the same deputies in each vote. Closer examination shows that ninety-three of the 200 deputies voted for moderation on all three occasions, i.e. for the appeal to the people, for some punishment less than the unconditional

[1] Eleven deputies were absent, and no vote is recorded for Gardien. Larivière, Rouzet and Valady questioned the competence of the Convention. Noël abstained, and Giroust voted ambiguously.

[2] Eleven deputies of the 200 were absent on this occasion also. Noël and Vallée abstained, and Asselin gave an ambiguous vote.

[3] Nine deputies were absent, Chevalier and Noël abstained, and Guyomer and Boucheroux voted ambiguously. Of the remaining 187 deputies, 129 voted for some punishment less than death, thirteen favoured death only if it were accompanied by a reprieve, and nine accepted Mailhe's amendment, by which the execution and a reprieve could be supported as separate issues.

[4] Fifteen deputies were absent. Chambon, Condorcet, Grangeneuve and Noël abstained, and Antiboul voted ambiguously.

death penalty, and for a reprieve. To these should be added those whose votes were essentially similar—ten who voted for death with a deferment of execution, eight who failed to vote on one of the three occasions, and Duchâstel, who only voted once, against immediate execution. The total of 112 deputies whose voting was consistently that of the majority of the 200 certainly gives us the hard core of moderates amongst these men. It is the more remarkable that hardly any of them were prominent deputies. Many of them, indeed, are scarcely known at all apart from these votes.

Examination of the way in which the better-known deputies amongst the 200 voted is even more revealing. In a table given in Appendix C at the end of this volume it is shown that if as a result of the evidence reviewed in previous chapters the names of sixty men who appear to have been associated in one way or another with Brissot are taken and sub-divided into groups according to their probable degree of intimacy with him, then unity of voting on these three occasions is patently in inverse proportion to the closeness of the relationship. In other words, the greatest political disunity is to be found, not on the fringe, but at the centre of the supposed Brissotin faction. Although of the seventeen men who may be assumed to have been closest to Brissot thirteen voted for the referendum, only seven voted for the reprieve, whereas seven opposed it. In the crucial vote concerning the penalty, the division amongst these seventeen was nine to eight in favour of execution,[1] and the number of them who voted consistently for moderation was only three— Brissot himself, Louvet and Valazé, all of whom, incidentally, were invariably rigid in resistance to Robespierre. That there should be such disunity on so critical an occasion, and that such men as Barbaroux, Ducos, Gensonné, Isnard, Lasource and Vergniaud should have favoured severity, is in itself a sufficient comment upon the view that a distinct Brissotin or Girondin party is to be found in the Convention in January 1793. Rather does the evidence that has been considered here suggest that Louis died because the majority of the assembly was disunited,

---

[1] The vote for the amendment by which execution and a reprieve could be simultaneously supported being taken, as it was in the Convention, as an unconditional vote for execution. Four of the seventeen voted in this way.

and that in this respect, as in others, the small Brissotin group which had come from the Legislative Assembly had become indistinguishable from that majority.

CHAPTER VII

The Victory of the Mountain

IN the Spring of 1793 the invasion which had been repulsed in
the previous autumn again threatened to overwhelm France.
This change of fortune made it imperative that the deadlock
which had developed in the Convention should be broken, for
although the opponents of the Mountain could still gain
majorities in the assembly, they could seldom translate resolu-
tions into effective executive action. The current belief in a
rigid separation of powers still forbade members of the legislature to exercise any direct control of government, and the
executive committees which eventually developed were still
only embryonic, their direction being a matter of bitter dispute
with the Mountain. Even a success in the Convention, usually
won only after sessions of endless filibustering, remained transient whenever it was opposed by the Commune and Clubs of
Paris. More than ever the leaders of the majority in the Convention were cursed with responsibility without real power.

To attempt to resolve this difficulty by having a new election
was barely possible even in theory, and quite impossible in
practice. The Convention was not officially a legislature, but
only an assembly called to create a new constitution. Until its
work was complete no legal electoral procedure could exist, and
talk of a dissolution while the enemy armies were advancing
seemed to savour of defeatism. In any event, an election was
impracticable: as Buzot later acknowledged,[1] the majority of
Frenchmen were at least passively royalist in sympathy. A
popular vote would at best produce a situation which no true
revolutionary could tolerate, and at worst it might lead to
disorder or even civil war. Thus tentative proposals for an
appeal to the people as a means of resolving the situation in the

[1] Buzot, *Mémoires, passim*, particularly pp. 10–21 in the edition of Guadet and
p. 31 in that of Dauban.

assembly merely provided the Mountain with ammunition for new accusations of federalism and treason.

So the Convention remained caught in its vicious circle of futility. Tumult in the Chamber became commonplace and even armed violence was not unknown. In contrast to the increasing national emergency all this appeared artificial, and deputies, already all too conscious of the power of the Montagnard pressure group, also became increasingly aware of the paramount need to establish some unity of leadership for the distracted nation. From January until June this note of necessity was heard, faintly at first and then more loudly and more deeply, until at length a sufficient number of obscure deputies were ready to acquiesce in the triumph of the Mountain. The story of how this came about may now be told.

The weeks following the death of the King were relatively peaceful, for the passionate conflict had left men both physically and emotionally exhausted. The drift to war with England, Spain and Holland was accepted almost as a matter of course. Indeed, even in the previous autumn, when France had been confronted by a serious dilemma, foreign affairs had not caused any clear division of opinion in the assembly.[1] In the period of success which followed the Prussian retreat, the logic of revolutionary doctrine had demanded that the territories which the French armies occupied should attain democratic self-government as sovereign states, but the national needs of France made it equally imperative that she should compensate herself for the costs of her revolutionary crusade and prevent the return of reactionary rulers to her borders. Roland's government had not given any clear lead on this problem, and after some confused debates it was left to La Revellière-Lépaux, hitherto an inconspicuous deputy, to propose the famous *Fraternité et secours* decree of 19 November.[2] Only one man opposed the vote which incorporated Savoy in the French republic, and Cambon's decree of 15 December, which in effect introduced the depreciated

---

[1] I cannot find that the debates support the interpretation of Michon, *Robespierre et la guerre révolutionnaire, 1791–1792*, p. 128 ff., that Robespierre consistently favoured the view that peace should be made as soon as it became practicable.

[2] *Moniteur*, xiv, 516, 588.

French *assignat* into all areas under French control, was also given general support.[1] Such expansion and its accompanying propaganda shattered all accepted principles of public law, and when this was made manifest by the opening of the River Scheldt the Dutch and the English alike were irrevocably antagonized. To France, however, a continued career of conquest seemed to hold the promise of security and financial stability, and no section of the Convention was wise or courageous enough to disillusion a people intoxicated by easy victories.[2]

So far as controversy had been aroused in the assembly about these matters it had been concerned with questions of administration. Early in November a Directory of Purchases had been created to supervise and eventually supplant the private contractors who had hitherto supplied the armies, and in its cumbrous working the Montagnards found a fruitful field for allegations that Roland's associates in the financial world were profiting from inefficiency. When Roland discovered that Pache, the War Minister he had himself recommended, had acquired Montagnard sympathies, he withdrew his own representative from the Directory, and blamed Pache for all the difficulties of supply encountered by the armies. Pache, for his part, repudiated the loans which Dumouriez, who had now resumed friendly relations with Brissot,[3] had been raising on his own initiative in Belgium.[4]

Behind all this lay the sterner struggle for control of the Convention and of the Executive Council. The Mountain's success in the campaign for the execution of the King had somewhat counter-balanced the hostility their violence aroused, and

---

[1] *Moniteur*, xiv, 755–8.
[2] The Convention unanimously declared war on England and Holland on 1 February 1793, and the declaration of war on Spain was accepted without discussion in the assembly on 7 March (*Moniteur*, xv, 330–2 and 639–40). Bancal's doubts about whether Britain would peacefully accept the status of a French Department are illuminating: *Henri Bancal à Anacharsis Cloots* (Paris, 1792), B.M., F.777.2.
[3] Temporarily broken after the dismissal of Roland by Louis XVI.
[4] *Jacobins*, iv, 344, 544; *Moniteur*, xiv, 550; Lefebvre, *La Convention*, i, 165–71; and on the relationship between Brissot and Dumouriez, Brissot, *Correspondance et Papiers*, p. 314 ff. and R. M. Brace, 'General Dumouriez and the Girondins, 1792–1793', *American Historical Review*, lvi, No. 3 (1951), pp. 497–9.

the assassination of a deputy, Lepelletier, apparently provided irrefutable proof of their argument that moderation merely provided a cover for the lawlessness of reaction. The incident led to the suppression of Roland's Information Service, and to a Montagnard victory in the elections for the renewal of the Committee of General Security.[1] On 24 January the rise in Montagnard influence was again revealed when Rabaut St. Etienne, one of those who had supported the proposal for a referendum about the King, was elected President only after two recounts, by 176 out of 355 votes, and the three new Secretaries were all men of Montagnard sympathies.[2] In the Executive Council, too, the change was obvious. Of those who had taken office in the previous August, only Clavière and Lebrun remained hostile to the Mountain. Pache, who had replaced Servan with Roland's recommendation in October, had become sympathetic to the Montagnards, while Garat, who had succeeded Danton as Minister of Justice, was moving steadily towards them. Monge, another of Roland's associates, had proved himself a nonentity, and on 22 January Roland himself was driven to resign, his office being taken over by Garat and his supporters being hard put to it even to win approval for the publication of his last official letter.[3]

What was really needed was a more effective means by which the Convention could supervise and control the executive, but moves in this direction usually degenerated into fights over the appointment of particular individuals. A scheme put forward by Sieyès for the reorganization of the Ministry of War was exploited by Buzot, Barbaroux and Salle as an opportunity for attacking Pache, and all that was achieved was the abolition of the Directory of Purchases, which had become obnoxious to all. In an attempt to restore harmony, Barère moved the resignation of both Pache and Monge, but Monge was re-elected and Pache replaced by a careerist, Beurnonville, both men being accepted only because they were too insignificant to be repugnant to any section of opinion.[4] Similarly, the creation of the Committee of General Defence on 1 January has the appearance of a vain attempt by the opponents of the Mountain to recover

---

[1] *Moniteur*, xv, 256, 265.   [2] *Moniteur*, xv, 265, 276.   [3] *Moniteur*, xv, 271–3.
[4] *Moniteur*, xv, 287–92, 311–15, 320–2, 328–30, 351–2, 356, 496.

influence. Although it was supposed to be a co-ordinating body, its members—including Brissot, Guadet, Gensonné, Pétion and Boyer-Fonfrède—remained preoccupied with the work of the committees from which they were drawn, and its meetings, being held openly, became miniatures of the Convention, so over-crowded and turbulent that neither private discussion nor public progress was possible.[1]

Thus although the extension of the war made military reform and greater executive efficiency essential, very little of value was achieved.[2] The Montagnards gained politically by the elimination of all but two of their opponents from the Executive Council, and they scored another success when Pache was elected Mayor of Paris by 11,881 votes to the 404 cast for Roland.[3] The real gainer, however, was Dumouriez. With a friendly and acquiescent War Minister and a free hand to arrange loans and supplies as he liked, he had acquired a dangerous degree of independence.

It was at this point that on 15 February Condorcet presented his long-awaited constitutional proposals to the Convention.[4] His Constitution was republican and superficially democratic, although a complex and protracted process of indirect election would have limited the effective exercise of power to the upper classes. It gave all men equality in citizenship, but its only concession to social aspirations was a promise of national assistance to the needy. In short, it gave political rights to the many and political power to the few, while trade and property rights remained absolutely free. The scheme has been regarded as representative of the political thought of a supposedly separate Girondin group,[5] but there is little evidence to support this view. Admittedly Gensonné and Vergniaud, Brissot[6] and Pétion,

---

[1] *Moniteur*, xv, 26; Aulard, *Recueil des actes du comité de salut public*, i, 376, 389. Pétion replaced Kersaint when he resigned, and other members of the Committee were Barère, Sieyès, Rouyer, Doulcet, Penières, Brunel, Lacaze and Defermon. For criticisms of its operation and membership, see *Jacobins*, v, 17, and *Moniteur*, xv, 647, and xvi, 111.

[2] See, e.g., Cambon's report on 7 May 1793 (*Moniteur*, xvi, 330).

[3] *Moniteur*, xv, 446.

[4] Duguit, Monnier, Bonnard, *Les constitutions . . . de la France depuis 1789*, p. 33 ff.; *Moniteur*, xv, 456–88.

[5] e.g., Lefebvre, *La Convention*, i, 272; Aulard, *Histoire politique*, ii, chapter v; Mathiez, *Girondins et Montagnards*, chapter iv.   [6] Later replaced by Barbaroux.

were members of the Constitutional Committee which was established soon after the Convention first met, but so too were Paine, Sieyès and even Barère, as well as Danton and Condorcet himself. It is generally agreed that in practice the Constitution was almost wholly the work of Condorcet, and he, despite his old friendship with Brissot, did not finally sever himself from the Montagnards until their hostility to his proposals drove him to do so.[1]

Like everthing else, the Constitution became a matter for political controversy. Those who opposed the Mountain did their best to accelerate its acceptance,[2] their somewhat sudden anxiety appearing explicable only in political terms. Its successful establishment would, no doubt, have restored to them the initiative which the Mountain had stolen, and done much to redeem reputations. A balance between Paris and the provinces might have been established, and revolutionary government made superfluous. Moreover, new elections under the new system would probably have led to the return of deputies and ministers who possessed national prestige and conservative support. These same reasons probably account also for the cold reception given to Condorcet by the Montagnards. They quickly gained an initial success by exposing a surreptitious attempt to include in the printed proposals a hitherto unknown minority report in favour of a Second Chamber, and they then concentrated their criticism upon the failure of the proposed Constitution to establish real political equality and upon the federalist tendencies which they claimed to detect in it.[3] Condorcet's plan did in fact include proposals apparently designed to strengthen local authorities against the central government and to strengthen the countryside against the towns. Small municipalities were to be integrated into larger *arrondissements* around single authorities; local authorities, both municipal and departmental, were to retain all their existing

---

[1] For criticism of the composition of the Committee, see *Jacobins*, iv, 380. For the position of Condorcet, see Lefebvre, *loc. cit.*—where a letter is cited in which Vergniaud asks Danton to join him at his address to correct proofs of the Constitution—and *Jacobins*, v, 30, and Chapter III above.

[2] *Moniteur*, xvi, 155, 381.

[3] *Moniteur*, xv, 516–17, and xvi, 213–16; *Jacobins*, v, 29–32; and see Chapter VIII below.

powers and to have a four-year term of office which would
make them the most stable elements in the new system. Whatever the theoretical merits of this plan, it was certainly inappropriate to the situation of France in 1793, which was one that
demanded some reversal of the decentralization established by
the Constitution of 1791.[1]

A major factor in this situation was the rapid deterioration of
the national economy.[2] In December 1792 the Convention had
hopefully abandoned the tentative and ineffective measures
taken for control of the economy by the Legislative Assembly,
reverting to complete freedom of trade. The repeated issue of
assignats, however, was accompanied by the steady depreciation
of currency, while the widening of the war increased the
demands of the armies for supplies even as it curtailed opportunities for foreign purchases. Prices rapidly outstripped pur-
chasing power, disorders occurred in the Departments, and in
Paris popular discontent was expressed by a group of extremists
known as the *Enragés*, whose first objective was effective price-
control, the *maximum*.[3]

The Convention, however, offered no remedies for the situation, pinning its faith to such palliatives as attempts to buy corn
from abroad and the offer of a limited amount of national
assistance for the poor in France. When on 12 February a deputation from the Sections of Paris came to the Convention to
demand the *maximum*, the whole assembly rejected their petition,
which even Marat condemned as excessive, outlandish and
subversive. Buzot, indeed, considered it politic to warn the
delegates that their conduct might make Paris, the cradle of
liberty, into its tomb.[4]

After similar petitions had been rejected on 22 and 24
February by both the Jacobin Society and the Convention, the
sans-culottes took the law into their own hands. Rioting broke out
in the capital on 25 February. Shops were raided and their
contents sold to the crowds at popular prices. The Convention
was united in deploring these disorders and in supporting the

[1] A. Cobban, 'Local Government during the French Revolution', *English
Historical Review*, lviii (1943), p. 24.
[2] See also Chapter VIII below.
[3] *La Vie chère*, p. 114 ff.; Lefebvre, *La Convention*, i, 278.
[4] *Moniteur*, xv, 430–6; *Jacobins*, v, 53.

efforts of the Commune to restore normal conditions, but
the disturbances naturally led to recrimination. On the day of the
riots Robespierre rose to condemn the failure of the executive
to deal effectively with the *émigrés*, whose return to France was,
in his view, responsible for the unrest reported from all quarters.
In his reply Pétion pleaded the difficulties of legislation, significantly remarking that the Convention was not a revolutionary
assembly. At the same time the opponents of the Mountain
accused Marat of instigating the disorders in an inflammatory
article which had appeared in the *Ami du Peuple*.[1] For the
moment neither side gained any advantage by these tactics, for
the Convention as a whole was unpopular in Paris. The reality
of the people's grievances had, however, been revealed, and the
spontaneity and extent of the rioting may well have suggested
to the Mountain that the future would lie with those who were
first to accept the necessity for drastic economic legislation.

From March until May 1793 the situation in the Convention
was increasingly dominated by events elsewhere—in the political clubs of Paris, in the villages of the Vendée, and particularly
on the battlefields of Belgium. Reverses in the field and economic difficulties at home revived the revolutionary ferment in
Paris. Emergency legislation shattered any hopes of stabilizing
the Revolution. The clash of personalities in the Convention
became at once more fierce and more inopportune. The growing discontent of the *sans-culottes* of Paris compelled deputies to
choose between repression and an alliance with the people, the
cost of which was to be price-control and a purging of the
Convention itself.

In the first week of March Dumouriez, who was in all probability already contemplating counter-revolutionary action,
began the belated French advance into Holland. As the Dutch
fell back before him, Coburg's Austrians struck hard at the
forces he had left to hold Belgium, routing them in the field and
forcing a general retreat to the line of the River Dyle. This sudden reverse precipitated disorders in Belgium so widespread

---

[1] *Moniteur*, xv, 544, 558–60, 568–72; *Jacobins*, v, 38.

that they amounted to a national revolt against the French forces of occupation.[1]

The Convention, meanwhile, had unanimously approved a proposal incorporating Brussels in the French Republic and had promulgated an optimistic address to the people of Holland. Even when, on 5 March, news arrived of the fall of Aix-la-Chapelle, and Choudieu proposed the immediate despatch of all federal forces in Paris to strengthen the front, fear of the Mountain took precedence over national needs. Buzot urged the supreme necessity of maintaining order in Paris and Isnard rated the Mountain for attempting to pervert parliamentary procedure. Louvet attempted to expose an assassination plot and Lanjuinais alleged that insurrection was imminent. After Barbaroux had warned deputies of the ever-present danger of anarchy, Boyer-Fonfrède succeeded in patching up a compromise by which the provincial troops were to be sent to guard their own Departments—a sterile solution which simultaneously deprived the Convention of its guardians and the generals of their reinforcements.[2]

The full extent of the reverses in Belgium only became known gradually, while wildly exaggerated rumours held sway in Paris. A blunt denial of official optimism on 8 March by Delacroix, who asserted that the French front had been broken and that a new national crisis was at hand, led to a rapid rise in public agitation. The sudden sounding of the alarm—Danton's call for an immediate levy of volunteers from Paris, a spirited call to arms from the Commune and a hasty recruiting campaign in the Sections—produced a situation similar to that of September 1792.[3] On 9 March, as volunteers paraded through the hall of the Convention, the people assembled outside. In the evening a crowd invaded the Jacobin Club, demanding a purge of the assembly, and later moving on to destroy the printing presses of Brissot's *Patriote français* and Gorsas's *Courrier*. Throughout the night many deputies hourly expected insurrection and massacre. According to Meillan, forty-three of them stayed in

---

[1] R. M. Brace, 'General Dumouriez and the Girondins, 1792–1793', *American Historical Review*, lvi, No. 3 (1951), p. 502.

[2] *Moniteur*, xv, 590, 607–8, 620–4.

[3] *Moniteur*, xv, 647, 651, 653–4.

their seats in the Convention, determined to die honourably at their posts of duty.[1]

The call for a clearance of deputies at this crisis need not occasion surprise. A clarification of the situation in the Convention was indeed one of the most urgent needs of France and one which the assembly itself seemed wholly unable to meet. Moreover, for months past the popular press, and even more the gutter press of the Revolution, had poisoned the public mind by consistently identifying criticism of the Mountain with moderation, reaction and treason, while wild accusations and demands for impeachment had become the common language of debate in clubs and Convention alike. On this occasion the populace sought scapegoats somewhat erratically. Some called for the removal from the Convention of all who had failed to vote for the execution of the King, others for that of all who had supported the 'appeal to the people' during the trial, and others again for the trial of such prominent opponents of the Mountain as 'Brissot, Pétion, Buzot, Guadet, Vergniaud, Gensonné, Barbaroux, Gorsas, Clavière, Rebecquy, Lanjuinais, etc.'[2] —to quote the resolution of the Bonconseil Section.[3]

As it happened, the storm subsided without bloodshed. The movement appears to have been a spontaneous one, which lost momentum when it failed to win the approval either of the Commune or of the Jacobin Society,[4] which remained in session throughout the night in order to disassociate itself from the rioting. A shower of rain and the vigilance of the volunteers from Brest—who had not yet left the capital—were sufficient to dispel any danger. Nevertheless those against whom the mob had demonstrated were convinced that they had again escaped assassination by a hair's-breadth, and their hatred of the Montagnard representatives of Paris was redoubled. They naturally made the most of their predicament, praising the restraint of the Commune but attacking the Montagnards as the 'Orleanist' instigators of murder.[5]

---

[1] *Moniteur*, xv, 662–3; Meillan, *Mémoires*, pp. 23–5.   [2] Author's italics.

[3] *Moniteur*, xv, 695; Lefebvre, *La Convention*, i, 307–8.

[4] At the Jacobins on 9 March Dubois-Crancé told the crowd that the massacre for which it called was a horrible measure, likely to lead to the overthrow of the Republic (*Jacobins*, v, 38).

[5] *Moniteur*, xv, 698, 700, 702–5, 730–1; Meillan, *Mémoires*, 23–5; Louvet, *A mes*

Military defeat and public unrest led also to the legislation which initiated the second Terror. Such emergency legislation, passed under popular pressure, was necessarily inimical to those who now had pretensions to moderation. At the same time, however, their opposition to these laws held up effective administration, and so brought further suspicions upon them.

On 9 March the Convention accepted two principles without much discussion—the extension of taxation on wealth, and the despatch of deputies to the Departments and the front as 'representatives on mission'.[1] By accident or design, these deputies were drawn almost entirely from the Mountain, and though this somewhat changed the balance of power in the Convention their actions in the Departments increased the influence of the Mountain where it had hitherto been weakest. On the same night the Montagnards also gained an advantage by compelling the Convention to postpone discussion about the destruction of the printing presses and by securing instead a decree forbidding any deputy to act as a journalist or an editor.[2]

The creation of the Revolutionary Tribunal was another blow to hopes of checking further revolutionary developments. This was accepted in principle on 9 March despite opposition from Birotteau and Lanjuinais, and the organization of the new court was completed in the next two days. The original proposals of the Montagnards were condemned by Vergniaud as inquisitorial, and Fonfrède's motion for the selection of jurymen from the Departments was accepted instead. In practice, however, the necessity of the hour limited the immediate choice to Paris and—by an amendment moved by Rabaut St. Etienne—its adjacent Departments. Nor could Lépaux and Vergniaud prevent, or Gensonné and Guadet repeal, the decision that jurymen should vote aloud and in public.[3]

But Danton's repeated appeals for a real reorganization of the machinery of government, even at the expense of the sacred separation of powers, remained fruitless. When the question was

---

commettans (*Mémoires*, ii, 219); *Lettre du citoyen Salle* and *Gustave Doulcet à Dominique Garat* (Paris, 1793), B.M., F.833.16 and F.R.63.29.

[1] *Moniteur*, xv, 662-3.

[2] Repealed on 1 April 1793 on the proposal of Boyer-Fonfrède, *Moniteur*, xv, 668.

[3] *Moniteur*, xv, 665-6, 671, 681-2, 684, 688.

first raised by Cambacères, Buzot rushed to condemn the idea as a move towards dictatorship, and when Danton implored the assembly not to rise without reaching a decision, the vital part of his proposals was ignored. Similarly Lépaux on 11 March condemned as dictatorial a proposal that ministers should be appointed from among the members of the assembly, and Robespierre's attempt to reopen the discussion was blocked by Bancal in terms which were little more restrained.[1] Thus the creation of what eventually became the Committee of Public Safety was delayed until the balance of forces in the Convention had been changed. Nevertheless, the futility of these perpetual recriminations was becoming more obvious. Danton roundly condemned inaction with the words 'These discussions are trivial: I see only the enemy', and Buzot's reiterated denunciations of dictatorship evoked the ominous cry 'We are here to act, not to trade in tittle-tattle'.[2]

The anxiety aroused in the Convention by military defeat yet remained but a shadow of the anger of the *sans-culottes* of Paris. On 12 March petitioners from the Section Poissonnière came to the assembly to require the resignation of Beurnonville, the Minister of War, and the impeachment of Dumouriez. Their demand was dismissed, and general indignation followed the revelations of Marat and Lesage about the current demand for a purge of the Convention itself. Lesage implied that the Mountain was fundamentally at fault for insisting on the creation of the Revolutionary Tribunal, an insinuation which provoked a reply in kind from Marat.[3] Opinion in the assembly was clearly lagging far behind that of the capital, and as yet no readiness to accept either popular policies or the necessity for repression was apparent.

Soon, however, more positive policies were enunciated. On 13 March Vergniaud delivered a speech, often quoted for its rhetoric alone, which was in fact an analysis of the situation and a demand for discipline.[4] In his view the whole Convention was

---

[1] *Moniteur*, xv, 681–2, 686.   [2] *Moniteur*, xv, 679–81.

[3] Marat had at first spoken of the demand for a purge as 'an atrocious crime, tending to destroy the National Convention' (*Moniteur*, xv, 696).

[4] He also revealed a further demand by the Quatre Nations Section for the expulsion of 'Roland, Brissot, Gensonné, Guadet, Pétion, Barbaroux, Louvet, *etc.*' [Author's italics] (*Moniteur*, xv, 700–4).

dangerously close to disaster. In the abortive insurrection of 10 March and the subsequent demands for the punishment of Dumouriez and prominent deputies he saw proof that every principle of law and justice was being threatened by a rising tide of disorder. The evil, he believed, sprang from counter-revolutionary activity, which flourished only because the Convention itself was divided into opposing groups, one of which regarded the Revolution as complete while the other thought that a measure of public unrest was a necessary attribute of national defence. This last view Vergniaud condemned, accusing the Montagnards of smoothing a path for sedition by their short-sighted sympathy for popular tumults which blinded the people to the distinction between true liberty and selfish license. If this 'new model of liberty' remained unchecked, despotism would inevitably follow. The Convention should therefore unite, and crush anarchy both by ordering the arrest of the 'revolutionary committee' which was active in Paris and by initiating a thorough investigation of the proceedings of the political organizations of the city.

Vergniaud's speech was an appeal for repression.[1] The reply of Marat[2] indicated the alternative. Deliberately avoiding 'polished discourse', he acknowledged that the Convention was indeed divided into two sections, but where he saw one as misguided by the secret sympathizers of royalism, he thought that the other, the Mountain, wished to save the republic without seeing clearly how it ought to do so. According to Marat, the way was plain—the Montagnards must show themselves to be the true allies of the people. Thus, and only thus, could the republic be preserved.

The sharp divergence of view apparent on this occasion had no immediate sequel.[3] A lengthy dispute led only to agreement that neither speech should be officially published lest the Departments be misled, and a characteristically rational speech by Boyer-Fonfrède caused the Convention to compromise on an order for the arrest of prominent agitators.[4] The military and

---

[1] It was nonetheless roundly condemned for its moderation by Louvet (*Mémoires*, i, 79).　　　　　　　　　　　　　　[2] *Moniteur*, xv, 705.
[3] There was apparently an abortive attempt at a *rapprochement* between those concerned at this time: see *Moniteur*, xvi, 105, and Meillan, *Mémoires*, p. 28.
[4] *Moniteur*, xv, 706, 711.

M

economic situation was not yet sufficiently critical for either policy to be acceptable.

Deterioration, however, was not long delayed. Recalled from Holland to restore order in Belgium, Dumouriez began by restricting the activities of Jacobin agents and by sending a letter to the Convention on 12 March which amounted to an attack upon the whole policy and administration of the Republic. He then gave the order for an advance, and was decisively defeated by the Austrians at Neerwinden on 17 March. After the frontier fortress of Louvain had also fallen to the Austrians, he notified their general, Coburg, of his readiness to lead his forces against the revolutionaries of Paris, and so was suffered to evacuate Belgium unmolested. On 27 March he reached an agreement with the Austrians by which the Constitution of 1791 was to be restored in France, with Louis XVII as King, and on 1 April he ordered the arrest of the Minister of War, Beurnonville, and the four deputies who had rushed from Paris to restore the situation, handing them over as prisoners to the enemy. Finally, after vain attempts to rouse his men to march against Paris, he galloped across the frontier and into the Austrian lines.[1]

Simultaneously, further misfortunes afflicted France. On 14 March Lasource reported the discovery of La Rouerie's conspiracy in Brittany, and Fauchet and Bancal told of similar troubles in their own Departments of Calvados and Puy de Dôme. Then on 18 March the Convention learnt of the rising in the Vendée, and heard that one of its representatives on mission had been seriously wounded in a scuffle at Orleans. Next day further unrest was reported from Lyons.[2] Everywhere, it seemed, local resistance to recruiting was providing a perfect field for royalist resistance movements, and there was a grave danger that the civil war which had already begun in the West would flare across France and destroy every obstacle in the path of the Austrian armies.

A reaction by the Convention to this long tale of trouble was delayed by the secrecy which shrouded Dumouriez's negotiations with the enemy. The news of his defeat in the field, however, could not be concealed, and a profound sense of malaise

---

[1] A. Sorel, 'Dumouriez: un général diplomate au temps de la Révolution', *Revue des deux mondes*, lxiv (1884), p. 308.   [2] *Moniteur*, xv, 714–15, 732, 743.

produced a familiar pattern of events in Paris. New revolutionary *journées*, averted only by the caution of the Montagnards, the Jacobins and the Commune, threatened on both 24 March and 1 April,[1] and new revolutionary laws were accepted by the Convention. On 19 March, for example, all armed demonstrators were placed under a ban of outlawry, and later in the month severe penalties were imposed upon priests and *émigrés*. On 21 March, too, local vigilance committees were created to supervise the activities of all foreigners[2]—committees which were to become powerful instruments of the Terror.[3]

These measures encountered little opposition in the Convention. Lasource and Fonfrède, indeed, supported the legislation against foreigners. The general willingness to bow to the prevailing wind may have been due in part to a particularly menacing address presented by the Jacobin Society of Marseilles,[4] but the principal reason was probably a deeper anxiety. The Committee of General Defence knew on 15 March of Dumouriez's letter of the 12th, a letter which afforded clear indications of his intentions.[5] No official comment was made to the Convention, but those in the know presumably saw even more clearly than their colleagues that the time was not opportune to oppose measures which might soon seem more necessary and become more popular than ever.

The gradual revelation of the full extent of Dumouriez's treachery exposed the appalling incapacity of the Convention as it was then constituted, and brought an alliance between the Montagnards and the people of Paris perceptibly closer. This was first apparent when Danton, who had hurried to the frontier for first-hand information, hesitated to give on his return an explicit account of his discoveries.[6] Ducos and Buzot questioned his conduct, suggesting that he was himself privy to the general's actions, and Danton in reply alleged that the real

---

[1] *Moniteur*, xv, 759.   [2] *Moniteur*, xv, 751, 762.

[3] See Sirich, *The Revolutionary Committees in the Departments of France, 1793–1794.*

[4] Leading Babey and Barbaroux to enunciate the policy of convoking the primary electoral assemblies, their panacea henceforward: *Moniteur*, xv, 765–7.

[5] The letter appears in the *Moniteur* of 25 March 1793 (xv, 779). See also R. M. Brace, 'General Dumouriez and the Girondins, 1792–1793', *American Historical Review*, lvi, No. 3 (1951), p. 502.

[6] For consideration of the controversial dates and motives of the movements of Danton, see Lefebvre, *La Convention*, i, 333–5.

liaison was between Dumouriez and Roland. This particular allegation, perhaps no more than a diversionary counter-attack by one who saw grave danger to his reputation, if not to himself, in any examination of his own recent relations with Dumouriez,[1] may have had a more personal cause, for it is sometimes suggested that Danton's antipathy to Roland—perhaps even his association of Roland with Dumouriez—may have sprung from a rebuff encountered by him in an attempt to obtain office in their Ministry of March 1792.[2] Certainly he now hastened to praise the Mountain, to condemn those who believed that the revolution was over and to proclaim his belief that 'The Revolution cannot exist, and can never be consolidated, without the people'. On the same occasion Robespierre, too, spoke in the same sense: 'It is imperative that we surround ourselves with the people . . . how can the Revolution be sustained if patriots cannot bring their strength to bear?'[3] On 1 April, too, a similar sequence of events occurred. After Marat had attacked the Committee of General Defence as the instrument of an incompetent faction, a report of all the known facts about Dumouriez's conduct was at last made, but even the knowledge that the only barrier before the armies of Austria might be about to burst asunder failed to unite the assembly. Lasource and Penières renewed the endeavour to incriminate Danton, who replied by reiterating his exhortation. Dramatically disowning moderation and those he called the feeble men who had tried to save the King, he acknowledged the superior wisdom of the Montagnards and called upon the Convention to enlist the aid of the people against the enemies of the revolution both at home and abroad.[4]

From all this there came no effective action to thwart Dumouriez,[5] whose plans were finally frustrated only by the

---

[1] 'Danton, during the first months of 1793, was more closely associated with the General than anyone else': Lefebvre, *Etudes sur la Révolution française*, p. 52.

[2] Lefebvre, *loc. cit.*, citing Mathiez, 'Danton sous la Législative', *Annales révolutionnaires* (1912). See also Pariset, *La Révolution*, ii, 67–9 (in Lavisse, *Histoire de France contemporaine*).

[3] *Moniteur*, xv, 807–8, 815.   [4] *Moniteur*, xvi, 14–16, 18–21, 25–6.

[5] Four deputies, including Bancal des Issarts, and the Minister of War, Beurnonville, were sent to arrest or dismiss Dumouriez, but were themselves arrested by him. Bouchotte, a Jacobin, subsequently became Minister of War. See *Moniteur*, xv, 840, and xvi, 21, 30, 64.

patriotism of the army he had commanded. At the time the Convention did little more than to approve the abolition of parliamentary immunity, a piece of panic legislation recklessly proposed by Birotteau, and soon afterwards the deputy Sillery was arrested as a supposed accomplice of Dumouriez, a precedent against which the Montagnard Charlier vainly protested.[1] Only later, when the danger had receded, were further steps taken to strengthen the executive. Then the status of representatives on mission was improved, a new measure of conscription introduced, and, despite opposition from Barbaroux, Lanjuinais, Lépaux and Fonfrède, the powers of the Public Prosecutor greatly increased.[2] There was also, on 25 March, some reorganization of the two principal committees of the Convention. That concerned with General Security remained under Montagnard control, while the Committee of General Defence, although still almost as inefficient as before, now included such men as Robespierre, Danton, Fabre d'Eglantine and Dubois-Crancé.[3] Moreover, on 6 April, a new instrument of government, the Committee of Public Safety, was created. Although it was Isnard who was most responsible for its formation, the men who were appointed to it were deputies sympathetic to the Mountain.[4] Their powers were as yet limited, but for the first time they held genuine executive authority as well as seats in the Convention.

Again, although the Montagnards, in common with the rest of the Convention, had given Dumouriez their confidence until his defection was self-evident,[5] they were also able to profit afterwards by deliberately emphasizing the earlier association with him of some of their own opponents. Those—particularly Gensonné—who had worked with him during his and Roland's ministry in 1792 had apparently forgiven him for his part in the dismissal of that administration, had supported his appointment as Commander of the Army of the North, pleaded his cause against Pache in the Convention and hesitated to expose him

---

[1] Mathiez, *La Conspiration de l'étranger*, pp. 294–6.

[2] *Moniteur*, xvi, 61–2, 69, 80.

[3] *Moniteur*, xv, 792, 795.

[4] Jean Debry was appointed, but refused to serve for reasons of health. *Moniteur*, xvi, 48, 52, 75, 83–4.

[5] e.g. *Jacobins*, v, 86; *Moniteur*, xv, 653, 673, 679, 693–4.

when he became suspect.[1] These things, with certain similarities of outlook common to both the general and his former friends— their dislike of the Jacobins of Paris and their tendency to appeal to the conservative elements in France—served to identify their courses and made it easy to allege that there had been clandestine collaboration between them. Particularly damaging was Dumouriez's statement of his intention to preserve 'the sound part of the Convention', a phrase which Marat never tired of quoting to discomfort his critics.[2] The accusation of complicity with Dumouriez was to remain a millstone round the necks of the Mountain's chief opponents and to be a capital charge in the indictment which eventually sent them to the scaffold.

The events of April again illustrate the deadlock which was paralysing the Convention at this time. After an initial attack by Robespierre, each side attempted to establish its own supremacy, and each in turn failed to do so. Deputies continued to abuse each other, and the rising anger of the people of Paris was expressed in further peremptory demands for a purge of the assembly.

Although on 27 March Robespierre had spoken in favour of the idea of alliance with the people, he and his supporters were not yet prepared to sanction insurrection. His speeches suggest that he was hoping rather to force his opponents from influence by mobilizing public opinion against them. On 10 April an opportunity arose for him to promote such a propaganda campaign by denouncing them to the Convention. Pétion had read an address to the Mountain from the Halle au Blé Section which called upon patriotic deputies to cleanse the Convention of Dumouriez's accomplices, Fonfrède had condemned this as an appeal to a minority, calculated to bring the whole assembly into disrepute, and Guadet had reiterated the old accusations about dictatorship and demanded a full investigation by the

---

[1] *Madame Roland*, i, 249–50; Brissot, *Correspondance et Papiers*, p. 314 ff.; *Lettres de J. P. Brissot à M. Dumouriez*, B.M., F.675.6; J. C. Renault, 'Clavière et Dumouriez', *La Révolution française*, i (1881), pp. 96–105; R. M. Brace, 'General Dumouriez and the Girondins, 1792–1793', *American Historical Review*, lvi, No. 3 (1951), *passim*.

[2] *Moniteur*, xvi, 52 (for Robespierre's speech of 3 April) and 57, 121, 136 (for Marat's use of Dumouriez's phraseology).

Revolutionary Tribunal. Robespierre then rose, and in a lengthy reply presented the recent history of the revolution as an indictment of mismanagement by what he called 'the faction'. His speech, however, was more than mere recrimination. It was an accusation of complicity by 'Brissot, Guadet, Vergniaud, Gensonné, and other hypocritical agents of the same coalition' in a criminal and treasonable conspiracy. The members of the faction were 'a profoundly corrupt coalition', participators in a plot against the Republic, 'links in a chain connecting all the hostile chancelleries of Europe'. Dexterously avoiding an open assault, he then demanded that the Tribunal should immediately institute proceedings against Marie Antoinette, against the followers of the Duke of Orleans and Dumouriez, 'without excepting even Messieurs Brissot, Vergniaud, Guadet, Gensonné'—if indeed the Convention was prepared to commit sacrilege by concerning itself with 'these illustrious gentlemen'.[1]

In contrast to Robespierre's collective accusation, the replies made in the course of the next two days by Vergniaud and Guadet were personal. Each as an individual denied particular charges against himself and presented a plausible self-justification. Even so they could not wholly extricate themselves from the net which Robespierre had spread. Vergniaud's concluding peroration derived its rhetorical force from his scornful repetition of the word 'We', and Guadet defied the Convention to deny deputies their rights of friendly association when they were 'linked, or nearly so, by the same sentiments and the same principles'.[2]

The attack and the replies it evoked illuminate the position in the Convention. Robespierre himself probably believed in the existence of a great conspiracy, although we need not assume him to have been regardless of the advantage to be derived from his vague but deliberate amalgamation of his enemies. Fundamentally, however, the situation was similar to that which had confronted the English House of Commons in its attacks upon the ministers of Charles I. As there was then no effective political expedient by which parliament could control the ministers or bring about a change of government, the

---

[1] *Moniteur*, xvi, 87, 100–4, for the preliminary speeches, and 104–9 for Robespierre.
[2] *Moniteur*, xvi, 112–19, 127–36.

political errors of men like the Duke of Buckingham had to be represented as criminal offences, and their authors proclaimed as traitors—a device so dangerous that only extreme emergencies could make it acceptable. In all likelihood Robespierre, too, could see no other way of eliminating his opponents and giving some unity of direction to the supreme authority of France. The Convention, however, was not under his control and was not convinced of the necessity for such drastic action. Guadet was able to maintain that 'a member of the national assembly can never be accused on account of erroneous opinions', and Danton doubted the wisdom of 'a denunciation based only upon political proofs'.[1] Robespierre's attack was a failure, and the stalemate in the assembly remained unaltered.

The renewed suspicions and the prevailing frustration nevertheless fostered a still more dangerous degree of violence in debate. On 10 April there was fighting at the tribune. On 11 April Deperret drew a sword in a general scuffle, later alleging that he had been threatened by a deputy armed with a pistol, and the acting President, Thuriot, eventually abandoned the chair, declaring 'I can do nothing against tyranny of this sort'. Similar episodes also occurred next day,[2] and in the circumstances it is scarcely surprising that each side should have resorted to somewhat dubious methods to silence opposition and make the work of the Convention more effective.

The opponents of the Mountain struck first, endeavouring to remove their most vulnerable foe, Marat. On 11 April Buzot won a delay for Guadet's reply to Robespierre, and when Guadet spoke next day he ended his defence by a counter-attack. Alleging in his turn that his opponents were allied to Dumouriez, he denounced in particular a circular which had been sent out by the Jacobin Society of Paris. Signed by Marat on 5 April, this summoned the people of the provinces to hurry to the defence of Paris and warned them that a 'sacrilegious cabal' was directing the counter-revolution from within the Convention itself.[3] During the debate which followed Danton warned the assembly of the danger of jettisoning parliamentary immunity, and endeavoured to ascribe all blame to the Duke

---

[1] *Moniteur*, xvi, 131, 136.   [2] *Moniteur*, xvi, 101, 121–3, 125–6.
[3] *Jacobins*, v, 126–8; *Moniteur*, xvi, 121, 135–6.

of Orleans. His advice was disregarded. Fonfrède's insistence that 'all France accuses Marat' brought a resolution for an *appel nominal* to decide upon an impeachment. Next day some seventy deputies of the Mountain defiantly signed a paper endorsing the Jacobin circular, while Gensonné moved constitutional proposals which might suffice to justify an appeal to the electorate. The impeachment alone was approved, by a substantial majority.[1]

The voting on this occasion is of considerable interest.[2] Of the 360 deputies who were present, forty-eight abstained from voting, 220 voted for the impeachment of Marat, and ninety-two opposed it. If the voting is analysed by the method already applied to that concerning the King, it appears that of the 200 deputies whom historians have since called Girondins 131 were present, of whom 110 voted with the majority, while eighteen abstained and only three opposed the impeachment. Thus where 61 per cent of the assembly favoured the proposal, 83 per cent of those later called Girondins did so. Again, however, closer examination shows clearly that deductions about an attack on Marat by a united party cannot be supported, for while the deputies whose association with Brissot seems slight and uncertain were virtually undivided on this occasion, those who were probably closer to him and more prominent in the Convention were also less determined and more disunited. The earlier resignation of Kersaint, and the absence at this time of Brissot, Condorcet and Vergniaud, reduce the number of these deputies to thirteen, of whom only five voted against Marat— Barbaroux being the only one of major importance amongst them. All the others—Buzot, Ducos, Gensonné, Guadet, Isnard, Lasource, Louvet and Pétion—abstained from voting. As in the votes cast to decide the fate of the King, unity appears only amongst the less important deputies, the principal speakers appearing divided and irresolute.

The defeat of the Mountain on this occasion was soon reversed, for Marat was acquitted by the Revolutionary Tribunal and was borne back to the Convention at the head of a

---

[1] *Moniteur*, xvi, 136–40, 148–51; *Appel nominal 13–14 avril 1793:* '*Y a-t-il lieu à accusation contre Marat?*' B.M., F.313.79.

[2] Appendix C, Part II.

triumphal popular procession. Even before this, however, his opponents had been attacked in their turn. On 15 April an address was presented to the Convention by a deputation from the Sections. This seemed a formidable document, for its demand for the exclusion of twenty-two deputies[1]—a figure which soon became symbolic—had been approved by thirty-three Sections and sanctioned by both the Jacobin Society and the Commune. Moreover, as more Sections gave notice of their support it became known that men from Marseilles were again on the march to Paris, and insurrection seemed imminent once more. But in fact the Sections had made a false move. Some days before, on 10 April, when the Halle au Blé Section had suggested to the Jacobin Society that those deputies who dared not defend the republic ought to be recalled, Robespierre had objected, foreseeing that the proposal might be made an excuse for an appeal to the electors. In accordance with his advice, representatives of the Sections had met to discuss a more specific plan. The address presented on 15 April, however, still retained the same defect: the twenty-two were to retire as soon as a majority of the Departments should adhere to it. This prospect of provincial disunity divided the Sections from their more cautious sympathizers. Robespierre again counselled calm, the Commune withdrew its support, and the Sections were left leaderless.[2]

In the Convention, Buzot, Lasource, Guadet and Gensonné—who had all been named in the petition—and Fonfrède, who drew a roar of sympathy from the assembly by deploring the fact that the Sections had not associated him with his colleagues, all tried to turn the address against the Mountain. They claimed that deputies' lives were being jeopardized by a campaign of deliberate scurrility and welcomed the idea of an appeal to the electorate of France. Vergniaud, however, recognized that that course might be disastrous, and the Convention eventually dismissed the address as a calumny.[3] Thus the assembly remained in the same situation as it was at the beginning of the month.

[1] Barbaroux, Birotteau, Brissot, Buzot, Chambon, Doulcet, Fauchet, Gensonné, Gorsas, Grangeneuve, Guadet, Hardy, Lanjuinais, Lanthénas, Lasource, Lehardi, Louvet, Pétion, Salle, Valady, Valazé, Vergniaud. See *Moniteur*, xvi, 155, and *Proscription*, p. 26.   [2] *Jacobins*, v, 132; *Moniteur*, xvi, 152.
[3] *Moniteur*, xvi, 157, 162, 190, 196, 198.

Succeeding developments nevertheless foreshadowed the ending of the impasse. While Robespierre had objected to the Sections' reliance upon the provincial electorate, the sympathy he showed towards their purpose is a clear indication that he and his supporters were moving steadily closer to them. Popular support for the Montagnards, however, was still dependent upon their acceptance and promotion of the principle of price-control. This decisive step was now to be taken.

By this time some move to curb inflation had become more necessary than ever. The British blockade and the outbreak of civil war in the West had aggravated the difficulty of food distribution, and the defection of Dumouriez had again shaken public confidence in the depreciating currency. Hoarding, a natural consequence of the shortages, had caused further shortages and still higher prices. Both evils were generally attributed to the machinations of reactionaries, and price-control, which would make hoarding profitless, seemed a good revolutionary solution. It is, however, unlikely that these considerations alone would have convinced the Montagnards. With the rest of the Convention they had rejected the measure only two months before, and later they were to do their best to disown their *volte-face* in accepting it at all. Political advantage apart, the real explanation of their conduct is that they realized that the Revolution was in such peril that domestic discontent could no longer be ignored. As Châsles told the Convention, 'Of all incentives to counter-revolution, the cost of living is the most potent'. Moreover, the apparent imminence of invasion made an appeal to popular enthusiasm seem essential. Jeanbon Saint André, on mission in Lot and Dordogne, had already grasped this in March when he wrote 'If we expect the multitude to help us to safeguard the Revolution it is very necessary indeed to keep them alive'.[1] In the words later used by Baudot in his Memoirs, 'only the masses could hurl back the foreign horde. Therefore we had to inspire them to support us by giving them a real interest in our success.'[2]

The course of events suggests that an understanding between the Montagnards and the local authorities in Paris about this

---

[1] *La Vie chère*, pp. 139, 163–6, 182 (St. André's letter, dated 26 March 1793, is quoted on p. 165).   [2] Baudot, *Notes historiques sur la Convention nationale*, p. 158.

matter may have been reached between 18 and 20 April.[1] On 18 April the Department of Paris convened a meeting of all the local authorities in the area, including the Commune, to discuss means of combating the rise in the cost of living. The result was the presentation of a petition to the Convention calling for price-control. That same afternoon Chaumette called upon the General Council of the Commune to swear 'an oath of brotherhood, unity and mutual protection with the Sections, popular Societies and all the people of Paris'. The Commune took the oath and unanimously accepted Chaumette's further proposal that it should declare itself 'in a state of revolution' until food supplies had been assured. On 20 April the Commune was attacked in the Convention, particularly by Buzot, Vergniaud, Guadet and Gensonné,[2] and was compelled to produce the minutes of its meeting for inspection. The Montagnards, however, welcomed the reading of Chaumette's oath with cries of 'Include us! We too swear to die for the safety of the people!' Later, after many deputies had left the hall, the Montagnard minority which remained granted the municipal officials the honours of the sitting, by 143 votes to six. Four days later Robespierre gave developments his guarded approval by advocating some legal limitation of property rights.[3]

The Convention was now compelled to consider the economic situation amidst great political excitement. On 18 April Vergniaud condemned the proposal as a measure ruinous to agriculture, to commerce and to the prosperity of the common people, while Buzot demanded that Creuzé's earlier justification of free trade should be officially read throughout the whole of Paris. After an interval of committee work, the debate was resumed on 25 April, when Creuzé condemned price-control as dangerously impolitic and Barbaroux anticipated a fall in

[1] Mathiez (*La Vie chère*, pp. 171-8) argues that the Montagnard acceptance of the *maximum* was precipitated by Dumouriez's defection and was apparent in Robespierre's speech on 10 April. The earlier speech on 27 March and St. André's letter of 26 March, with the brevity of the relevant part of the speech of 10 April, would appear to indicate a more gradual evolution of Montagnard thought. Cp. Lefebvre, *La Convention*, ii, 33.

[2] On this occasion Gensonné urged every provincial town to imitate Paris by proclaiming itself in revolt and preparing to march against the capital. *Moniteur*, xvi, 191.

[3] *Moniteur*, xvi, 176, 190-1, 196-200, 213.

production and the appearance of an army of inspectors. The most that seemed likely to be acceptable to the assembly was a measure for compulsory corn-sales, and the public in the galleries became increasingly exasperated. When Ducos forecast that price-control would be followed by famine, tumult raged, and Guadet's call to the Convention to leave Paris for Versailles, where it could debate freely, was taken up by Viger with an exhortation to deputies to be ready to cut their way out with the sabre.[1]

On 1 May a crisis was reached. Some 8,000 men of the Faubourg St. Antoine surrounded the building, calling, under the threat of immediate insurrection, for heavier taxation of wealth, the conscription of the rich, and the acceptance of the *maximum*. Although Masuyer seized the opportunity to read a prepared speech proposing that a shadow Convention should meet at Tours or Bourges against a sudden emergency, the assembly remained surprisingly calm on this occasion. Fonfrède and Buzot contented themselves with a vain demand for the arrest of the ringleaders, and even the Montagnards disavowed the address as subversive. The imminence of insurrection and the failure of every other expedient nevertheless led to the enactment of both price-control and compulsory corn-sales on the next day. Ducos and Vernier opposed these measures to the last, but the majority of deputies were silent, probably feeling with Buzot that they must resign themselves to 'a law of circumstance'.[2]

In practice the legislation proved cumbersome and inadequate. Politically, however, its importance was considerable. Price-control had become an article of faith for the people of revolutionary Paris, and its acceptance was hailed as a popular triumph. By giving it their support the Montagnards had become the acknowledged leaders of the people, and the alliance so sealed heralded the coming of the Terror, the expulsion of the enemy armies from French territory, and the final triumph of the Montagnards over the majority of the Convention.

Their victory was brought appreciably closer by the ill-advised efforts of their adversaries to exploit the nation-wide

[1] *Moniteur*, xvi, 176, 179, 238, 243–8, 271–2, 280.
[2] *Moniteur*, xvi, 289–92, 298, 300–5.

unrest caused at this time by conscription. Although the military danger was not so great as it seemed, the war having become an affair of sieges, men were urgently required in the Vendée, where the situation was grave. The Convention, which had ordered the conscription of 300,000 men without specifying any method of enlistment, adopted on 27 April a plan proposed by Cambon, who had been impressed by its operation in his own department, the Hérault. Committees composed of representatives of local authorities and popular societies were to select conscripts from amongst those eligible for military service. This plan was never universally enforced, but it nevertheless caused widespread unrest, for if it was followed the group predominating in a particular area had a free hand to conscript its chief political opponents, and if it was not, confusion and controversy prevailed. The common result was violent conflict for control of local assemblies,[1] and this discord seemed to some deputies in the Convention to be a heaven-sent opportunity to rally public opinion against the Jacobins and to sustain the efforts of the more conservative elements to gain control of the Sections of Paris. In doing this they were able to steal the thunder of the Montagnards by alleging that they were acting at the behest of the people.

In Paris controversy centred on a decree issued by the Commune on 1 May, which ordered the enlistment of 12,000 men by methods analogous to those used in the Hérault. Subsidiary issues—the taxation of wealth and the inadequacy of maintenance grants given to the families of serving soldiers—also aggravated unrest. Pétion, who had already represented price-control to be a threat to property and urged the bourgeoisie to attend and direct the Sectional assemblies, was now followed by others. The *Patriote français* praised free enlistment and called upon its readers to accept the challenge of anarchy and fight it to a finish—language which roused the Commune to a formal denunciation of Girey-Dupré, Brissot's assistant editor. In the Convention Fonfrède and Vergniaud on 5 May welcomed a deputation from the Section Bonconseil, which had been won by the better class citizens and had sworn 'no longer to allow a handful of intriguers, posing as patriots, to crush good citizens

---

[1] *Moniteur*, xvi, 239, 243; Lefebvre, *La Convention*, ii, 114–16.

under a popular despotism'.[1] Next day, when it became known that the leaders of this deputation had been arrested, Vergniaud, Guadet and Lidon fought hard for their release, alleging that a new form of crime, *lèse-municipalité*, had been invented. Again, when groups of young men paraded through Paris on 6 May chanting 'Down with the anarchists! Marat to the guillotine! To the devil with Robespierre, Marat and Danton!', and some were arrested, Isnard, Buzot, Vergniaud and others tried hard to persuade the Convention to intervene on their behalf.[2]

This attempt to support bourgeois resentment proved a costly failure. The Hérault system of recruiting was indeed abandoned, but conscription continued to be arranged in Sectional assemblies where the middle-class opposition was overcome by the illicit transfer of radical voters from one Section to another. The complacency of the Commune may have been temporarily shaken, but the deputies who attacked it suffered the greater harm by identifying themselves at a critical time with an essentially selfish and unpatriotic movement.[3] The disturbances in Paris seemed to be substantially the same as the more serious strife in the Vendée, and to the Montagnards protection of the one appeared identical with protection of the other. To Robespierre on 8 May it seemed that 'There are now only two parties in France, the people and the enemies of the people', and Marat told those who opposed him in the Convention that 'it is not possible that there can ever be any accord between you and the patriots of the Mountain'.[4]

The position was the more serious since provincial agitation akin to that which had disturbed Paris also received encouragement from the benches of the Convention. In the provinces the Montagnards, monopolizing the posts of representatives on mission, had raised recruits, levied taxes, stirred popular sentiments and initiated the Terror despite efforts in the Convention to cancel their appointments or to curb their powers, and some

---

[1] *Moniteur*, xvi, 294, 319, 342; *Patriote français*, 4 and 8 May 1793; *Lettre de Jérôme Pétion aux Parisiens* (Paris, 1792), B.M., F.665.5.

[2] *Moniteur*, xvi, 322, 347–9, 414.

[3] It was at this time that Desmoulins's highly successful and damaging pamphlet, *Histoire des Brissotins*, appeared (B.M., F.1103.5).

[4] *Jacobins*, v, 180; *Moniteur*, xvi, 422 and 478.

deputies tried to exploit the resentment their proceedings inevitably aroused. In mid-May a new influx of petitions from the provinces appeared, with many strident protests about the powers of the commissioners, and there was even talk in the Convention of the vengeance of France being visited upon the Mountain.[1] Some speakers did not hesitate to incite local resistance to the commissioners. Salle and Birotteau urged their constituents to be defiant, Guadet demanded that local provincial assemblies should protect themselves by remaining in permanent session, and Chasset called upon respectable citizens in Lyons to ensure that they dominated that city. Even Vergniaud now appealed to the men of the Gironde to rise and arm themselves in defence of their own representatives.[2]

Whatever their purpose, exhortations like these were of obvious encouragement to the widening royalist counter-revolution. They were matched by renewed intransigence in the Convention. On 11 May Salle and Barbaroux led prolonged opposition to the continuation of the Committee of Public Safety, and on 13 May Condorcet proposed an ultimatum: if the Constitution could not be accepted, the electoral assemblies ought to meet on 1 November to elect a new Convention. Allegations of injustice by the Revolutionary Tribunal proved particularly galling to the Montagnards, and after one had caused two hours of disorder on 17 May speakers on both sides deplored the prevailing deadlock.[3] The occasion provided one of the last opportunities to solve the fundamental problem.

The Montagnard view was put by Couthon, who maintained that the legitimate rights of a large body of members were being ignored. He proposed that any hundred deputies should have the formal right to force a division by *appel nominal*—a method of holding up proceedings which has had a distinguished history in later French assemblies. Vergniaud, on the other hand, insisted that the *appel nominal* should be strictly limited to constitutional questions. In all others, deputies who were dissatisfied should be content to record and sign the minority view in the official minutes, for the minority must bow to the general

[1] *Jacobins*, v, 138; *Moniteur*, xvi, 387, 392, 405.
[2] *Moniteur*, xvi, 4–5, 191; Vatel, *Vergniaud*, ii, 151–3.
[3] *Moniteur*, xvi, 202, 259, 403, 406–8.

will. If orderly debate on this basis could not be enforced, he and his colleagues would withdraw from the assembly, and the Department of the Gironde would disassociate itself from Paris.[1] Next day proposals similar to these were presented by the Legislative Committee, but only prolonged dispute followed. Guadet, theatrically but with unhappy accuracy, prophesied a cutting of the Gordian knot by a *coup d'état* analogous to Pride's Purge of the Long Parliament in England.[2] The fleeting opportunity of establishing some efficient standing orders, which might at least have contributed to more peaceful and more useful debate, was lost.

During the last two weeks of May an insurrection against the majority of the Convention was being prepared in the streets of Paris. The deputies were aware of this, Valazé's anxiety being so great by 20 May that he sent an urgent message to many of his friends warning them to carry arms when next they came to the Convention.[3] Yet, dangerous as was their situation, they made no attempt to compromise. Indeed, it was a desperate attempt to assert their authority which precipitated the revolution of 2 June.

On 18 May, after the reckless and provocative Isnard had been elected as President of the Convention, Guadet renewed the demand for a shadow Convention at Bourges[4] and proposed that the Commune of Paris should be dissolved and municipal administration provisionally entrusted to the presidents of the Sections. These proposals were rejected in favour of Barère's demand for a full inquiry into the situation in Paris, and by agreeing to the appointment of a Commission of Twelve for this purpose the Convention provided its majority with an instrument for a final offensive against its opponents.[5]

---

[1] The use the Montagnards would have made of the *appel nominal* may be gauged by their demand for an *appel nominal* to determine whether 150 deputies were sufficient to make an *appel nominal* compulsory.

[2] *Moniteur*, xvi, 408, 411–13, 415. [3] See above, p. 96, n. 1.

[4] Cp. Paine's letter to Danton, 6 May 1793: 'I see but one effectual way to prevent a rupture . . . to fix the residence of the Convention, and future assemblies, at a distance from Paris.' Conway, *Life of Thomas Paine*, ii, p. 53.

[5] *Moniteur*, xvi, 411, 425.

N

The Commission, elected on 20 May by less than 200 deputies, contained only two prominent men, Boyer-Fonfrède and Rabaut St. Etienne.[1] Fonfrède only attended its meetings occasionally, and he was later exempted from the Montagnards' purge because he was said to have tried to restrain his colleagues. Rabaut, however, acted as secretary to the Commission and was probably its moving spirit. Of the others, the president, Mollevaut, and Gardien, Viger and Larivière were the most notable.[2] They may have had some association with the deputies of the Gironde, but on the whole the probability is that the Commission was representative of the moderate majority of the assembly.

The Twelve first used their powers to question Pache, now Mayor of Paris, and Garat, the Minister of the Interior. They endeavoured to inspect the registers of the Sections, and on 24 May their spokesman, Viger, told the Convention that plans for an insurrection had been discovered. He recommended as preliminary preventive measures a reinforcement of the National Guard near the Convention and the compulsory closure of Sectional assemblies at 10.0 p.m. Further, only authorized persons ought to be allowed to move from one assembly to another. Vehement speeches by Boyer-Fonfrède and Vergniaud won approval for these proposals, and the Commission proceeded to take the law into its own hands by issuing warrants for the arrest of the more notable leaders of the people, including Varlet and Hébert, who were in fact imprisoned in L'Abbaye.[3]

This high-handed action[4] brought immediate repercussions, for Hébert was an official of the Commune as well as being the editor of the scurrilous but popular journal *Père Duchesne*. On 25 May a deputation from the Commune appeared at the bar of the Convention, but its protest only evoked the threat from Isnard which was to become notorious: 'I tell you in the name of the whole of France that if these perpetually recurring

[1] Appendix A, List II. Voting ranged from 197 for Boyer-Fonfrède to 104 for Gardien.

[2] Chaumette later alleged that Barbaroux and Pétion had unofficially attended some of the meetings of the Commission: *Moniteur*, xviii, 234.

[3] *Moniteur*, xvi, 464, 467–70. For justifications of the Commission, see, e.g., *Précis tracé à la hâte par Rabaut St. Etienne*, and *Bergoeing à ses commettans* (Paris, 1793), B.M., F.334.18 and F.991.16.

[4] The right of the Commission to make the arrests was not challenged, although their manner and motives were.

insurrections ever lead to harm to the parliament chosen by the nation, Paris will be annihilated, and men will search the banks of the Seine for traces of the city.'[1]

Such language naturally infuriated the people of Paris, who particularly resented the arrests as a violation of the sovereignty of the Sections. The next day, 26 May, sixteen Sections protested to the Convention. Their protest, however, was simply referred to the Commission, which went boldly forward, ordering the arrest of Dobsen, a civic official and the president of the Cité Section, and instructing several of the more conservative Sections to hold armed men in readiness for its defence on the morrow. The next session of the Convention was therefore one of almost continuous uproar. When a delegation from the Cité Section appeared and demanded that the Twelve should be sent before the Revolutionary Tribunal, Isnard rebuked them for childish presumption and the Montagnards accused Isnard of partiality, chanting in chorus 'We are oppressed, we will resist oppression'. As Vergniaud and Lépaux called for the convocation of the primary electoral assemblies—'which alone can save France'—and as Larivière, Guadet and Isnard were successively shouted down, the *sans-culottes* invaded the hall and some two hundred armed men from the Butte des Moulins Section arrived on the orders of the Commission to disperse the crowd. Amidst the excitement Garat addressed the assembly, accusing the opponents of the Mountain of promoting disorder in a peaceful city in order to provide some excuse for repression. Tumult continued late into the night, until the Montagnards outnumbered other deputies. The dissolution of the Commission and the liberation of its prisoners was then decreed.[2]

Had the majority of deputies been content to accept this situation, insurrection might still have been averted. On 28 May, however, Lanjuinais contested the minutes of the previous session, alleging amongst other things that members of the crowd had taken their places in the hall and voted with the Montagnards. After further violent controversy the Commission was reinstated by 279 votes to 238,[3] the closeness of the division

[1] *Moniteur*, xvi, 479–80.
[2] *Moniteur*, xvi, 486, 491–6, 500; Lefebvre, *La Convention*, ii, 163.
[3] Appendix C, Part III.

foreshadowing the approaching triumph of the Mountain. It is also remarkable that 146 deputies, apart from the ninety-two who were recorded as 'absent on mission', were marked as absent from the assembly. Of the 200 later to be called Girondins, 135 voted for the re-establishment of the Commission, which only nine opposed. This virtual unanimity is again apparent in the voting of the deputies grouped for purposes of analysis as being associated in varying degrees with Brissot, for of these forty-one voted for the motion, fourteen were either absent or abstaining—the record does not distinguish between these negatives—and only one, Condorcet, opposed. These figures, the first to show effective unity at the centre of the supposed group, certainly indicate the critical nature of the division. They tend to confirm the view that the group became an entity only in the hour of its downfall, if indeed the existence of a group can be postulated at all from the evidence of a voting list which shows the deputies in question to be at one with the majority of their colleagues.

The Mountain again refused to accept the decision of the majority. Rabaut's attempts to present the Commission's report were so consistently howled down that he concluded by offering its resignation, and the assembly was harried into renewing the order for the release of those who had been imprisoned.[1] Apparently the activities of the Commission had convinced the Montagnards that the danger of counter-revolution triumphing if moderation was allowed to prepare its path was real and urgent. To contain the moderates by endless filibustering, while awaiting some manifestation of public opinion, no longer seemed sufficient. As the votes were being counted in the *appel nominal* on 28 May Robespierre warned the assembly that what he called the chicanery of the Right would produce a royalist reaction, and when the Gardes Français Section presented an address demanding the abolition of the instruments of revolutionary government, Danton virtually appealed to the *sans-culottes* to redress the balance of forces in the Convention.[2] Robespierre's personal note-book[3] shows that at the end of May

---

[1] *Moniteur*, xvi, 500–4, 509.   [2] *Moniteur*, xvi, 503, 509–10.
[3] *Rapport fait au nom de la commission chargée de l'examen des papiers trouvés chez Robespierre par E. B. Courtois* (Paris, 1795).

he too believed that disaster could only be averted if the *sans-culottes* restored unity to the Convention and to the government. Where Danton is reputed to have said 'Things cannot continue like this. One side or the other must resign',[1] Robespierre wrote that the first need of the nation was 'a single will'. The entry in the note-book outlined the methods by which the people were to be roused to action. In public, however, Robespierre limited himself to a tacit sanction of insurrection, telling the Jacobin Society on 29 May 'It is not for me to tell the people the means they should take to save themselves . . . I have no other duty to fulfil at this moment'—a comment so well comprehended that his audience broke into vociferous cheering.[2] Thereafter the centre of political gravity lay in the emergency committee of public safety formed at the Evêché to direct a larger assembly of representatives of the Sections known as the Central Revolutionary Committee.[3] Here the Revolution of 31 May was prepared, while in the Convention the supporters of the Commission of Twelve tried to decide whether that body still retained any legal position.

On 31 May the deputies assembled to the sound of the tocsin and their hall was gradually surrounded by a considerable but comparatively quiescent crowd. The Montagnards then moved for the formal abolition of the Commission, to which Buzot, Vergniaud and Valazé replied by calling for the immediate investigation of the insurrection that was obviously impending outside. Amidst prolonged disorder, efforts were made to effect some settlement in the assembly. Danton attempted to offer peace in return for the abolition of the Commission, but opposition drove him to conclude with the abrupt cry 'Scorn not my counsels'. Rabaut St. Etienne later vainly suggested that a compromise might be reached if the Committee of Public Safety were charged with the completion of the work of the Commission. Later again, a deputation from the Commune tacitly disavowed the insurrection and asked for closer co-operation with the Convention in dealing with the crisis, and Vergniaud responded to Couthon's appeal for unity by proposing that the assembly should record its recognition of the

[1] *Mémoires de Meillan*, p. 49. [2] *Jacobins*, v, 213.
[3] Lefebvre, *La Convention*, ii, 171–2, 180–90.

vigilance, patriotism and restraint shown by the Sections. All these attempts at moderation were however rejected in favour of an enquiry into the insurrection, and as the day drew to a close it became clear that the majority were not prepared to pacify the insurgents or to conciliate the Mountain.[1]

Equally it became apparent that disparity of purpose between the Revolutionary Committee of the Sections and the deputies of the Mountain—who still feared that the use of force would alienate the country at large—had helped to frustrate popular victory in an insurrection already inadequately organized. In the course of the evening, however, Robespierre gave the movement more positive purpose. As a measure of protest against pressure from outside, Vergniaud had left the hall, hoping that his colleagues would follow, but finding himself unsupported he returned, interrupting Robespierre in a lengthy speech with the cry 'Well, come to some conclusion!' To this Robespierre replied 'Yes! I will conclude, and against you!', and he then gave his support to the insurgents by demanding the impeachment of his opponents.[2] Whether he spoke in sudden anger or whether the ignominious failure of Vergniaud's walk-out revealed the opportunity open to him, his action was decisive. Impeachment implied arrest, a move which could be made within the letter of the law and which might also prevent the accused from fleeing from Paris to seek the aid of the provinces. The step was sufficient to unite the various elements in revolutionary Paris—the *sans-culottes*, the municipality and the Jacobins—with the Montagnards, and the next stage of the insurrection was almost wholly successful.

Stimulated by the news of rebel victories in the Vendée and in Lyons, and profiting from the lessons learned on 31 May,[3] the Central Revolutionary Committee ringed the Convention on 2 June with armed men. Lanjuinais fearlessly denounced all whose actions or acquiescence made this new outrage possible, but the assembly had no option but to consider the impeachment, which had been formally demanded against twenty-four deputies in the name of the people by Hassenfratz on the

---

[1] *Moniteur*, xvi, 523–4, 528–9, 531–2.   [2] *Moniteur*, xvi, 537.

[3] 'The Revolution of 2 June may be considered the most carefully prepared of the period': Lefebvre, *La Convention*, ii, 217.

previous evening,[1] and which was now reiterated by a new delegation. Barère, speaking for the Committee of Public Safety, tried to preserve some semblance of constitutional independence by suggesting first that the accused should resign voluntarily, and then that the Convention should continue the debate outside, amidst the people. Some deputies accepted the first proposal, but others refused to bow to force.[2] The second suggestion was accepted, and a procession of deputies marched behind the new President, Mallarmé, in a vain endeavour to pierce the silent circle which enclosed the Convention, minatory and immobile. Defeated, they returned to their chamber and decreed the provisional arrest of twenty-nine of their number, including ten members of the Commission of Twelve, and the two ministers who had not become reconciled to the Mountain, Clavière and Lebrun.[3] The insurrection failed in only one particular: some of the accused, forewarned, had already effected their escape, and others were soon to elude their guards.[4]

The contest could only be continued on a wider stage, in the towns and villages of France. In the Convention the fight had been fought to a finish, and its echoes died away amid ineffectual protests from the friends of the fallen. Although those who had led the majority in the Convention had long had a legitimate cause of grievance in the Montagnards' refusal to accept majority decisions, they had themselves led many attempts to crush the Montagnards, consistently calling them anarchists and scorning all attempts at compromise. The cause of their collapse was inherent in their political position: rebels to the royalists and royalists to the revolutionaries, their intransigent and unconstructive concern in a period of national crisis with their own political interests alienated even that moderate section which might have saved them. Those who, like Barbaroux and Buzot, escaped to the provinces found some short-lived support, but they did not find men prepared to die in their defence. Only a girl, Charlotte de Corday, was ready to sacrifice herself, and by a final irony of fate her assassination of Marat was to do more than anything else to send her heroes to the scaffold.

[1] Appendix A, List I.

[2] Isnard, Lanthénas, Fauchet, and Dusaulx offered to resign or accept suspension, Barbaroux and Lanjuinais refused to do so. *Moniteur*, xvi, 544, 547, 553.

[3] Appendix A, List III.   [4] *Mémoires de Meillan*, 52–4; *Proscription*, 42–3.

CHAPTER VIII

Was there a Girondin Party?

As we have seen, once the twenty-nine deputies had been expelled from the Convention on 2 June they and all those who dared for any reason to question the authority of the Mountain soon became the victims of Montagnard attacks. These attacks subsequently provided historians with material for the creation of a legendary Girondin party, just as the proscription lists drawn up by the Montagnards provided a convenient nominal roll of supposed party members. All this extraneous material can now be disregarded, and the question of the existence of a Girondin party decided by consideration of facts more relevant to the period before the Revolution of 2 June.

I

In the first place, the sustained association of any large number of deputies in any single group seems unlikely to have been either politically practicable or theoretically justifiable in France in 1793. In the eighteenth century party was not a respectable form of association. Even in England it was still regarded as factious opposition to the King's Government. In pre-Revolutionary France, where the royal power was held to be absolute, there was no parliament, much less any parliamentary party. The Revolutionaries, therefore, had neither experience nor the tradition of political organization to guide them, and to suppose that by 1793 any but the most rudimentary form of party could have been created is to postulate a rapidity of practical political development inherently improbable in so short a period as four years. The chaotic conditions which prevailed during those years in the successive parliaments of France—a land in which political groups are even now much more important than parties—make such progress seem still more unlikely.

These considerations apart, the intellectual atmosphere of the Revolution was inimical to the growth of political parties.[1] The Revolutionaries inherited the absolutist belief that the State must be directed towards a single ultimate good by the single will which alone could comprehend that ideal. The Revolution identified this single will with that of the people, and to recognize and give expression to the will of the people was the function of the people's deputies in the national assemblies. It was assumed that if each deputy independently voiced the will of his constituents, the assembly as a whole would automatically express the will of the people as a whole. Hence there arose what Sorel has called 'the terrible postulate of unanimity, which all desired and all judged necessary'.[2] Dissidence could only mean that the will of the people was being misunderstood or perverted by the selfish interests of some particular group, and this implied defiance of the sovereignty of the people. Thus to differ from the opinion of the majority, once it had been established by freely-expressed individual opinions, was to commit the crime of *lèse-nation*, as heinous an offence as *lèse-majesté* had been in the days of the monarchy. To all these conceptions the idea of party as a desirable form of political association is entirely alien.

Because these beliefs were accepted as axiomatic, the conflicts in the Convention were regarded as scandalous by all concerned,[3] and were only to be accounted for in terms of downright villainy. Thus in 1792 Robespierre wrote that the political quarrels of the day represented only the conflict of private interests with the general interest, of cupidity and intrigue with justice and humanity, and in May 1793, as has been said, he told the Jacobin Society that there were only two parties in France, the people and the enemies of the people.[4] Similarly,

---

[1] e.g., Condorcet, 23 February 1793: 'Constitutions based on a balance of powers presuppose or cause the existence of two parties, and one of the first needs of the French Republic is to avoid party altogether.' (*Moniteur*, xv, 460.)

[2] Sorel, *L'Europe et la Révolution française*, iii, 70.

[3] The only exception known to me is Dulaure, who wrote: 'It is a particular proof of ignorance to pretend that in a large assembly opinions are unanimous, and it is still more unjust for men to accuse each other of treason because their varying temperaments produce varying views' (*Observations à mes commettans*, Paris, 1793, B.M., F.1000.9).

[4] *Le Défenseur de la Constitution*, No. 4; *Jacobins*, v, 180.

Louvet began a pamphlet attacking Robespierre with an English sentence: 'In politics there exist onless (*sic*) two parties in France, the first composed of philosophers, the second of robbers and murderers.'[1] In such an atmosphere sustained and united action by any considerable number of deputies is not to be expected, although personal friendships and possibly temporary combinations to attack or defend particular proposals would not be unnatural.

II

The differences of opinion which disrupted the unanimity which theory demanded of the Convention did not derive from social distinctions amongst the deputies. The Convention was a remarkably homogeneous body, and no difference of social origin distinguishes the 200 so-called Girondins either from the Mountain or from the rest of their colleagues. The 749 deputies in the assembly were almost all of the middle-class, the great majority of them being professional men. At least 215 of them were lawyers, and 379 had participated in the work of local administration, work which called for, and could be combined with, legal practice. Only two deputies in the whole assembly, Noel Pointe of the Rhône-et-Loire and Armonville of the Marne, can be considered as working-men.[2] This social uniformity is equally apparent among the 200, of whom at least eighty were men of the law, while more than 100 had been members of local administrative bodies. The 200 also included smaller groups of similar social status: seven were doctors or surgeons, fifteen were—or had been—priests, fifteen were naval or military men, and at least fifteen were small proprietors. There is also a fringe of men whose social position is less easy to define. A few, including Isnard, were business men or merchants. Others, of an importance ranging from that of Condorcet to that of Carra, may be described as literary men. At least one,

---

[1] Louvet, *A Maximilien Robespierre et à ses royalistes* (Paris, 1792), B.M., F.849.8. Cp. also Billaud Varenne, *Moniteur*, xvii, 199.

[2] Lefebvre, *La Convention*, i, 6; Mathiez, *La Révolution française*, ii, 44; *La Convention telle qu'elle fut et telle qu'elle est* (Paris, 1793), B.M., F.1277.1; Daunou, *Mémoires*, p. 186. This section in general is based upon the biographical records of the deputies concerned: see Chapter III above, and bibliography.

Girault, had been a successful diplomat. With such rare exceptions as the inn-keeper Lozeau, however, the 200 may fairly be
described as typical members of the Convention so far as their
social background is concerned, and if it be objected that the
deputies of the Gironde themselves were lawyers of much
greater renown than their rival Robespierre, the closeness of
their association with Brissot, the youngest son of a small provincial shopkeeper, indicates the impossibility of sustaining
classification on such lines.

The repeated Montagnard allegation that their opponents
were federalists suggests that a more successful distinction might
be derived from an analysis of the constituencies represented by
the 200, but a map showing these constituencies tells us little.[1]
Certain Departments and even certain regions were strongly
represented amongst the 200, whilst others were represented
weakly or not at all, but to account for these differences in
other than personal and political terms is more than difficult.
The Seine-Inférieure, the Gironde and the Bouches du Rhône,
which were strongly represented, were areas of economic importance, but Morbihan and the Hautes Alpes, equally strongly
represented, were the reverse. Regional loyalties, which might
appear to account for the apparent unity of Brittany and the
Alpine area, do not appear to have influenced the Pyrénées.
The outlying parts of France were perhaps more fully represented than the central plateau, yet everywhere strongly represented Departments stand in juxtaposition to those without
representation, while individuals or small groups of deputies
appear in apparently illogical places. No correlation is apparent
between a distribution map and the geography or economic
and historical development of France. Nothing more emerges
than the not unnatural fact that the miscellany of deputies who
happened to incur the wrath of the Mountain represented a
miscellaneous assortment of constituencies.

[1] This is clearly apparent in the representative area illustrated overleaf.

A map of Western France showing the distribution by *Départements* of the deputies from that area who have been said to have been Girondins

III

The negative conclusion to this attempt to find some distinguishing characteristic or bond of unity among the 200 without reference to ideas seems to force us back to an explanation in terms of policy. Some historians have suggested that the most fundamental distinction between the 'Girondins' and the Jacobins was their differing attitudes towards economic and social problems. In Mathiez's view, the former weakly sought in war a solution to all the economic ills of France, and vacillated between the free-trade interest of their own class, the bourgeoisie, and their need to recruit popular support; Robespierre, however, represented the small man, and voiced the popular demand for the only true solution to economic evils, a return to the system of state-control which had been enforced by the old monarchy and destroyed by the Constituent Assembly.[1]

Not only does the indiscriminate use of the name 'Girondins' in this argument gloss over many differences of opinion, but the existence of well-defined differences in economic and social policy between the Jacobins and the remainder of either the Legislative Assembly or the Convention is itself questionable.

In the time of the Legislative Assembly, Brissot certainly argued that war would restore the national credit of France, and he was supported on occasion by Gensonné, Condorcet and Lasource.[2] This, however, was only an incidental argument, and the first economic crisis which the Assembly encountered, the sugar shortage of January 1792, reveals those who have been called Girondins as perplexed politicians rather than doctrinaire economists. Fauchet, a preacher of evangelical socialism, urged the Committee of Commerce to draft a scheme 'which will reconcile freedom of trade with measures for the prevention of hoarding'. Ducos claimed that the shortage would solve itself without state intervention, yet urged careful study so that a law could be drafted which would meet the situation without infringing property rights.[3] Lasource echoed this indecision,

---

[1] *La Vie chère*, 29, 67, and *passim*; cp., e.g., Michon, *Robespierre et la guerre révolutionnaire 1791–1792*, and *Valazé*.

[2] *Moniteur*, xi, 118; *Chronique de Paris*, 11 January 1792; Lasource, *Discours tendant à réfuter les orateurs* (Paris, 1791), B.M., F.338.6.

[3] *Moniteur*, xi, 181, 204.

while exhorting the Assembly to act promptly. Réal, at that time sympathetic to Brissot, thought that free-trade must be sacrificed unless the situation improved, and Manuel and Louvet fell back upon the curious expedient whereby all the Jacobins agreed to abstain from sugar and coffee until the shortage was over.[1] This evidence does not suggest more than general irresolution in a situation in which the obvious solution conflicted with a generally accepted belief in economic freedom, nor is there any evidence to suggest that the problem was a party issue at this date.

A second economic crisis later in the year shows the beginning of a distinction between Robespierre and the deputies in the Assembly, but according to Mathiez's own analysis of the situation, Robespierre was almost alone among leading politicians in his economic views. In the late spring of 1792 there was a recrudescence of the local shortages of corn which had long troubled France. Two of the more revolutionary sections of Paris presented petitions demanding measures of price-control, and disorders occurred in many places, disorders which Mathiez regards as manifestations of a vast but unorganized social movement by the peasantry and workmen. After a brief period of appeasement, the Assembly resorted to repression.[2]

This general crisis was crystallized by the murder by rioters of Simmoneau, the Mayor of Étampes, in March. The Assembly and the Jacobin Club joined in condemnation of this crime. Guadet and Isnard, Chabot and Thuriot, all agreed that counter-revolutionaries were responsible. The Jacobins sent a letter of consolation to the Mayor's son, and Jean Debry proposed that a monument be erected to his memory.[3]

A different attitude was apparent in Robespierre's speeches. On 26 March he opposed a proposal that the Mayor be posthumously awarded a civic crown, and on 9 April the Jacobins ignored, at his instigation, a proposal that a fête should be held in honour of the murdered man. When the Assembly undertook the organization of the fête, Robespierre again opposed the

---

[1] Walter, *Histoire des Jacobins*, 234–8.

[2] *La Vie chère*, 50, 63, 66; Sagnac, *La Révolution*, i, 346 (in Lavisse, *Histoire de France contemporaine*).

[3] *Moniteur*, xi, 557, 563, 566, 573, 578, 666; *Jacobins*, iii, 431.

proposal, and censured the policy of repression by saying that there was one law for the powerful and another for the poor. The importance of his attitude is undeniable, but he was not in this respect representative of opinion in the Legislative Assembly, which, as Mathiez himself says, 'remained devoted to the dogma of free-trade with an unshakable stubbornness'.[1] No separate Girondin party can be discerned on this issue at this time.

The further economic troubles which occurred in the autumn of 1792 show that the balance of opinion had remained unchanged. In spite of a good harvest and the extension of democratic measures after 10 August, the lower classes of France remained distressed and discontented. Inflation had continued to augment the cost of living, while the invasion and the needs of the army had dislocated the distribution of corn. In these circumstances, the Legislative Assembly authorized local authorities to requisition supplies. Unaccompanied by any central direction or measures of price-control, the legislation proved ineffective in practice, and was eventually replaced by a reversion to free-trade and the repression of all disturbances.

Mathiez has suggested that one reason for the failure of this first attempt to control the economic situation was the fundamental hostility of the Girondins towards any form of state interference in economic matters. Certainly many of the leaders of the Legislative Assembly and the Convention again appeared as convinced free-traders. Vergniaud proposed the introduction of requisitioning as an extraordinary measure dictated by the supreme needs of the army. Roland, although Minister of the Interior, opposed the operation of the law, and repeatedly preached economic liberalism to the Convention. Amongst others, Pétion, Gardien and Serre supported his arguments, and Creuzé-Latouche, speaking for those who wanted 'complete freedom for commerce', secured the decree of 8 December 1792 which repealed the earlier regulations and announced that 'the most complete liberty will continue'.[2]

But again these views do not afford a criterion to distinguish a Girondin party. As always, the deputies spoke as individuals.

---

[1] *Jacobins*, iii, 452, 477; Sagnac, *op. cit.*, i, 356; Hamel, *Histoire de Robespierre*, ii, 276; *La Vie chère*, p. 29.

[2] *La Vie chère*, 100–6; *Moniteur*, xiii, 727, and xiv, 517, 599, 619, 642, 682, 694–6.

Where Valazé and Roland urged an increase in foreign purchases by the Government, Boyer-Fonfrède believed that even
this would prove injurious, and recommended a mild measure
of tariff control, while Barbaroux objected to even the limited
degree of compulsion which Serre supported. When Roland and
Pétion urged repression of disorders in the Eure et Loire, Buzot
joined Robespierre in proposing that civil commissioners should
accompany the troops in order to prevent injustices. By
Mathiez's own account, the only deputy who really understood
the situation and favoured price-control was Louis Viger—who
has also been accounted a Girondin.[1]

The deputies of the Gironde were no more alone in supporting free-trade in the autumn than they had been in the spring
of 1792. The great majority of the Convention took this view,
and the Mountain silently disavowed the principle of price-
control.[2] The publication of Saint Just's speech in support of
free-trade, which began with the words 'Violent legislation
about trade does not appeal to me', was agreed to without dis-
sent, and both Robespierre and Danton recognized the necessity of restoring order, even by force. It is true that Robespierre
again showed himself in advance of other deputies by his insistence that the first duty of the State was to ensure that the means
of existence were within the reach of all, but even his attitude
was full of caution. In his speech on 2 December he approved of
free-trade in principle, limiting his criticism to those responsible
for monopolies and exploitation and saying that such men should
be forced to be honest; he refused to propose any specific decree,
and simply promised to support any measure against exploitation.[3] His views may contain the seeds of later action, but in
December 1792 he was decidedly non-committal.

In this matter, as in others, a situation which was not in itself
a cause of dissension seems to have been used both by the
Montagnards and by their opponents for the purpose of securing
political advantage. At first the Montagnards attacked Roland
and his friends as the pawns of the financiers and speculators

---

[1] *La Vie chère*, p. 107; *Moniteur*, xiv, 236, 499, 614, 619–20, 642, 694.

[2] This point is accepted by Mathiez (*La Vie chère*, p. 103), and indicated by
Lefebvre (*La Convention*, i, 16) also.

[3] *Moniteur*, xiv, 610, 620, 629.

they alleged to be behind the crisis,[1] while the opponents of the Mountain alleged that the disorders were being fomented by the Jacobins, by agents of the Commune or of Orleans, and that the demand for price-control was part of a plan to establish the dreaded *loi agraire*.[2] Later, as we have already seen, the Montagnards had the political acumen to see that the masses must be rallied to the Revolution if the invader were to be repulsed, and they then, in April 1793, purchased popular support by accepting that price-control from which they, in common with the rest of the Convention, had shrunk in horror only two months before. In this matter it is the Montagnards who are distinct, and that by their political initiative rather than by their economic policy.

The same contention, that the differences which appeared between the Montagnards and their opponents in economic policy were dependent upon and secondary to political developments, seems equally true of Mathiez's assertion that the Girondins can be distinguished by their tendency to support the economic interests of the provincial bourgeoisie.[3] Until price-control had been adopted these interests were favoured by a Convention preponderantly sympathetic to free-trade, and the adoption by both the Montagnards and their opponents of partisan attitudes in the social strife subsequently occasioned by such questions as recruitment had a clear political purpose, that of gaining or retaining effective control of local assemblies, and so ultimately of the Convention. Thus while we can agree that Robespierre was more advanced in his views than most deputies, and that the Mountain was peculiar in adopting a popular policy at an earlier stage than the rest of the assembly, Mathiez's more general thesis must be considered, at best, unproven. The economic and social problems which confronted the Convention do not furnish evidence to distinguish a Girondin party

[1] The account given of Clavière by Jean Bouchary, *Les Manieurs d'argent à Paris à la fin du XVIII*[e] *siècle*, does not support the view that his relationships with financiers had political significance.

[2] e.g., *Patriote français*, 17 September 1792, or Brissot, *A tous les Républicains* (Paris, 1792), B.M., F.353.8.

[3] *La Vie chère*, e.g. p. 189: 'Economic federalism duplicated political federalism', or Mathiez, *Girondins et Montagnards*, pp. 87–90, where the decentralization of Condorcet's constitution is treated as a deliberate attempt to enhance the power of the provincial middle-classes in order to check social changes.

O

from the body of the Convention, a distinction which must still be sought elsewhere.

IV

Another assertion is that all the differences between Robespierre and his opponents sprang from a fundamental difference of philosophy.[1] The 'Girondins' have been said to represent the critical and pragmatic philosophy of Voltaire and the Encyclopaedists, a philosophy based on the hypothesis that all problems can be solved by knowledge and by reason, and one which had little place for any personal deity, whereas Robespierre is said to represent the more emotional and romantic philosophy of Rousseau, a philosophy which, however theoretical, was nevertheless coherent and constructive, deriving its strength from the conception of a benevolent Deity, the God of Nature and of Natural Man.

Evidence to support this explanation of the difference between Robespierre and his opponents is abundant. In the Legislative Assembly the attitude of the deputies of the Gironde was particularly apparent in their views on the problems created by the hostility of the non-juring priests to the Civil Constitution of the Clergy. In his report on the situation in the Vendée, Gensonné revealed a complete lack of sympathy for the religious issues involved, deploring both the intolerance of the priests and the incipient intolerance of the State and recommending the complete separation of civil and religious affairs as the rational solution of the problem.[2] Later Ducos called upon God and good sense to preserve him from treating the same question from a theological standpoint. His view that a diversity of religious opinions was both inevitable and politically desirable seems a distinct echo of Voltaire. Guadet, too, said that the problem must be approached in the light of reason and not in that of theology, for the one was eternal and the other transient, while Vergniaud expressed the opinion that civil government

---

[1] e.g.: Blanc, *Histoire de la Révolution française*, vi, 311 ff.; Aulard, *Orateurs*, i, 172 ff.; Thompson, *Robespierre*, i, 215 ff.; Walter, *Robespierre*, 561 ff.

[2] *Moniteur*, x, 328, 386.

bore no relation to heavenly dogma, for every man was free to turn East or West, as he chose, to worship the Divinity.[1]

These deputies of the Gironde appear to be of one mind in their vague Deism, in their dislike of dogma and of clericalism, and in their attitude of reasoned secular toleration. They did not however lead anything approaching a party on this issue, for their anti-clericalism did not differ from that of the great majority of their colleagues in the Assembly and in the Jacobin Club. They were not even wholly agreed with those who were associated with them in other matters: Ducos and Gensonné both rebuked Fauchet for his intemperate and inflammatory language, which was nevertheless voiced as violently by such men as Isnard and Jean Debry.[2]

The distinction between this general cynicism and the attitude of Robespierre became apparent in the Jacobin Club on 26 March 1792.[3] Speaking of the effect on France of the death of the Emperor Leopold, Robespierre said: 'The most resolute were beginning to despair, and then Providence, which watches over us far better than our own wisdom, struck down Leopold and disrupted the plans of our adversaries.' Guadet seized upon this point, saying that he could see no meaning in such a conception and suggesting that Robespierre, having laboured to destroy the despotism of monarchy, was now resurrecting the despotism of superstition. In a long and unprepared[4] reply Robespierre renounced all sympathy for a corrupt and degenerate priesthood, but proclaimed his heart-felt faith in the existence of God, the Eternal Creator of man and nature, the Providence 'which is an essential influence on the destinies of nations and which seems to me to watch over the French Revolution with very particular care'.

In sharp contrast to this speech, which Thompson considers to have been 'the momentary unveiling of a fundamental difference of mind and outlook' between Robespierre and the easy-going intelligentsia of the Assembly,[5] is Brissot's defence of Condorcet at the Jacobins on 25 April. Brissot attributed the

---

[1] *Moniteur*, x, 215, 471, and xii, 92 and 406.
[2] *Moniteur*, x, 252, 308, 389, and xii, 5; *Journal*, 30 October and 7 November 1792.
[3] *Journal*, 26 March 1792.
[4] Blanc, *Histoire de la Révolution française*, vi, 316; Michelet, *Histoire de la Révolution française*, vi, 405. [5] Thompson, *Robespierre*, i, 217.

freedom which France had won to the untiring energy and burning genius of Condorcet and his collaborators, Voltaire and d'Alembert: 'The most durable monument to our Revolution is philosophy. The patriot *par excellence* is a philosopher.'[1]

Three days later Robespierre agreed that 'the mathematicians and the members of the Academy that M. Brissot holds up to us as models' had indeed destroyed the credit of the clergy, but he condemned them as sycophants of royalty and persecutors of Jean-Jacques Rousseau, 'who in my opinion is alone among the celebrities of his time in meriting public honour, prostituted as it is to political charlatans and trumped-up heroes'.[2]

These speeches, with the later conduct of Robespierre in condemning the 'philosopher' Helvetius as a persecutor of Rousseau and in promoting the worship of the Supreme Being,[3] justify the assumption that a profound difference of philosophy existed between him and the great majority of the deputies both in the Legislative Assembly and in the Convention. The difference is important, for philosophies may be regarded as the mainsprings of political action, but it does not serve to distinguish a Girondin party in either assembly. The views expressed by Brissot and the deputies of the Gironde were those most commonly held at the time, and those of Robespierre mark only his own isolation from all but a few of his colleagues.[4]

V

The other characteristic commonly attributed to the supposed Girondin party is that of federalism. As we have seen, this was a charge constantly levelled by the Montagnards against those who opposed them, until by the summer of 1793 the term 'federalist deputies' had come into use as a generic description of all those whom the Montagnards had driven from the Convention. Since by that time considerable parts of France were in open revolt against the Revolutionary government, the name

[1] *Jacobins*, iii, 529; Blanc, *op. cit.*, vi, 323.
[2] Buchez and Roux, *Histoire parlementaire*, xiv, 153–5.
[3] *Jacobins*, iv, 550; Walter, *Robespierre*, p. 561.
[4] An exception to this generalization may be Bancal des Issarts, who also spoke of Providence as watching over the Revolution: Mège, *Le Conventionnel Bancal des Issarts*, p. 263.

had high emotional significance and was more damning than definite. As one of the imprisoned deputies wrote, it was one of several 'hateful terms of denunciation . . . which, constantly repeated but never explained, always seem to indicate great crimes but in reality mean only "marked for execution"'.[1]

The denigratory usage of the word federalism apparently coincides with the first meetings of the Convention. In the earlier days of the Revolution federalism had often been advocated by men of advanced views as a means of checking excessive centralization, and it was discussed quite dispassionately by Chabot at the Jacobin Society as late as 10 September 1792.[2] At this point, however, an interesting sequence of events occurs. On 17 September, just as the Legislative Assembly was approaching dissolution, its deputies heard a letter from Roland urging them to institute an armed force to guard themselves and their successors.[3] The following day as we have seen, Gensonné embodied this proposal in a formal motion, which was accepted as a decree, but never really effected. On 24 September, when Kersaint and Buzot launched the first attack upon Robespierre in the Convention, the proposal reappeared, but now it referred explicitly to the formation of a force to be recruited in the provinces, the notorious 'departmental guard'. The same evening Chabot again addressed the Jacobin Society, saying of those whom he called 'our biggest busy-bodies' that 'The most dangerous scheme of this tedious set is that of establishing a federal system of government'. It was, moreover, on the next day, 25 September, that Danton broke the force of Buzot's attack by successfully calling on the Convention to proclaim as a capital offence any attempt to destroy the unity of France.[4]

Thus those who first broke the peace in the Convention exposed themselves to counter-attack and made 'federalism' a potent accusation by attempting to rally provincial support against Paris at a time when the newly formed republic still

---

[1] *Les Douze Représentants du Peuple détenus à Porte Libre* (Paris, 1794), B.M., F.843.17.

[2] *Jacobins*, iv, 259, 273-8; A. Cobban, 'Local Government during the French Revolution', *English Historical Review*, lviii (1943), p. 24.

[3] A letter occasioned by the theft of the Crown Jewels from the Garde Meuble (*Moniteur*, xiii, 722, 736).

[4] *Moniteur*, xiii, 722, 736, and xiv, 11, 36, 39-40, 42; *Jacobins*, iv, 329. See Chapters V and VI, above.

seemed in mortal peril—for Valmy was not fought until 20 September. Thereafter the charge took rapid root, aided by Danton's revelation on 29 September that Roland had contemplated leaving Paris when the Prussian army was advancing in August, and by Cloots's allegations in the pamphlet *Ni Marat ni Roland* that those who attended Madame Roland's receptions were contemplating the division of France into a federation of small states. Later still, when such deputies as Barbaroux and Kervélegan called provincial troops to Paris without the authority of the Convention and when an appeal to the people about the sentencing of the King was proposed, the charge seemed substantiated, and when in the spring of 1793 the renewed Austrian advance coincided with provincial unrest and rebellion it became synonymous with counter-revolution and treason.

That anyone in Brissot's circle of friends ever seriously contemplated federalism in its literal sense is unlikely. Roland and his friends had certainly considered the advisability of leaving Paris in the critical days of June and July 1792, when Barbaroux, finding Roland and Clavière reviewing a plan whereby the Revolution might take refuge in the South of France if reaction should triumph in Paris and the North, had joined them in a study of the map and in visualizing the armies of the Revolution fighting on the line of the Loire. The practical outcome of the meeting, according to Barbaroux, was his summons to the *fédérés* of Marseilles, who symbolize for ever the spirit which drove Louis from the Tuileries and the invader from French soil. But even if Barbaroux misleads us in ascribing this revolutionary and patriotic measure to this particular occasion, there is no reason to suppose that the idea of a 'Republic of the South' ever merited more than Madame Roland's description of it as a 'trivial and hypothetical' plan, conditional upon complete disaster in the North.[1] It cannot be regarded as federalism, for the idea of the ultimate unity of France, even by reconquest from Corsica, was implicit in the discussion.[2]

---

[1] Above, Chapters III and IV. See Barbaroux, *Mémoires*, p. 122: *Madame Roland*, i, 84, 160, and ii, 292.

[2] 'We had no intention of deserting Paris and the North; on the contrary, it was agreed that we would try every possible means of saving them': Barbaroux, *Mémoires*, p. 122.

This is not to say that the episode is wholly without significance, for the idea of calling upon provincial troops to defend
the Revolution against reaction may have been the origin of
later efforts to enlist their aid against the turbulent elements in
the capital. Moreover, when Danton referred in the Convention
to Roland's readiness to abandon Paris he spoke not of July,
but of the end of August. By that time some anxiety about Paris
was probably complicating Roland's worries about the approach
of the invading armies, so that if the idea of consolidating the
Revolution in the South was indeed revived in August there
may have been some separatist implications.[1]

Conclusions about Cloots's allegations of federalist talk at
Madame Roland's table need not be quite so speculative as this.
Cloots himself believed that the revolution in France would be
imitated throughout the world, until all men were united in a
single democratic republic. On 3 September 1792 he expounded
his beliefs to Madame Roland's guests, and it seems as if after
some academic discussion his asseverations became boring.
Apparently he was snubbed by his hostess and departed in
dudgeon to compose his pamphlet. Damaging as this was at the
time, dispassionate examination of it in the light of the replies
which it evoked suggests now that some of those present, particularly Buzot, were perplexed by the problem of how a single
unified republic could be established in a state as large as
France.[2] Such perplexity is understandable. The writings of
Rousseau and the general knowledge educated men had of the
ancient world had made them familiar with small republics,
but the only large republic in the contemporary world, the
United States of America, had a federal government, as indeed
had Switzerland and the United Provinces. Cloots's extrava-
gances may have led Roland and his friends to extol the virtues

---

[1] Barbaroux's friend Deperret condemned on 17 September 1792 'those who
plan to unite the Midi while abandoning the North to its own devices' (*Jacobins*,
iv, 302).

[2] Miss Williams later said that her friends sometimes considered creating small
republics as models for the rest of France (*Souvenirs de la Révolution française*, p. 63).
See also: *Madame Roland*, i, 107; *Ni Marat ni Roland*; *A mon tour la parole*; *Un mot
d'Anacharsis Cloots* (Paris, 1792 and 1793); B.M., F.775.3 and F.776.1 and 5;
Réponses au Prussien Cloots par Roland, Guadet, Kersaint et Brissot and *Henri Bancal à
Anacharsis Cloots son collègue* (Paris, 1792), B.M., F.776.6 and F.777.2; Dulaure, *Du
fédéralisme en France* (Paris, 1793), B.M., F.1103.3.

of the small society, but their written replies to him are convincing evidence that it was his huge world-state to which they really objected. Brissot, for example, explained his hope that France would expand to her natural frontiers and then content herself with promoting the formation of a surrounding band of associated but independent republics. Bancal, too, deliberately disassociated himself from Cloots, proclaiming his faith in the eventual evolution of a world of free but federated nations. So far as the unity of France is concerned, an academic anxiety about the future was the root of the offence on this occasion.[1]

True federalism apparently appealed to no one in Roland's circle except Buzot, and it is possible that his views and actions— for he was particularly prominent in the agitation for a departmental guard for the Convention—represent the heart of all the Montagnards' allegations and exaggerations. Cloots's attack was particularly concerned with him, and in his own memoirs,[2] written after his flight from Paris, he strenuously maintained that federalism was at least a legitimate form of government and one which could be supported without criminal intent. He even asserted that in view of the moral weaknesses he saw in France it might well prove to be the only form of republicanism suitable for the country.

Although Buzot reiterated the claim that he spoke only for himself and that he and his friends had never attempted to effect any move towards federalism, his disclaimers disregard the vital fact that by the autumn of 1792 the term had acquired a significance much more far-reaching than its literal meaning. In Cloots's allegation that Madame Roland's guests had disparaged Paris and in Kersaint's proud assertion in his reply of his own record of opposition to the Commune appears the real meaning of the word as it was understood by the Montagnards— suspicion, distrust and even hatred of the power of Paris. Some such feeling would be natural enough among any group of provincial deputies. It is still apparent in its simplest form even as late as the spring of 1793, when Barbaroux and Boyer-

---

[1] Cp. Paganel, *Essai historique*, ii, 366: 'by drawing attention and suspicion to a vague plan . . . the Commune itself created this monster', i.e. federalism.

[2] Buzot, *Mémoires* (ed. Guadet), pp. 49, 151–3, 156–7, 194. Cp. *Madame Roland*, i, 107.

Fonfrède, both representatives of large provincial ports, demanded that these, like Paris, should be granted state subsidies for the purchase of food.[1] Its evolution into the form called federalism, however, requires some historical explanation.

At the time of the Legislative Assembly, when Brissot and the deputies of the Gironde were still the spokesmen of the Revolution, Paris was their potential ally against the power of the Court, and jealousies remained latent. Once they had attained power and gained their immediate ends, a divergence of interests appeared, for Robespierre was profoundly distrustful of their sincerity and strength of purpose and the *sans-culottes* of the capital were still far from satisfied. Before 10 August 1792 this divergence was to some extent concealed by the necessity for presenting a united front to Louis and Lafayette, but when the power of the Crown was irretrievably broken by the storming of the Tuileries, Brissot and his friends came face to face with the hostility of Paris and its militant municipality.

The appearance of the Convention should have remedied this situation, for in theory it provided a new focal point for all patriotic loyalties. In practice, however, the quarrel between Robespierre and the Brissotins had been embittered to the point of consuming hatred by the September Massacres,[2] and the Brissotins, in their brief and hazardous period of power during the last weeks of the Legislative, had learnt what it was like to attempt to govern while facing constant pressure from the various municipal and popular authorities of Paris. They therefore entered the Convention as deputies, or met it as Ministers, with a fully formulated point of view in mind. According to this, the Convention represented the sovereignty of the whole French people, and obstruction or undue influence from any quarter was quite intolerable; Paris, in particular, must bow before its master, abandon its pretensions to leadership, and accept complete equality with the other Departments; the Convention alone was the capital of France.

These were the ideas which inspired the proposals for the

---

[1] *Moniteur*, xvi, 4. Cp. Paganel, *Essai historique*, ii, 344: 'the interests of a few big cities suggested the thought to them.'

[2] Cp. Baudot, *Notes historiques sur la Convention nationale*, p. 147, where the clash with the Commune is treated as 'an accidental consequence' of the conflict with Robespierre.

enforcement of law and order with which Buzot first broke the
unity of the Convention three days after its assembly, and they
were given full and coherent expression by Roland in his letter
to the deputies on 30 September.[1] In practice, they implied
both the subordination of Robespierre and an attempt to
strengthen the Convention against the capital by enlisting the
aid of the provinces, and these policies are undoubtedly identical with what was loosely called federalism. The demand for a
departmental guard, the illicit summoning of provincial troops,
the inspired addresses of provincial loyalty, the proposal for a
referendum on the fate of the King, even the strengthening of
local authorities in Condorcet's abortive Constitution, all can
be considered as aspects of this effort to redress the balance of
power between Paris and the rest of France.

The deep roots of this wide antagonism can no doubt be
traced to the fundamental difference of philosophy which, as
we have seen, separated Robespierre from most of his contemporaries. That which was manifest, however, was hostility to
Robespierre and to the delegation and city of Paris. It is
federalism, in this limited sense, which is of all the various
characteristics attributed to the supposed Girondin party that
which has the greatest verisimilitude.

VI

Of other alleged characteristics, this may be said: differences of
policy in many matters divided Robespierre from his opponents
as the course of the Convention proceeded, but these were
rather incidental than fundamental, consequences of the personal quarrel and the clash over Paris but not in themselves
first causes of controversy. Much of the obscurity that has concealed the position has certainly arisen because historians have
sought for first principles in the stormy story of the conflicts in
the Convention, but have disregarded the fact that the deputies
who led that assembly were themselves dominated by their
experience of the immediate past, and so were primarily concerned to avenge old wrongs and to prevent the reappearance
of known perils.

---

[1] *Moniteur*, xiv, 88. Cp. *ibid.*, 41, 153, or Buzot's first letter to his constituents
(Paris, 1793), B.M., F.1033.10.

For this reason, if we are now to decide whether there was in the Convention anything that can legitimately be described as a Girondin party, some recapitulation of our earlier conclusions about the period of the Legislative Assembly is necessary. At that time a group of some seven deputies—Brissot, Condorcet, Gensonné, Guadet, Isnard, Lasource and Vergniaud—and Roland, their Minister, is clearly apparent. These men shared common friendships and a common hostility to the Court, and they may even have co-ordinated some of their actions by prior consultation at Vergniaud's apartment. In 1791–2 they stimulated and led the attack on the newly established constitutional monarchy in a way that was wildly irresponsible, so gaining prestige, place, and some degree of power. Then, to retain these things, they were prepared to compromise with the Court, and the ambiguity of their conduct during the critical days of July and August 1792 roused the implacable hostility of Robespierre and the revolutionary authorities of Paris, a hostility which they reciprocated after they had experienced the perils of the September Massacres and the dogmatic defiance of the Commune.

This antagonism was clearly transferred to the Convention, in which these same deputies sat in the same hall that the Legislative Assembly had used. It is even probable that some of them at least participated in what may be regarded as a determined bid to consolidate with the new assembly the power they had precariously held in the Legislative. There seems to have been an effort to attract those deputies who were strangers to Paris to the Club which favoured Brissot, the Reunion, and so to limit the influence of the Jacobin Society and Robespierre. There were certainly attempts during the first ten days of the Convention to circumscribe the power exercised by the Commune and Sections of Paris, and to implicate Robespierre in charges of conspiracy, intrigue and wholesale slaughter. The fact that many new deputies, particularly Barbaroux and Buzot, who were already close to Brissot, joined Lasource and Vergniaud in leading the attack upon Robespierre and his supporters can easily suggest that the beginning of the Convention marks a substantial increase in the size of the Brissotin connection.

The deduction, however, seems unsound. It is, for one thing, a curious fact that the Brissotins of the Legislative Assembly took very little part in debates in the Convention between September 1792 and the beginning of March 1793, seldom speaking except for their occasional presentation of committee reports. Brissot himself would seem to have been as preoccupied with diplomatic issues as was Condorcet with the preparation of his Constitution. Isnard and Lasource were absent on missions to the Departments for much of the period, and even the principal deputies of the Gironde, Vergniaud, Guadet and Gensonné, only intervened in discussion at irregular intervals. The initiative in the campaign against Robespierre came from the new deputies, and if some of the more prominent of these, like Barbaroux and Buzot and, to a lesser degree, Louvet, had previous associations with Brissot, others, like Lanjuinais and Valazé, did not. It is also a point of much significance that when on 30 September 1792 the new assembly heard Roland's letter, enunciating the theory of the supremacy of the Convention over the Commune, they welcomed it with prolonged applause. Antagonism towards Paris, supposedly the peculiar characteristic of a group in the Convention, is in fact apparent in almost every quarter of it from its earliest days. Nor is this surprising, for the deputies were meeting in the heart of a turbulent city which had a bare fortnight before been the scene of outrages which can still shock scholars in our present case-hardened century. It is at least arguable that even as early as September the Brissotin group had merged with the majority of the Convention. The fact that the initial assault upon Robespierre could not be pressed to a conclusion does not invalidate this interpretation of the situation, for when Danton asserted that the attack implied a federalist threat to the unity of France he appealed to his hearers' patriotism, the one sentiment which consistently proved powerful enough to outweigh the general fear of Paris.

To reject this view, and to grant greater credibility to the theory that the attack upon Robespierre and Paris was monopolized by an enlarged but distinct Brissotin group, is but to defer recognition of the identification of that group with the great majority of the assembly. As we have seen, the Montagnards alleged that in October a measure of equilibrium was reached in the Convention and that in November some sort of centre party was appearing—assertions, incidentally, which tend to confirm an initial picture of a Montagnard minority in an overwhelmingly hostile chamber. Whatever measure of truth there may be in these comments, any such development was certainly no more than a brief period of transition—or, more probably, reversion—to a position in which the Montagnards opposed, and were opposed by, the remainder of the deputies, a position which was to remain unaltered until the beginning of June 1793. The cardinal characteristic of the autumn of 1792 is not the establishment of any third force, but the steady increase in the force and vehemence of the Montagnard minority, which drove many men into active opposition to it. Of this, many examples could be given, but it may suffice to mention only two: Fauchet, whose exclusion from the Jacobin Society in September for his supposed part in the escape of Narbonne from Paris, may stand for the exclusion of all leading critics of the Mountain by January 1793 on the technical charge of failure to renew their membership cards;[1] and Pétion, who at first affected a benevolent neutrality, but became by his assumption of superiority a perfect target for Montagnard attacks and cries of 'No more lectures!' and 'Long live King Pétion!'[2]

In the great affair of 1792, the trial of the King, the Montagnard minority was able to carry the day for the same reason as before: the ruthlessness demanded of the assembly by Saint Just and Robespierre was reluctantly accepted as a patriotic necessity, imperative to the survival of the Revolution and the Nation. At the same time, fear of Paris was a general and ever-present consideration. According to a story told by the Earl of Lauderdale to an Englishman visiting Paris in 1803,[3] he had at

[1] *Jacobins*, iv, 316–17; *Claude Fauchet à trente Jacobins qui s'intitulent la Société* (Paris, 1792), B.M., F.246.1; *Le Journal des Amis* (which Fauchet established early in 1793 and which was violently anti-Jacobin), B.M., F.1579.1; and Charrier, *Claude Fauchet*, ii, 187–92.

[2] *Moniteur*, xiv, 791, 852. See also *Lettre de Jérôme Pétion à la Société des Jacobins* and *Observations de Jérôme Pétion sur la lettre de M. Robespierre* (Paris, 1792), B.M., F.665.9 and F.662.12. He was excluded from the Society on 27 April 1793: *Jacobins*, v, 48.

[3] *An Englishman in Paris, 1803: The Journal of Bertie Greatheed*, p. 39 (28 January 1803).

the time of the trial entertained Brissot and a large party of
'Brissotinis' (*sic*) at his house, and when one of them commented
on a brace of pocket pistols on the chimney-piece, and drew his
own for comparison, it was discovered that every man save
Brissot himself was carrying arms. Moreover, the violence dis-
played by the Mountain in these debates again swelled the
numbers of those who opposed them. Some, like Kersaint and
Manuel, were driven to the point of resignation, and when
Dusaulx threatened to resign also he was answered only with a
cry of 'So much the better!'[1] Others again, like Salle and
Serre, were included in the wholesale expulsion from the Jacobin Society of all supporters of the proposed referendum. The
true position in the Convention at this time may be gauged by
the position of Rabaut St. Etienne, who in November was named
by Desmoulins as one of the *phlegmatics* but who in January supported Buzot's proposals for a departmental guard[2]—proposals, it is worth repeating, which were accepted by the majority
before Boyer-Fonfrède of the Gironde caused them to be
abandoned.

After the comparatively quiet period which lasted from the
execution of the King until the early days of March 1793, political strife became increasingly intense, and the names of deputies of prominence appear more and more frequently in the
record of debates. In the conflicts of mid-April, for example,
Barbaroux and Buzot continued their incessant attacks upon
the Mountain; Pétion and Fonfrède denounced the address
presented by the Section Halle au Blé, as Vergniaud, Guadet,
Gensonné and Lasource condemned that of the united Sections
of Paris; Vergniaud and Guadet made lengthy replies to Robespierre, and even Brissot appeared to refute the allegations made
about his relationship with Dumouriez. Only Condorcet remained aloof, confining himself to the defence of his constitutional proposals.

Obviously such men as these were more prominent in their
opposition to the Mountain than were others. Their number,
estimated from the evidence of the debates and of personal

---

[1] *Moniteur*, xv, 85. (For the resignations of Kersaint and Manuel see *Moniteur*,
xiv, 233, 255, 267. Manuel was excluded from the Jacobin Society on 26 December
1792: *Jacobins*, iv, 623.)   [2] *Moniteur*, xv, 69, 114.

friendships, may be put at about fifteen or sixteen. Barbaroux, Brissot, Buzot, Gensonné, Guadet, Isnard, Lasource, Louvet, Pétion, Salle and Vergniaud would seem to have pride of place on both counts, with the possible addition of Boyer-Fonfrède, Condorcet and Fauchet, while the names of Lanjuinais and Rabaut St. Etienne might be added on the evidence of the debates alone. By the same standards some twenty-five other men might be considered the most consistent supporters of these leading figures. Bergoeing, Birotteau, Carra, Chambon, Deperret, Doulcet, Ducos, Duprat, Dusaulx, Gorsas, Grangeneuve, Hardy, Lacaze, Lehardy, Lesage, Lidon, Masuyer, Minvielle, Mollevaut, Valady and Valazé all appear to have had some personal tie with one or more of the sixteen and were fairly consistent in their support. Larivière, Rabaut Pommier, Rouyer and Serre might also be added to this list on the evidence of debates alone, and even Madame Roland's neglected admirer, Lanthénas, showed signs of sympathy for his first friends at the close of their careers.[1]

A side-light on the relative importance of these men is provided by the denunciations launched before 2 June by the Jacobins and the Sections of Paris. The Jacobin circular of 26 March named Brissot, Gensonné, Guadet and Vergniaud as the particular accomplices of Dumouriez; that of 19 April repeated these names with the addition of that of Pétion; and the Cordeliers's address to the Jacobin Society on 19 May also accepted these same five men as the 'chiefs-of-staff of the counter-revolutionary army'.[2] A similar picture is presented by the various Sectional lists of traitors presented to or denounced in the Convention. According to Marat on 12 March, the Section Poisonnière had demanded the heads of the three deputies of the Gironde, Gensonné, Guadet and Vergniaud;[3] the first two of these were also named by the Section Bonconseil on the same day, by the Section Quatre Nations (according to Vergniaud's statement on 13 March), by Bonconseil again on 8 April, by the united Sections on 15 April, and by Hassenfratz on 1 June.[4] The names of Brissot and Barbaroux also occur in

---

[1] Lanthénas, *Motifs de faire du 10 août un jubilé fraternel* (Paris, 1793), B.M., R.109.9.   [2] *Jacobins*, v, 106, 146, 198.   [3] *Moniteur*, xv, 693.
[4] *Moniteur*, xv, 695, 704, and xvi, 87, 156, 544.

all these; Pétion, Vergniaud and Buzot appear four times, and Louvet, Lanjuinais and Gorsas three times. Lasource—whose conduct seems to have been fairly restrained until one of these denunciations drove him to accuse Robespierre of personal vindictiveness,[1] was named only twice, on 15 April and 1 June. The naming of Fonfrède and Rabaut St. Etienne only in the final list is an interesting indication of their probable restraining influence on their colleagues, while Isnard, in the same category, was long almost more Montagnard than the Mountain in his efforts to establish a strong Committee of Public Safety. In general the lists and even the last minute alterations to the final list again suggest that the figure 15 is a fair estimate of the number of the principal opponents of the Mountain.[2]

The debates nevertheless show that even these men seldom acted in concert. Indeed their opinions were often in conflict, even at times which in retrospect appear of considerable importance to themselves. In the important conflict with the Mountain about the composition and powers of the Sections, for example, the efforts made by Pétion and Brissot were offset by Vergniaud's condemnation of the strife as a deplorable division, artificially excited, and by Lanjuinais's reproachful reminder that 'There is but one People'. Independence of this sort is particularly apparent in the *appels nominaux*, which show clearly that even in the most vital votes the centre of the so-called Girondin party was quite inchoate. As the deputy Mennesson wrote in 1792, the leading figures in the Convention were essentially egotists.

Equally any attempt to decide the composition of a party by tabulating the names of deputies who supported policies favoured by the principal speakers is vain. The policies, such as hostility to the Revolutionary Tribunal or to the *maximum*, may be stated easily, but differences of opinion between individuals make classification futile. On the other hand, much evidence

---

[1] 'I have spoken of a man, it is enough, I am denounced', *Moniteur*, xvi, 171.

[2] Distinctive plotting of these more prominent deputies in their constituencies on the map referred to earlier in this Chapter shows that some are grouped together, as in the Gironde, and that some, like Condorcet in Aisne, probably attracted the loyalty of the more obscure deputies who appear in the same constituency. The distribution still remains explicable only in terms of common friendships and a common proscription.

indicates that the standard view that the Convention consisted of a Girondin party, the Montagnards and a substantial Centre, the 'Plain' or 'Marsh', is unsound. The considerable influence of such moderate men as Boyer-Fonfrède, Rabaut St. Etienne and Lanjuinais, who fought courageously for the authority of the assembly as a whole; the fact that Valazé's associates at the salon in the Rue d'Orléans were both numerous and comparatively obscure; the frequent references in writing and in debate to the two parties which existed in the Convention; and, above all, the evidence of the *appels nominaux*: all suggest that the Plain, if it ever had reality,[1] soon became divided into two sections, one of which was remarkably unanimous in its opposition to the Mountain while the other—more influenced, perhaps, by considerations of national security—was increasingly prepared to accept Montagnard leadership. Marat could not have been impeached, nor the Commission of Twelve re-established after its first dissolution, unless a considerable number of the rank and file of the assembly had not supported the views of more prominent anti-Montagnards. Certainly any serious effort to isolate a Girondin party from the body of the Convention breaks down through the impossibility of distinguishing between a Right and a Centre.

Careful examination of the frequency and tenor of individual deputies' speeches provides some indication of their relative importance and casts some light upon the general course of events, but it does not furnish any adequate criteria by which a Girondin party can be distinguished from the majority of the Convention. The Montagnards alone appear as a distinct entity, having a fair measure of unity imposed upon them by the public debates and frequent purges of the Jacobin Club and having their separatism justified in their own eyes by the conviction that they represented, not a party, but the true voice of the sovereign people. The only distinction between them and their principal opponents which has any consistent validity is that of their divergent attitudes towards Paris, and in this essential matter the attitude of the so-called Girondin deputies was that of the majority of the Convention. Had it not been so, the

---

[1] Cp. Brissot's assertion that 'the same principles prevailed there . . . sometimes in different forms'. J. P. Brissot, *A ses commettans* (Paris, 1793), B.M., F.674.2.

P

insurrection of 2 June 1793 would not have taken place, for it would not have been necessary.

CHAPTER IX

Conclusion

THE attempt that has been made in these pages to draw closer to Brissot and his friends has shown that current generalizations on the subject need some revision, and this revision in its turn is not without importance in the interpretation of the general course of the Revolution.

The closer approach, originally suggested by the doubts and differences which are apparent in the historians' views about the unity and policy of the supposed Girondin party, has revealed that its very existence is a remarkable historical legend, originating in contemporary propaganda and subsequently accepted by historians as a matter of convenience. Under examination, the party disintegrates. Proscription by the Montagnards, which has long been accepted as a criterion of membership of the party, has proved to be a fortuitous process from which no valid deductions can be drawn. In practice, there was neither a recognized party leader nor an accepted policy. The supposed Girondin deputies consistently asserted their independence, speaking and acting as individuals even at the most critical moments of the conflict with Robespierre. As for the alleged party headquarters, they have appeared as irrelevant to the main question. When the *Club de la Réunion* was influential it was as much Robespierrist as Brissotin in composition, and a subsequent attempt by Brissot's friends to capture and maintain or develop it was a complete failure. The *Comité Valazé*, the nearest approach to an attempt at party organization, represents nothing more than an ineffectual effort by a comparatively unimportant deputy to rally even more obscure men against the threat of domination by the Montagnard minority. In short, the only people in the Convention to bear any resemblance to a coherent party were the Montagnards, who were opposed by most of the amorphous majority of the assembly.

Brissot and his friends should be regarded as a small and loose-knit group or coalition of individualists who rapidly became representative of the resistance of the majority to Robespierre, their personal independence remaining unqualified. Evidence even of collaboration between them during the time of the Convention is extremely slight, for the meetings at Madame Roland's salon lacked any precision of purpose and ended when her husband resigned his office in January 1793. They appear in the Legislative Assembly as a fairly coherent group, but one of only some seven or eight prominent radicals, a coterie which increased little in size in the Convention. Even in May 1793, when Montagnard pressure was greatest, the 'faction' was no more than a frail alliance of some fifteen deputies, men whose outlook was so identical with that of the majority of their colleagues that they can be distinguished only as personalities, individuals whose reputation, powers of oratory or personal courage marked them out above others as enemies of the Mountain.

A group of this sort can scarcely be said to have had any specific policy. The men concerned, however, may be regarded as representing in some respects a great many of the revolutionaries. Most of them were clearly *arrivistes*, drawn together even before 1789 by their profound dissatisfaction with the society in which they lived. In their letters, in Brissot's *Patriote français* and at Madame Roland's first receptions, they had expressed their discontent with the existing order and anticipated the opening of a new era. When their opportunity occurred in 1791–2 they showed themselves avid and irresponsible in their pursuit of place and power, even to the extent of encouraging incipient insurrection in order to gain political advantage. Then, when leadership had been won, they proved irresolute in everything but the endeavour to retain it, vacillating at all critical times and showing determination only in their efforts to crush Robespierre, the man who impugned their integrity and challenged their authority.

Yet even in these, their most unpleasing characteristics—which were of course by no means peculiar to them—Brissot and his friends were not altogether unpardonable. They seem to have sought power more for its social advantages than from any desire to dominate. Some of them indeed acted as demagogues, stimulating forces which they were quite unable to control, but they were not themselves serious enemies of society. Rather were they men of considerable culture and professional ability, who had hitherto been excluded from their appropriate place in the political and social life of the nation. Before the Revolution, their political energies were confined to impracticable plans for philanthropy in France and to participation in the remote cause of negro emancipation overseas, while their social aspirations could only be expressed by the assumption of such trivial territorial titles as Brissot *de Warville*, Pétion *de Villeneuve*, and Roland *de la Platière*. By 1792, however, they had gained the social status appropriate to their new political position. They were, for a time, cultivated by the liberal nobility. Pétion became Mayor of Paris. Ministers of State sat at Madame Roland's table. Their salons seemed to stand at the centre of French affairs. It is understandable if for them the Revolution was, in a sense, consummated.

Although Robespierre's quarrel with Brissot began when he refused to acknowledge the expediency of an attack upon Austria, the root of his hostility towards the Brissotins lay in his recognition of their readiness to accept the Revolution as completed, to consort with men of rank and reputation, and so to sever themselves from the still unsatisfied lower ranks of the people. The quarrel, in its turn, revealed a second respect in which Brissot and his friends represented a common contemporary attitude: as ample evidence, particularly that of the debate at the Jacobin Society on 26 March 1792, indicates, their philosophy was a somewhat cynical deism. In this they were sharply distinguished from Robespierre, who regarded the Revolution as one through which Providence was working to eradicate every evil from society and to bring about the complete regeneration of mankind.

This distinction had far-reaching consequences in the development both of the Revolution and of France. At first their lack of a more positive faith merely encouraged Brissot and his friends to procrastinate in emergencies and, instead of seeking positive solutions, to resort to the repression of social and political unrest. Later, however, the very limitations of their outlook acquired a positive value. Although they themselves lived precariously from day to day, having no immediate object save the elimination of Robespierre, their opposition to him made them, almost inadvertently, the champions of two fundamental principles. They came to represent both the Rule of Law and the right of the individual to resist oppression by the State.

After the insurrection of 10 August 1792, revolutionary authority, exercised in the name of the sovereign people, was retained by the Commune of Paris in defiance of the rump of the Legislative Assembly. The friends of Brissot, particularly the deputies of the Gironde, then attempted to restore some sort of constitutional authority by calling for a national Convention and by attempting to dissolve the Commune. The Convention, however, was in its turn confronted by the refusal of the Paris radicals to acknowledge its authority. This may have been in some measure a consequence of the Brissotins' exploitation of their influence in the new assembly in their effort to discredit and destroy Robespierre, but it was nevertheless a clear instance of the defiance of a legally constituted authority by a dissident minority of the people, even if it was adopted after provocation and in support of what were believed to be progressive principles. Robespierre himself did not finally sanction the forcible seizure of power by the radical minority of Paris until he considered that the nation stood in such danger that the action was justified, yet he had long lent his prestige to a parallel course—the systematic perversion of parliamentary procedure by the Montagnard minority. Both the Montagnards, in their defiance of majority decisions, and the Brissotin leaders of the majority, in their attacks upon Robespierre and their appeals to the provincial electorate, were putting into practice a conception of democracy not compatible with the Rule of Law, but as the Brissotins' fight to maintain their position against the threats of the Jacobins, the Commune and the crowd became increasingly futile, they became increasingly conscious of the virtues of legality and the iniquity of the appeal to violence.

Their failure to deal effectively with the radicals of Paris must yet stand as the most serious failure of these men. The opening of the Convention appears in French history as a moment of great opportunity, which constructive statesmen might have employed to reconcile the people of Paris to the rule of an assembly lawfully elected by a more conservative countryside. Far from attempting this difficult task, those who led the majority first antagonized Paris by persecuting its delegates, and then fostered the latent hostility between the capital and the provinces by futile attempts to enlist provincial aid in their own interest. The ensuing crisis was checked by the Terror and by the Montagnards' alliance with the radicals of Paris, but this alliance was but a temporary incident, and Robespierre himself was to be overthrown in his turn in part because he too tried to restrain the radicals. The conflict between the national assembly and the *sans-culottes* was not again resolved until Napoleon did what Brissot and the deputies of the Gironde had lacked the power or the decision to do, and dispersed the mob with his 'whiff of grapeshot'. But even Napoleon could not wholly heal the wounds which these events inflicted upon France, and subsequent struggles kept them open and angry throughout the nineteenth century.

On the other hand, those who led the Convention before Robespierre's advent to power deserve praise for their refusal to recognize the validity of the doctrines which were implicit in the *coup d'état* which drove them from the assembly. In the end they took their stand upon principle, though they only became conscious of it when their own lives were at stake and they were faced with the consequences of the contrary principle. For Robespierre's eventual decision to sanction revolutionary action by the *sans-culottes* was in large measure a consequence of his personal philosophy. By May 1793 he had come to the conclusion that the Revolution was being endangered by a self-interested clique. From his philosophy it followed that this same clique was frustrating the purposes of Providence, of which, by approving the purge of the Convention, he made himself the arbiter. Thereafter, by refusing to recognize the legality of Robespierre's victory, the deputies who were driven from their seats were really resisting the doctrine that an *élite* has the right to rule by virtue of its understanding of the way in which the State may bring men spiritual salvation as well as material welfare. Eventually those deputies who died in 1793-4 died in defence of a vital principle: by challenging the authority of the court which condemned them in the sinister name of the security of the State, they really proclaimed their faith in a Republic which would approve and defend individual freedom of conscience.

They did not die in vain. After only a year, the ruthless rule of Robespierre's *élite* proved as unnecessary as it was intolerable, and when the survivors of those who were proscribed in 1793 returned to the Convention after Thermidor, France had resumed the line of political development most natural to her people. Some later historians have indeed paid lip-service to Michelet's interpretation of the Revolution as Justice incarnate, and said as he did of those who died that 'the divine fire of the Revolution was not in them': but since the days of the Jacobins no such *élite* has obtained power in France, and the nation's most serious weakness has remained that so apparent among the leaders of the Convention—an excess of individualism.

Chronological Table

October 29	Second attack upon Paris and the Montagnards.
November 6	*Jemappes: French conquest of Belgium.*
19	*Decree of 'fraternité et secours'.*
20	Discovery of the *armoire de fer*.
December 3	Decision to try the King.
11	Interrogation of the King.
27	Proposal of a referendum on the Convention's verdict.

1793

January 17	Condemnation of the King.
21	Execution of the King.
22	Resignation of Roland.
February 1	*Declaration of War on Great Britain and Holland*
15	Condorcet presents his proposed Constitution.
25	Food riots in Paris.
March 1–7	*Revolt in Belgium.*
7	*Declaration of war on Spain.*
9–10	Further rioting in Paris.
11	Creation of the Revolutionary Tribunal.
16	Revolt in La Vendée.
18	*Neerwinden: defeat of Dumouriez in the Netherlands.*
25	Reorganization of the Committee of General Defence.
April 5	Desertion of Dumouriez.
6	Creation of Committee of Public Safety.
12	Impeachment of Marat.
15	The Sections demand a purge of the Convention.
May 4	Enactment of the first *maximum*.
20	Creation of the Commission of Twelve.
31	Attempted Revolution.
June 2	THE REVOLUTION OF 2 JUNE—arrest of Brissot and others.
6 and 19	The 'Protest of the Seventy-five'.
July 28	Eighteen deputies named as traitors.
August 10	Fête to inaugurate Montagnard Constitution.
October 3	Impeachment of Brissot and forty-four others.
24	Opening of the trial of Brissot '*et ses complices*'.
31	Execution of Brissot and nineteen others.

APPENDIX A

The Proscribed Deputies

The full names and Departments of all the deputies named in Lists I-X are given in alphabetical order in List XI.

LIST I

The twenty-four deputies named in the petition presented by Hassenfratz on 1 June 1793

Barbaroux	Fauchet	Lasource
Birotteau	Gensonné	Lehardi
Boyer-Fonfrède	Gorsas	Lesage
Brissot	Grangeneuve	Lidon
Buzot	Guadet	Pétion
Chambon	Isnard	Rabaut St. Etienne
Ducos	Lanjuinais	Salle
Dusaulx	Lanthénas	Vergniaud

Moniteur, xvi, 544, a partial list only; *Proscription*, p. 37; *Procès-verbal*, xiii, 16, where Gorsas is omitted. The more famous petition of 15 April also contained the names of Doulcet, Hardy, Louvet, Valady and Valazé, but not those of Boyer-Fonfrède, Ducos, Dusaulx, Isnard, Lesage, Lidon or Rabaut St. Etienne. See *Moniteur*, xvi, 157; *Proscription*, p. 26.

LIST II

The members of the Commission of Twelve

Figures show the number of votes cast in support of each deputy.

Bergoeing, 175	Kervélegan, 191
Bertrand LaHosdinière, 182	Henri-Larivière, 180
Boilleau, 182	Mollevaut, 180
Boyer-Fonfrède, 197	Rabaut St. Etienne, 191
Gardien, 104	St. Martin Valogne, 188
Gommaire, 184	Viger, 186

Moniteur, xvi, 439, which omits Bergoeing, and Mavidal and Laurent, *Archives parlementaires*, lxv, 138. The Editor's footnote in the *Moniteur* is misleading, since he regards Bertrand LaHosdinière as two men.

LIST III

The twenty-nine deputies who were placed under guard on 2 June 1793

Barbaroux	Gommaire	Lesage
Bergoeing	Gorsas	Lidon
Bertrand LaHosdinière	Grangeneuve	Louvet, J.
· Birotteau	Guadet	Mollevaut
Boilleau	Henri-Larivière	Pétion
Brissot	Kervélegan	Rabaut St. Etienne
Buzot	Lanjuinais	Salle
Chambon	Lasource	Valazé
Gardien	Lehardi	Vergniaud
Gensonné		Viger

Procès-verbal, xiii, 29; *Moniteur*, xvi, 555; *Proscription*, p. 38. For details of the alterations which were made to the list before it attained this final form, see note 3, page 40 above.

LIST IV

The fourteen deputies named in the decree proposed by Saint Just on 8 July 1793

(a) Named as traitors	(b) Named as suspect
Barbaroux	Gardien
Bergoeing	Gensonné
Birotteau	Guadet
Buzot	Mollevaut
Gorsas	Vergniaud
Lanjuinais	
Louvet	
Pétion	
Salle	

Procès-verbal, xv, 313; *Moniteur*, xvii, 157; *Proscription*, p. 70. The Convention accepted the recall of Bertrand LaHosdinière, but postponed discussion of the main decree. Brissot and Duchâstel had been impeached as individuals on 15 and 23 June 1793.

LIST V

The twenty-nine deputies named in the decree of 28 July 1793

The names in italics are those of deputies who were not included in earlier proscription lists.

(a) *Named as traitors*	(b) *Named as suspect*
Barbaroux	Boilleau
Bergoeing	*Cussy*
Buzot	*Fauchet*
Chambon	Gardien
Chasset	Gensonné
Defermon	Grangeneuve
Gorsas	Lasource
Guadet	*Meillan*
Henri-Larivière	Mollevaut
Kervélegan	Valazé
Lanjuinais	Vergniaud
Lesage	
Lidon	
Louvet	
Pétion	
Rabaut St. Etienne	
Salle	
Valady	

Procès-verbal, xvii, 333; *Proscription*, p. 78 ff.; Wallon, *Le Tribunal révolutionnaire*, i, 116. The *Moniteur*, xvii, 268, varies considerably and is not accurate.

LIST VI

The eighteen deputies proscribed before, but not included in, the decree of 28 July 1793

The dates of proscription—all 1793—are given in parentheses.

(a) *Fugitives*

Birotteau (12 July)	Duchâstel (15 July)
Condorcet (14 July)	Masuyer (23 July)
Deverité (14 July)	Vitet (11 July)

(b) *Prisoners*

Brissot (2 and 23 June)	Lauze-Deperret (14 July)
Couppé	Magniez
(Arrested without a decree)	(Arrested without a decree)
Coustard (18 July)	Michet (11 July)
Forest (11 July)	Patrin (11 July)
Gommaire (2 June)	Serre (21 July)
Lehardi (2 June)	Viger (2 June)

Proscription, p. 84.

The forty-five deputies (excluding Philippe-Egalité) named by Amar on 3 October 1793

The twenty-eight names in italics are those of deputies who were not included in earlier proscription lists. The twenty-one names denoted by asterisks are those of the deputies who appeared with Brissot before the Revolutionary Tribunal.

Andrei	*Doulcet*	*Lesterp-Beauvais**
*Antiboul**	*Duchâstel**	Lidon
Boilleau*	*Ducos**	Lehardi*
Bonet	*Duprat**	*Masuyer*
Boyer-Fonfrède*	*Duval*	*Minvielle**
Bresson	Fauchet*	Mollevaut
Brissot*	*Gamon*	*Noel*
*Carra**	Gardien*	*Rouyer*
Chambon	Gensonné*	*Savary*
Condorcet	Grangeneuve	*Sillery**
Coustard	Guadet	Valady
Defermon	*Hardy*	Valazé*
Delahaye	*Isnard*	*Vallée*
*Deperret**	*Lacaze**	Vergniaud*
Deverité	Lasource*	Viger*

Procès-verbal, xxii, 118; *Moniteur*, xviii, 32; *Proscription*, p. 102. The statement in Kuscinski that Duval and Hardy were proscribed for signing the protest against the events of 2 June would appear to be an error: cp. List VIII below.

LIST VIII

The seventy-five deputies who signed the protest of 6 and 19 June 1793

The names in italics are those of deputies who were not included in earlier proscription lists.

Amyon	*Dugue D'Assé*	Masuyer
Aubry	Duprat	*Mercier*
Babey	*Dusaulx*	*Moysset*
Bailleul	*Estadens*	*Obelin*
Blad	*Faure*	*Olivier-Gerente*
Blanqui	*Fayolle*	*Peries*
Blaux	*Ferroux*	*Peyre*
Blaviel	*Fleury*	*Quinnec*
Bohan	Gamon	*Rabaut Pommier*
Bresson	*Garilhe*	*Ribereau*
Cazeneuve	*Girault*	*Rouault*
Chasset	*Grenot*	*Rouzet*
Chastelain	*Guiter*	*Royer*
Corbel	Hecquet	*Ruault*
Couppé	*Jary*	*Saladin*
Dabray	Lacaze	*Salmon*
Daunou	*Laplaigne*	*Saurine*
Defermon	*Laurence*	Savary
Delamarre	*Laurenceot*	*Serre*
Deleville	*Lebreton*	*Soubeyran de Saint Prix*
Deperret	*Lefebvre, J. U. F.*	*Tournier*
Derazey	*Lefebvre, P. L. S.*	Vallée
Descamps	*Maisse*	*Varlet*
Doublet	*Marbos*	*Vernier*
Dubusc	*Massa*	*Vincent*

Procès-verbal, xxii, 57; *Moniteur*, xviii, 60, and xxii, 386; *Proscription*, p. 54—where it is said that Boissy D'Anglas withdrew his signature—and p. 115; Mortimer-Ternaux, vii, 545. The two deputies Dabray and Doublet are sometimes wrongly written as one, 'Dabray-Doublet'. Saladin and Serre were proscribed individually on 21 August and 21 July: see *Moniteur*, xvii, 457 and 193.

Deputies who signed other protests to their Departments about the events of 31 May and 2 June 1793

THE SOMME PROTEST

Asselin, Delecloy, Deverité, Dufestel, François, Gantois, Louvet, P., Martin, Rivery.

(Mortimer-Ternaux, vii, 546–8)

THE HAUTE VIENNE PROTEST

Faye, Lacroix, Lesterp-Beauvais, Rivaud, Soulignac.

(Mortimer-Ternaux, vii, 553; not now known in full)

THE AISNE PROTEST

Belin, Bouchereau, Condorcet, Fiquet, Lecarlier, Loysel, Petit.

(Mortimer-Ternaux, vii, 549. Debry associated himself with this letter in a separate clause; Dupin withdrew his name)

THE MAINE ET LOIRE PROTEST

Leclerc, Lemaignan, Pilastre, La Revellière-Lépaux.

(*Mémoires*, La Revellière-Lépaux, i, 150; not now known in full)

THE HAUTES ALPES PROTEST

Barêty, Borel, Cazeneuve, Izoard, Serre.

(Wallon, *La Révolution du 31 mai et le fédéralisme en 1793*, i, 488)

THE MORBIHAN PROTEST

Michel.

(Mortimer-Ternaux, vii, 561)

LIST X

Other deputies who have been called Girondins

(*a*) *List of eleven deputies named by Aulard, with his reasons for their inclusion.*

Dechezeau, guillotined as a federalist
Dulaure, arrested as a Girondin
Kersaint, arrested as a Girondin
Manuel, arrested as a Girondin
Paine, arrested as a Girondin
Richou, arrested as a Girondin
Rebecquy, denounced as a Girondin
Bancal des Issarts, personal friend of the Rolands
Casenave, A., friend of the Girondins, letter of protest to the President of the Convention (Mortimer-Ternaux, vii, 570)
Lathénas, exempted from arrest on 2 June
St. Martin Valogne, exempted from arrest on 2 June

See Aulard, *Orateurs de la Législative et de la Convention*, i, 155.

(b) *List of twenty-five deputies named by Perroud, with his reasons for their inclusion.*

Camboulas, protested individually, 7 June
Chevalier, protested individually, 12 June
Grégoire, protested individually, 4 June
Lozeau, protested individually, 4 June
Bernard, arrested individually, 19 September
Brunel, arrested individually, 2 August
Couhey, arrested individually, 9 July
Despinassy, arrested individually, September, in Var
Forest, arrested individually, 11 July
Magniez, arrested individually, 22 July
Michet, arrested individually, 11 July
Patrin, arrested individually, 11 July
Vitet, arrested individually, 11 July
Audrein, named by the Central Revolutionary Committee, 31 May
Penières, named by the Central Revolutionary Committee, 31 May
Daubermesnil, resigned his seat, 2 May
Moreau (Meuse),[1] resigned his seat, 16 August
Sanadon, resigned his seat, 13 August
Soulignac, resigned his seat, 15 August
Tocquet, resigned his seat, 14 August
Chénier, poems in praise of the Girondins
Chiappe, support for the deputies attacked on 15 April 1793
Creuzé-Latouche, friend of the Rolands
Giroust, seat declared forfeit, 15 July
Guyomer, an avowed Girondin

(Proscription, p. 49 ff.)

(c) *List of eight other deputies included in the list compiled by Morse Stephens, no specific reasons being given.*

Casabianca	Girard
Corenfustier	Larroche
Devars	Mennesson
Duplantier	Personne

(Morse Stephens, *A History of the French Revolution*, i, 522)

[1] The identity of this deputy is obscure. Both J. F. Moreau (Saône et Loire) and M. F. Moreau (Meuse) resigned, or attempted to do so, on 15 and 16 August 1793. See: *Procès-verbal*, xviii, 410, and xix, 2; P. Montarlot, 'Les députés de Saône et Loire', *Mém. Soc. Eduenne*, xxxv (1907), p. 70; Guiffroy, *Les Conventionnels*; Kuscinski; Robert, etc., *Dictionnaire des Parlementaires*, iv, 426.

Q

LIST XI

The 200 deputies who have been called Girondins

1	AMYON, Jean Claude	Jura
2	ANDREI, Antoine François	Corse
3	ANTIBOUL, Charles Louis	Var
4	ASSELIN, Eustache Benoît	Somme
5	AUBRY, François	Gard
6	AUDREIN, Yves Marie	Morbihan
7	BABEY, Pierre A. Marie	Jura
8	BAILLEUL, Jacques Charles	Seine Inf.
9	BANCAL DES ISSARTS, Jean Henri	Puy de Dôme
10	BARBAROUX, Charles J. Marie	Bouches du Rhône
11	BARÊTY, Pierre	Hautes Alpes
12	BELIN, Jean François	Aisne
13	BERGOEING, François	Gironde
14	BERNARD, Marc A. François	Bouches du Rhône
15	BERTRAND, DE L'HOSDINIÈRE, Charles A.	Orne
16	BIROTTEAU, Jean Baptiste	Pyrénées Or.
17	BLAD, Charles A. Augustin	Finistère
18	BLANQUI, Jean Dominique	Alpes Maritimes
19	BLAUX, Nicolas François	Moselle
20	BLAVIEL, Antoine Innocent	Lot
21	BOHAN, Alain	Finistère
22	BOILLEAU, Jacques d'Ausson	Yonne
23	BONET DE TRYCHES, Joseph B.	Haute Loire
24	BOREL DE BEZ, Hyacinthe Marcelin	Hautes Alpes
25	BOUCHEREAU, Augustin François	Aisne
26	BOYER-FONFRÈDE, Jean Baptiste	Gironde
27	BRESSON, Jean Baptiste M. F.	Vosges
28	BRISSOT, Jean Pierre	Eure et Loire
29	BRUNEL, Ignace	Hérault
30	BUZOT, François Nicolas L.	Eure
31	CAMBOULAS, Simon d'Esparou	Aveyron
32	CARRA, Jean Louis	Saône et Loire
33	CASABIANCA, Luce	Corse
34	CASENAVE, Antoine	Basses Pyrénées
35	CAZENEUVE, Ignace de	Hautes Alpes
36	CHAMBON, Aubin Bigérie	Corrèze
37	CHASSET, Charles Antoine	Rhône et Loire
38	CHASTELAIN, Jean Claude	Yonne
39	CHÉNIER, Marie Joseph Blaise de	Seine et Oise

40	CHEVALIER, Jacques	Sarthe
41	CHIAPPE, Ange	Corse
42	CONDORCET, Marie Jean, Marquis de Caritat	Aisne
43	CORBEL, Vincent Claude	Morbihan
44	CORENFUSTIER, Simon Joseph	Ardèche
45	COUHEY, François	Vosges
46	COUPPÉ, Gabriel Hyacinthe de Kerennou	Côtes du Nord
47	COUSTARD, Anne Pierre de Massy	Loire Inf.
48	CREUZÉ-LATOUCHE, Jacques Antoine	Vienne
49	CUSSY, Gabriel de	Calvados
50	DABRAY, Joseph Séraphin	Alpes Maritimes
51	DAUBERMESNIL, François A.	Tarn
52	DAUNOU, Pierre Claude F.	Pas de Calais
53	DEBRY, Jean Antoine Joseph	Aisne
54	DECHEZEAU, P. C. D. Gustave	Charente Inf.
55	DEFERMON, Jacques	Île et Vilaine
56	DELAHAYE, Jacques Charles G.	Seine Inf.
57	DELAMARRE, Antoine	Oise
58	DELECLOY, Jean Baptiste J.	Somme
59	DELLEVILLE, Jean F. Philippe	Calvados
60	DEPERRET, Claude R. Lauze	Bouches du Rhône
61	DERAZEY, Jean J. Eustache	Indre
62	DESCAMPS, Bernard	Gers
63	DESPINASSY, Antoine Joseph M.	Var
64	DEVARS, Jean	Charente
65	DEVERITÉ, Louis Alexandre	Somme
66	DOUBLET, Pierre Philippe	Seine Inf.
67	DOULCET, Louis Gustave, Comte de Pontécoulant	Calvados
68	DUBUSC, Charles François	Eure
69	DUCHÂSTEL, Gaspar Sévérin	Deux Sèvres
70	DUCOS, Jean François	Gironde
71	DUFESTEL, Jean François	Somme
72	DUGUÉ D'ASSÉ, Jacques Claude	Orne
73	DULAURE, Jacques Antoine	Puy de Dôme
74	DUPIN, André (le jeune)	Aisne
75	DUPLANTIER, Jacques P. Fronton	Gironde
76	DUPRAT, Jean (cadet)	Bouches du Rhône
77	DUSAULX, Jean	Paris
78	DUVAL, Jean Pierre	Seine Inf.
79	ESTADENS, Antoine	Haute Garonne
80	FAUCHET, Claude	Calvados
81	FAURE, Pierre Joseph D. G.	Seine Inf.

82	FAYE, Gabriel	Haute Vienne
83	FAYOLLE, Jean Raymond	Drôme
84	FERROUX, Etienne Joseph	Jura
85	FIQUET, Jean Jacques	Aisne
86	FLEURY, Honoré Marie	Côtes du Nord
87	FOREST, Jacques	Rhône et Loire
88	FRANÇOIS, Landry François	Somme
89	GAMON, François Joseph	Ardèche
90	GANTOIS, Jean François	Somme
91	GARDIEN, Jean François Martin	Indre et Loire
92	GARILHE, François Clément Privat	Ardèche
93	GENSONNÉ, Armand	Gironde
94	GIRARD, Antoine Marie Anne	Aude
95	GIRAULT, Claude Joseph	Côtes du Nord
96	GIROUST, Jacques Charles	Eure et Loire
97	GOMMAIRE, Jean René	Finistère
98	GORSAS, Antoine Joseph	Seine et Oise
99	GRANGENEUVE, Jean Antoine	Gironde
100	GRÉGOIRE, Henri	Loire et Cher
101	GRENOT, Antoine	Jura
102	GUADET, Marguerite Élie	Gironde
103	GUITER, Joseph A. Sébastien	Pyrénées Or.
104	GUYOMER, Pierre Marie A.	Côtes du Nord
105	HARDY, Antoine François	Seine Inf.
106	HECQUET, Charles Robert	Seine Inf.
107	HENRI-LARIVIÈRE, P. F. Joachim	Calvados
108	ISNARD, Maximin	Var
109	ISOARD, Jean F. Auguste	Hautes Alpes
110	JARY, Marie Joseph	Loire Inf.
111	KERSAINT, Armand G. S. Coetnempren	Seine et Oise
112	KERVÉLEGAN, A. B. F. Le Goazre de	Finistère
113	LACAZE, Jacques (Aîné)	Gironde
114	LACROIX, Jean Michel	Haute Vienne
115	LANJUINAIS, Jean Denis	Île et Vilaine
116	LANTHÉNAS, François	Rhône et Loire
117	LAPLAIGNE, Antoine	Gers
118	LA REVELLIÈRE-LÉPAUX, Louis Marie de	Maine et Loire
119	LAROCHE, Jean Félix Samuel	Lot et Garonne
120	LASOURCE, Marc David Alba	Tarn
121	LAURENCE, André François	Manche
122	LAURENCEOT, Jacques Henri	Jura
123	LEBRETON, Roch Pierre François	Île et Vilaine

124	LECARLIER, M. J. François Philbert	Aisne
125	LECLERC, Jean Baptiste	Maine et Loire
126	LEFEBVRE, Julien U. F. de la Chauvière	Loire Inf.
127	LEFEBVRE, Pierre L. Stanislas	Seine Inf.
128	LEHARDI, Pierre	Morbihan
129	LEMAIGNAN, Julien Camille	Maine et Loire
130	LESAGE, Denis Toussaint	Eure et Loire
131	LESTERP-BEAUVAIS, Benoît	Haute Vienne
132	LIDON, Bernard François	Corrèze
133	LOUVET, Jean Baptiste de Couvrai	Loiret
134	LOUVET, Pierre Florent	Somme
135	LOYSEL, Pierre	Aisne
136	LOZEAU, Jean François	Eure et Loire
137	MAGNIEZ, Antoine Guillain	Pas de Calais
138	MAISSE, Marius Félix	Basses Alpes
139	MANUEL, Pierre Louis	Paris
140	MARBOS, François	Drôme
141	MARTIN, Jean B. St. Romain	Somme
142	MASSA, Ruffin	Alpes Maritimes
143	MASUYER, Claude Louis	Saône et Loire
144	MEILLAN, Arnaud	Basses Pyrénées
145	MENNESSON, J. B. Augustin	Ardennes
146	MERCIER, Louis Sébastien	Seine et Oise
147	MICHEL, Guillaume	Morbihan
148	MICHET, Antoine	Rhône et Loire
149	MINVIELLE, Jean Pierre A.	Bouches du Rhône
150	MOLLEVAUT, Etienne	Meurthe
151	MOREAU, Marie François	Meuse
152	MOYSSET, Jean	Gers
153	NOËL, Jean Baptiste	Vosges
154	OBELIN, Matherin J. F. de Kergal	Île et Vilaine
155	OLIVIER-GERENTE, Joseph Fiacre	Drôme
156	PAINE, Thomas	Pas de Calais
157	PATRIN, Eugène Melchior L.	Rhône et Loire
158	PENIÈRES, Jean A. Delzors	Corrèze
159	PERIES, Jacques (cadet)	Aude
160	PERSONNE, Jean Baptiste	Pas de Calais
161	PÉTION, Jérôme de Villeneuve	Eure et Loire
162	PETIT, Michel Edmé	Aisne
163	PEYRE, Louis François	Basses Alpes
164	PILASTRE, Urbain R. de la Brardière	Maine et Loire
165	QUINNEC, Jacques	Finistère

166	RABAUT POMMIER, Jacques A.	Gard
167	RABAUT ST. ÉTIENNE, Jean P.	Aube
168	REBECQUY, François Trophime	Bouches du Rhône
169	RIBEREAU, Jean	Charente
170	RICHOU, Louis Joseph	Eure
171	RIVAUD, François	Haute Vienne
172	RIVERY, Louis	Somme
173	ROUAULT, Joseph Yves	Morbihan
174	ROUYER, Jean Pascal	Hérault
175	ROUZET, Jean M. de Folmon	Haute Garonne
176	ROYER, Jean Baptiste	Ain
177	RUAULT, Alexandre Jean	Seine Inf.
178	ST. MARTIN, Charles Valogne	Aveyron
179	ST. PRIX, Hector de Soubeyran	Ardèche
180	SALADIN, Jean Baptiste Michel	Somme
181	SALLE, Jean Baptiste	Meurthe
182	SALMON, Gabriel René Louis	Sarthe
183	SANADON, Jean Baptiste	Basses Pyrénées
184	SAURINE, Jean Baptiste Pierre	Landes
185	SAVARY, Louis Jacques	Eure
186	SERRE, Jean Joseph	Hautes Alpes
187	SILLERY, Charles Alex. Pierre, Brulart de Genlis	Somme
188	SOLOMIAC, Pierre	Tarn
189	SOULIGNAC, Jean Baptiste	Haute Vienne
190	TOCQUOT, Charles Nicolas	Meuse
191	TOURNIER, Jean Laurent Germain	Aude
192	VALADY, J. G. C. S. J. J. Yzarn de, Marquis de Fraissinet	Aveyron
193	VALAZÉ, Charles Eléonore Dufriche-	Orne
194	VALLÉE, Jacques Nicolas	Eure
195	VARLET, Charles Zachée Joseph	Pas de Calais
196	VERGNIAUD, Pierre Victurnien	Gironde
197	VERNIER, Théodore	Jura
198	VIGER, Louis François Sébastien	Maine et Loire
199	VINCENT, Pierre Charles Victor	Seine Inf.
200	VITET, Louis	Rhône et Loire

The Attendance of Deputies Associated with Brissot at Private Meetings

	The salon of Vergniaud	The Reunion Club	The salon of Madame Roland (1792 and 1793)	The salon of Valazé
Barbaroux			*	*
Bancal des Issarts			*	
Bergoeing				*
Brissot	*	*	*	*
Buzot			*	*
Chambon				*
Condorcet	*		*	
Chasset			*	
Ducos	*	*		
Duchâstel				*
Deperret			*	*
Fauchet		*		
Duprat			*	*
Gensonné	*	*	*	*
Girard				*
Gorsas			*	*
Grangeneuve		*		*
Guadet	*		*	*
Hardy				*
Isnard		*		
Lacaze				*
Lanthénas	*		*	
Lasource		*		
Lehardy				*
Lesage				*

	The salon of Vergniaud	The Reunion Club	The salon of Madame Roland (*1792 and 1793*)	The salon of Valazé
Lidon				*
Louvet			*	*
Mollevaut				*
Meillan				*
Pétion			*	*
Rabaut St. Etienne				*
Rebecquy			*	
Salle				*
Valazé			*	*
Vergniaud	*		*	

Note: Based on the evidence reviewed in Chapter IV, this table has a total of only thirty-five names. Of these, two (Brissot and Gensonné) are common to all four groups; one (Guadet) appears three times; and thirteen appear twice. Of the nineteen deputies whose names occur once only, sixteen were elected in September 1792, and so had little opportunity to attend more than one meeting-place.

APPENDIX C

An Analysis of the Voting of the Deputies Associated with Brissot

In making this analysis, I have selected the names of sixty men, including Brissot himself, and sub-divided these into three groups according to their probable proximity to Brissot. *Group A* consists of the closer and more prominent of Brissot's associates, *Group B* of less prominent and more remote associates, and *Group C* of men whose relationship with him is still more debatable. The classification is based upon the survey of personal relationships which appears in Chapter III, upon that of the salons—see Chapter IV and Appendix B—and upon the frequency and importance of the deputies' interventions in debates. It is in the last resort a subjective classification, but both its broad divisions and the implications of the voting analysis are in my view indisputable.

The analysis will be applied to all the occasions for which detailed records of the voting in the Convention during the relevant period are available, i.e., the trial of Louis XVI, the attempted impeachment of Marat, and the attempt to re-establish the Commission of Twelve.

Group A (17 deputies)			Group B (18 deputies)			Group C (25 deputies)
Barbaroux			Bancal			Babey
Brissot			Bergoeing			Bailleul
Buzot			Boilleau			Birotteau
Condorcet			Boyer-Fonfrède			Bresson
Ducos			Chambon			Carra
Gensonné			Deperret			Chasset
Gorsas			Doulcet			Chiappe
Grangeneuve			Duprat			Creuzé-Latouche
Guadet			Fauchet			Duchâstel
Isnard			Lanthénas			Dusaulx
Kersaint			Larivière			Gamon
Lanjuinais			Lehardy			Girard
Lasource			Lesage			Grégoire
Louvet			Lidon			Hardy
Pétion			Masuyer			Lacaze
Valazé			Mollevaut			Manuel
Vergniaud			Rebecquy			Meillan
			Salle			Mercier
						Minvielle
						Noel
						Rabaut St. Etienne
						Rouyer
						Savary
						Valady
						Vallée

1. THE EXECUTION OF THE KING

Votes Cast:	Group A (17 men)	Group B (18 men)	Group C (24 men)[1]
For a referendum	13	13	16
Against this:	3	5	4
Absent:	1	—	3
Abstained:	—	—	1
Against execution:	12(8)	13(11)	19
For death:	5(9)	5(7)	3
Absent:	—	—	—
Abstained:	—	—	2
For a reprieve:	7	10	14
Against this:	7	7	4
Absent:	1[2]	—	6
Abstained:	2	1	—

TOTALS:

	Group A	Group B	Group C
(1) *For Leniency*			
Three votes:	7(3)	9(7)	11
Two votes:	5	2	6
(2) *For Severity*			
Three votes:	2	2	1
Two votes:	3	4	2

NOTES:

Figures in brackets apply if the 'amendment Mailhe' votes, for death and a reprieve, are counted as they were in the Convention, as votes for execution; in the main table, however, anything less than an unqualified vote for death has been taken as a vote for leniency.

SOURCE:

Appels nominaux sur le jugement de Louis XVI (Paris, 1793), B.M., F.1276.1.

[1] In Group C, Minvielle had not taken his seat at this time.
[2] In Group A, Kersaint, who resigned, has been shown as absent.

2. The Impeachment of Marat

	Group A	Group B	Group C
Strength of the group by 13 April 1793:	16	16	23
Absences on that day:	3	2	7
Present in the assembly:	13	14	16
Votes for the impeachment:	5	12	16
Votes against:	—	1	—
Abstentions:	8	1	—

NOTES:

In *Group A:* Kersaint had resigned, and Brissot, Condorcet and Vergniaud were absent.

In *Group B:* Rebecquy had resigned, Bancal had been arrested by Dumouriez. Salle abstained and Lanthénas opposed the impeachment.

In *Group C:* Minvielle had not yet taken his seat, and Manuel had resigned.

SOURCE:

Appel nominal 13–14 avril 1793: '*T a-ti-il lieu à accusation contre Marat?*' (Paris, 1793), B.M., F.313.79.

3. The Reinstatement of the Commission of Twelve

	Group A	Group B	Group C
Strength of the group by 28 May 1793:	16	16	24
Votes in favour of reinstating the Commission:	14	11	16
Votes against this:	1 (Condorcet)	—	—
Absent or abstaining (not distinguished):	1 (Gorsas)	5	8

NOTES:

In *Group A:* Kersaint had resigned.

In *Group B:* Bancal had been arrested and Rebecquy had resigned. Bergoeing, Doulcet, Lanthénas, Lesage and Lidon were either absent or abstained.

In *Group C:* Manuel had resigned and Minvielle had joined the assembly. Bailleul, Carra, Creuzé, Girard, Grégoire, Lacaze, Rabaut St. Etienne and Savary were either absent or abstained.

SOURCE:

Appel nominal . . . : '*Le décret qui a cassé la Commission des Douze, sera-t-il rapporté, oui ou non?*' (28 May 1793) Mavidal and Laurent, etc., *Archives parlementaires de 1787 à 1860,* lxv, 496 and 520 ff., citing A.N., c.253, ch. 460, *dossier spécial.*

BIBLIOGRAPHY

PRIMARY SOURCES

1. MANUSCRIPT SOURCES

Archives Nationales

Série w. *Tribunaux Révolutionnaires*

w.290.167. (Interrogation of Gorsas.)

w.292.204. *Part 2*, No. 67 (Letter by Bertrand LaHosdinière).

Part 3, Nos. 11, 18, 19, 20, 22, 23, 24, 27, 29, 32, 33, 38, 49 (Letters and memorials written in prison or in court by the deputies who appeared with Brissot before the Revolutionary Tribunal).

Part 5, Nos. 1, 2, 3, 4, 6, 7, 8, 9, 10, and 12 to 23 inclusive (Interrogations of the deputies who appeared with Brissot before the Revolutionary Tribunal).

w.300.297. (Interrogation of Kersaint.)

w.300.308. (Interrogation of Noël.)

w.300.308 *bis*. (Interrogation of Clavière.)

Série BB³. *Versements du ministère de la justice: affaires criminelles.*

BB³.72. No. 10 (Denunciation of meetings at Saint Cloud).

Série F⁷.4386–4824: *Police générale: comité de sûreté générale.*

F⁷.4443. *Part 3*, Nos. 154, 157, 158, 176.

Part 4, Nos. 179, 197, 198, 199, 205, 207, 209, 210, 235, 236, 259, 282.

Part 5, Nos. 283, 352, 354, 358, 359, 360.

Part 7, Nos. 449, 450, 452, 479, 480.

Part 8, No. 535.

Part 10, Nos. 586, 587, 593, 594, 597, 619, 695, 697, 700, 702. (All numbers relate to various notes and correspondence concerning the proscribed deputies.)

Bibliothèque Nationale

MSS. Nouv. Acq. Fr., 3534.

Nos. 36–69 (Correspondance de Dumouriez avec Gensonné).

2. PRINTED SOURCES

I. Pamphlets

Bibliothèque Nationale

8 Lc?.646. *Journal des Amis de la Paix.* Paris, 1791 (one issue only).

British Museum

935.b.13.10. Petit, Michel Edmé, *Le Procès des 31 mai, 1 et 2 juin.* Paris, 1794.

Croker Collections (catalogued by G. K. Fortescue, 1899)

These collections of pamphlets, a valuable source of material for the history of the Revolution, may be approached either through their Index (e.g., Série F.981–1033: *Justifications*) or through the General Catalogue (e.g., Bernard, Marc A. F., *Précis de la conduite civique du citoyen Bernard*, F.1023.10). A considerable number of these pamphlets have been referred to in this book, but since nearly all of them are concerned only with the particular opinions of individual deputies, reference should be made to the titles and index numbers cited in the footnotes. The following are among those particularly important and relevant to the argument advanced in the text:

Série F

313.79. *Appel nominal 13–14 avril 1793: Y a-t-il lieu à accusation contre Marat?* Paris, 1793.
334.18. *Précis tracé à la hâte par Rabaut St. Etienne.* Paris, 1793.
666.4. *Opinion de J. Pétion sur la question de savoir s'il existe une Convention Nationale.* Paris, 1793.
673.6. J. P. Brissot, *A tous les républicains de France.* Paris, 1792.
674.2. J. P. Brissot. *A ses commettans.* Paris, 1793.
826.2. *Tableau comparatif des sept appels nominaux fév.–10 août 1792.* Paris, 1792.
843.17. *Les douze représentans du peuple détenus à Porte-Libre.* Paris, 1794.
848.16. *Les représentans du peuple détenus à la maison d'arrêt des Carmes.* Paris, 1794.
917.1. *Opinion de M. E. Guadet sur le jugement de Louis.* Paris, 1793.
917.12. *Opinion de citoyen Gensonné sur le jugement de Louis.* Paris, 1793.
918.16. *Opinion de A. G. Kersaint sur le jugement de Louis.* Paris, 1793.
918.32. *Opinion de Lanjuinais sur Louis le dernier.* Paris, 1793.
1023.16. *Les représentans du peuple détenus à la maison d'arrêt des Ecossais.* Paris, 1794.
1023.17. *La défense de C. E. Dufriche-Valazé.* Paris, 1793.
1026.9. Gustave Doulcet, *Sur la pétition présentée contre vingt-deux représentans du peuple.* Paris, 1793.
1103.3. J. A. Dulaure, *Du fédéralisme en France.* Paris, 1793.
1103.5. C. Desmoulins, *L'histoire des Brissotins.* Paris, 1793.
1276.1. *Appels nominaux sur le jugement de Louis XVI.* Paris, 1793.

Série F.R.

61.28. J. A. Dulaure, *Physionomie de la Convention Nationale.* Paris, 1793.
64.11. *Les députés de la Manche: A nos commettans.* Paris, 1793.

II. *Correspondence*

MICHON, G. *Correspondance de Maximilien et Augustin Robespierre.* 2 vols., Paris, 1926.

PERROUD, C. *Correspondance et Papiers de J. P. Brissot.* Paris, 1911.
—— *Lettres de Madame Roland.* Paris, 1900.
—— with CHABAUD, A. *Correspondance de Barbaroux.* Paris, 1923.

III. *Journals*

Réimpression de l'Ancien Moniteur. 31 vols., Paris, 1854.
CONDORCET, M. J., RABAUT ST. ETIENNE and others. *Chronique de Paris.* 5 vols., Paris, 1789–1793.
GORSAS, A. J. *Le Courrier des LXXXIII Départemens.* 12 vols., Paris, 1791–2 (Continued from 22 Sept. 1792 to 8 mars 1793 in 6 vols as *Le Courrier des Départemens*).
Journal des Débats de la Société des Amis de la Constitution séante aux Jacobins. Paris, 2 juin 1791–24 Frimaire an II.
ROBESPIERRE, M. *Le Défenseur de la Constitution* (in Vol. iv of G. Laurent, *Œuvres complètes de Robespierre*, Paris, 1939).
BRISSOT, J. P. *Le Patriote français, journal libre.* Paris, 28 juillet 1789–2 juin 1793.

IV. *Memoirs*

BARBAROUX, C. *Mémoires*, ed. A. Chabaud. Paris, 1936.
BAUDOT, M. A. *Notes historiques sur la Convention Nationale.* Paris, 1893.
BRISSOT, J. P. *Mémoires*, ed. C. Perroud. 2 vols., Paris, 1904.
BUZOT, F. N. L. *Mémoires*, ed. (1) J. Guadet, Paris, 1828; (2) C. A. Dauban, Paris, 1866.
CHAMPAGNEUX, L. A. *Discours préliminaire ou Notice sur J. M. Ph. Roland.* Paris, 1800.
CHOUDIEU, P. R. *Mémoires et notes, 1761–1838*, ed. V. Barrucand. Paris, 1897.
DAUNOU, P. C. F. 'Mémoires pour servir à l'histoire de la Convention Nationale' in A. H. Taillandier, *Documents biographiques sur P. C. F. Daunou.* Paris, 1841.
DESGENETTES, R. N. DUFRICHE. *Souvenirs de la fin du xviiie siècle ou Mémoires de R. D. G.* 2 vols., Paris, 1835.
DUMONT, E. *Souvenirs sur Mirabeau et sur les deux premières assemblées législatives*, ed. J. Bénétruy. Paris, 1951.
DUMOURIEZ, Général. *Vie et Mémoires*, ed. J. F. Barrière. 2 vols., Paris, 1848.
DULAURE, J. A. 'Mémoires' in L. Duchesne de la Sicotière, *Notice historique et littéraire sur Dulaure.* Paris, 1862.

GRANDCHAMPS, Sophie. 'Souvenirs inédits de Sophie Grand-champs', C. Perroud, *La Révolution française*, xxxvii (1899), pp. 65–7.

GREATHEED, B. *An Englishman in Paris, 1803: The Journal of Bertie Greatheed*, ed. J. P. T. Bury and J. C. Barry. London, 1953.

GREGOIRE, H. B. *Mémoires recueillis par Hypollyte Carnot*. 2 vols., Paris, 1837.

LACRETELLE, J. C. D. *Précis historique de la Révolution française: Assemblée législative*. Paris, 1801.

LANJUINAIS, J. D. 'Fragment' in J. F. Barrière, *Bibliothèque des Mémoires*. Vol. xxx, Paris, 1832.

LA REVELLIERE-LEPAUX, L. M. *Mémoires* publiés par son fils. Paris, 1873.

LOUVET, J. *Mémoires*, ed. F. A. Aulard. 2 vols., Paris, 1889.

MEILLAN, A. *Mémoires de Meillan, député par le Département des Basses Pyrénées*. Paris, 1823.

PETION, J. *Mémoires*, ed. C. A. Dauban. Paris, 1866.

ROLAND, Madame J. M. *Mémoires*, ed. (1) C. A. Dauban, Paris, 1864; (2) C. Perroud, 2 vols., Paris, 1905.

WILLIAMS, H. M. *Souvenirs de la Révolution française*, trans. C. Coquerel. Paris, 1827.

V. *Other Primary Sources*

Almanach National, 1793. Paris, 1793.

AULARD, F. A. *La Société des Jacobins: Recueil des Documents*. 6 vols., Paris, 1889–97.

—— *Recueil des actes du comité de salut public*. 28 vols., Paris, 1889 onwards.

BUCHEZ, P. J. B. and ROUX-LAVERGNE, P. C. *Histoire Parlementaire de la Révolution française depuis 1789 jusqu'à l'Empire*. 43 vols., Paris, 1834 onwards.

COURTOIS, E. B. *Rapport fait au nom de la commission chargée de l'examen des papiers trouvés chez Robespierre*. Paris, 1794.

DUGUIT, L., MONNIER, H., and BONNARD, R. *Les constitutions et les principales lois politiques de la France depuis 1789*. 7th edn., Paris, 1952.

MAVIDAL, J., and LAURENT, E. *Archives Parlementaires, première série, 1787–1799*. 82 vols., Paris, 1868–92.

MORTIMER-TERNAUX, L. *Histoire de la Terreur, 1792–1794*. 8 vols., Paris, 1868–81.

Procès-verbal de la Convention Nationale: séances depuis le premier juin 1793. Vols. 13–72, Paris, 1793–5.

SECONDARY SOURCES

I. General Works of Reference

ARNAULT, A. V. and others. *Biographie nouvelle des contemporains.* 20 vols., Paris, 1820.

BALTEAU, J., and others. *Dictionnaire de biographie française.* 8 vols., Paris, 1933, in progress.

CARON, P. *Bibliographie des travaux publiés de 1866–1897 sur l'histoire de France depuis 1789.* Paris, 1912.

—— *Manuel pratique pour l'étude de la Révolution française.* Paris, 1947.

—— BRIERE, G., and MAISRE, H. *Répertoire méthodique de l'histoire de la France.* 9 vols., Paris, 1898–1912.

—— and STEIN, H. *Répertoire bibliographique de l'histoire de France.* 6 vols., Paris, 1923, in progress.

COURTEAULT, H. *Etat des inventaires des Archives nationales, départementales, communales et hospitalières au premier janvier 1937.* 2 vols., Paris, 1938.

GUIFFREY, J. *Les Conventionels.* Paris, 1889.

HATIN, E. *Bibliographie historique et critique de la presse périodique française.* Paris, 1866.

KUSCINSKI, A. *Les députés à l'Assemblée Législative de 1791.* Paris, 1900.

—— *Dictionnaire des Conventionels.* Paris, 1917.

MARTIN, A., and WALTER, G. *Catalogue de l'histoire de la Révolution française.* 5 vols., Paris, 1936.

ROBERT, A., and others. *Dictionnaire des parlementaires français.* Paris, 1891.

TOURNEAUX, M. *Bibliographie de l'histoire de Paris pendant la Révolution française.* 5 vols., Paris, 1890–1913.

TUETEY, A. *Répertoire général des Sources manuscrits de l'histoire de Paris pendant la Révolution française.* 11 vols., Paris, 1890–1914.

WALTER, G. *Répertoire de l'histoire de la Révolution française: travaux publiés de 1800 à 1940: Personnes.* 2 vols., Paris, 1941.

VILLAT, L. *La Révolution et l'Empire, 1789–1815.* 2 vols., Paris, 1936.

II. General Histories

AULARD, F. A. *Histoire politique de la Révolution française.* 2 vols., Paris, 1905.

BLANC, L. *Histoire de la Révolution française.* 12 vols., Paris, 1864–66.

GAXOTTE, P. *La Révolution française.* Paris, 1928.

JAURES, J. *Histoire socialiste de la Révolution française* ed. A. Mathiez. 8 vols., Paris, 1922 onwards.

LAMARTINE, M. L. A. de. *Histoire des Girondins.* 5 vols., Paris, 1870.

LAVISSE, E. *Histoire de France contemporaine: La Révolution.*
Vol. i: SAGNAC, P. *La Révolution, 1789–1792.*
Vol. ii: PARISET, G., *La Révolution, 1792–1799.* Paris, 1920–2.

LEFEBVRE, G. *La Révolution française* (in L. Halphen and P. Sagnac,
Peuples et Civilisations). Paris, 1951.

—— *Les Cours de Sorbonne: La Révolution française (La chute du roi; La
première terreur; La Convention,* parts 1 and 2). Paris, 1944–5.

MATHIEZ, A. *La Révolution française.* 3 vols, Paris, 1927.

MICHELET, J. *Histoire de la Révolution française.* 9 vols., Paris, 1849.

MIGNET, F. *Histoire de la Révolution française depuis 1789 jusqu'à 1814.*
2 vols., Brussels, 1828.

MORSE STEPHENS, H. *A History of the French Revolution.* 2 vols.,
London, 1891.

QUINET, E. *La Révolution.* 2 vols., Paris, 1865.

SOREL, A. *L'Europe et la Révolution française.* 8 vols., Paris, 1908.

STAËL, Madame G. de. *Considérations sur les principaux événemens de la
Révolution française.* 3 vols., London, 1818.

TAINE, H. *Les origines de la France contemporaine: La Révolution* (particularly Vol. ii: *La conquête Jacobine*). 6 vols., Paris, 1885.

THIERS, L. A. *The History of the French Revolution.* Trans. F. Schorberl,
5 vols., London, 1838.

TISSOT, M. P. F. *Histoire de la Révolution française depuis 1789 jusqu'à
l'Empire.* 6 vols., Paris, 1839.

TOULONGEON, F. E. *Histoire de France depuis 1789.* 4 vols., Paris,
1801–10.

III. BIOGRAPHIES AND BIOGRAPHICAL NOTICES

A great many of these have been written about the deputies who have been
called Girondins, but some are general eulogies and others have little to say
of the period 1791–4. The following have been more useful in the preparation
of this book:

ALENGRY, F. *Condorcet, guide de la Révolution française.* Paris, 1904.

BOUDET, M. *Les Conventionnels d'Auvergne: Dulaure.* Paris, 1874.

BOUGLER, E. *Le mouvement provincial en 1789 et biographies des députés
de l'Anjou.* 2 vols., Paris, 1865.

CAHEN, L. *Condorcet et la Révolution française.* Paris, 1904.

CHARRIER, J. *Claude Fauchet, évêque constitutionnel de Calvados, député
à l'Assemblée Législative et à la Convention, 1744–1793.* 2 vols., Paris,
1909.

CLAUDE, A. *Etienne Mollevaut et la vie politique en Lorraine.* Clamecy,
1933.

R

COMBES DE PATRIS, B. *Des Gardes françaises à la Convention nationale: Valady, 1766–1793.* Paris, 1930.

CONWAY, M. D. *The Life of Thomas Paine.* 2 vols., London and New York, 1892.

DAUBAN, C. A. *Etude sur Madame Roland et son temps, suivie des lettres inédites de Madame Roland à Buzot.* 2 vols., Paris, 1864.

DAVY, J. N. *Etudes sur la Révolution française: Les Conventionnels de l'Eure, Fr. Buzot, Duroy, etc.* Evreux, 1876.

ELLERY, E. *Brissot de Warville: a study in the history of the French Revolution.* Boston and New York, 1915.

GUILLAME, M. 'Marie-Joseph Chénier et Robespierre', *La Révolution française,* xliii (1902), pp. 347–57.

HAMEL, E. *Histoire de Robespierre.* 3 vols., Paris, 1865.

HEMON, P. *Audrein, Yves-Marie, député du Morbihan.* St. Briac and Paris, 1903.

HERISSAY, J. *Un Girondin, François Buzot, député de l'Eure à l'Assemblée Constituante et à la Convention, 1760–1794.* Paris, 1907.

LAFONT, E. 'Le Conventionnel Michel Edmé Petit', *La Révolution française,* lv (1908), pp. 403–23.

LEMAS, T. 'Ignaze de Cazeneuve, évêque constitutionnel des Hautes Alpes, membre de la Convention', *La Révolution française,* xviii (1890), pp. 317–34, 412–32.

LEVOT, P., and others. *Biographie Bretonne: recueil des notices sur tous les Bretons qui se sont fait un nom.* 2 vols., Vannes and Paris, 1852.

LINTILHAC, E. *Vergniaud, Le drame des Girondins.* Paris, 1920.

LOTH, J. *Les Conventionnels de la Seine inférieure.* Rouen, 1883.

MEGE, F. *Le Conventionnel Bancal des Issarts.* Paris, 1887.

MIRABAUD, R. *Un Président de la Constituante et de la Convention, Rabaut St. Etienne.* Paris, 1930.

MONTARLOT, P. 'Les députés de Saône et Loire aux assemblées de la Révolution,' *Mémoires de la Société Eduenne, Nouv. Série,* Autun, xxxiii (1905), pp. 217–73 (for Carra); and xxxii (1904), pp. 204–33 and xxxiii (1905), pp. 193–216 (for Masuyer).

NICOLLE, P. *Valazé, député de l'Orne à la Convention nationale.* Paris, 1933.

PERROUD, C. 'Notice sur la vie de Sieyès', *La Révolution française,* xxiii (1892), p. 160 ff.

—— 'Brissot et les Rolands', *La Révolution française,* xxxiv (1898), pp. 403–22.

PINGAUD, L. *Jean de Bry: Le Congrès de Rastatt, une préfecture sous le premier Empire.* Paris, 1909.

RENAUT, J. C. 'Clavière et Dumouriez', *La Revolution française*, i (1881), pp. 96–105.

SOUBEYRAN DE SAINT PRIX, Humbert de. *Hector de Soubeyran de Saint Prix, député de l'Ardèche à la Convention nationale, 1756–1838.* 2 vols., Paris, 1904.

THOMPSON, J. M. *Robespierre.* London, 1935.

TREILHES, A. *Etude sur le triumvirat Girondin.* Bordeaux, 1891.

VATEL, C. *Vergniaud: MSS., lettres et papiers.* 2 vols., Paris, 1873.

VERMOREL, A. *Œuvres de Vergniaud.* Paris, 1867.

WALTER, G. *Robespierre.* Paris. 1946.

IV. OTHER SPECIAL STUDIES

AULARD, F. A. *Orateurs de la Législative et de la Convention.* 2 vols., Paris, 1906.

—— 'Le comité de salut public', *La Révolution française*, xviii (1890), p. 5 ff.

—— 'Le détrônement de Louis XVI, 1792', *La Révolution française*, xxxvi (1899), pp. 25–67.

—— 'Evolution des idées politiques entre le 10 août et le 22 septembre 1792', *La Révolution française*, xxxvi (1899), pp. 133–60.

—— 'L'opinion républicain et l'opinion royaliste sous la première république avant le 9 thermidor', *La Révolution française*, xxxvi (1899), pp. 481–99.

BIRE, E. *Légendes Révolutionnaires.* Paris, 1893.

BOUCHARY, J. *Les manieurs d'argent à Paris à la fin du xviiie siècle*, Vol. i. Paris, 1939.

BRACE, R. M. *Bordeaux and the Gironde, 1789–1794.* New York, 1947.

—— 'General Dumouriez and the Girondins, 1792–1793', *American Historical Review*, lvi (1951), p. 493 ff.

CARON, P. *Les massacres de septembre.* Paris, 1935.

CASSAGNAC, A. de GRANIER. *Histoire des Girondins et les massacres de septembre.* 2 vols., Paris, 1860.

CHALLAMEL, A. *Les clubs contre-révolutionnaires.* Paris. 1895.

COBBAN, A. 'Local Government during the French Revolution', *English Historical Review*, lviii (1943), p. 17 ff.

DELVILLE, P. ST. CLAIRE. *La Commune de l'an II.* Paris, 1946.

FARMER, P. *France surveys her Revolutionary Origins.* New York, 1944.

GLAGAU, H. *Die französische Legislative und der Ursprung der Revolutionskrieg, 1791–1792.* Berlin, 1896.

GOOCH, G. P. *History and Historians in the Nineteenth Century.* London, 1913.

GUADET, J. *Les Girondins, leur vie privée, leur vie publique.* 2 vols., Paris, 1861.

LEFEBVRE, G. *The Coming of the French Revolution.* Trans. R. Palmer, Princeton, 1947.

—— *Etudes sur la Révolution française.* Paris, 1954.

—— *Les Thermidoriens.* Paris, 1946.

LINTILHAC, E. 'Le salon de Madame Dodun', *La Révolution française*, lxxi (1918), pp. 6–19.

MATHIEZ, A. *La conspiration de l'étranger.* Paris, 1918.

—— *Girondins et Montagnards.* Paris, 1930.

—— *La Réaction Thermidorienne.* Paris, 1929.

—— *La Révolution et les étrangers.* Paris, 1918.

—— *La Vie chère et le mouvement social sous la Terreur.* Paris, 1927.

—— 'Les Girondins et la Cour à la veille du 10 août', *Annales Historiques de la Révolution française.* 1931, pp. 193–212.

MICHON, G. *Robespierre et la guerre révolutionnaire, 1791–1792.* Paris, 1937.

PAGANEL, P. *Essai historique et critique sur la Révolution française.* 3 vols., Paris, 1810.

PERROUD, C. *Recherches sur la proscription des Girondins, 1793–1795.* Paris, 1917.

—— 'Le premier ministère de Roland', *La Révolution française*, xlii (1903), pp. 511–27.

—— 'Recherches sur le salon de Madame Roland en 1791', *La Révolution française*, xxxvi (1899), pp. 336–44.

—— 'Un projet de Brissot pour une association agricole', *La Révolution française*, xlii (1902), p. 260 ff.

SIRICH, J. B. *The Revolutionary Committees in the Departments of France, 1793–1794.* Harvard U.P., 1943.

SOREL, A. 'Dumouriez: un général diplomate au temps de la Révolution', *Revue des Deux Mondes*, lxiv (1884), pp. 302–33, 575–606, 797–829.

VATEL, C. *Charlotte de Corday et les Girondins.* 3 vols., Paris, 1864.

WALLON, H. A. *Histoire du Tribunal Révolutionnaire de Paris.* 2 vols., Paris, 1900.

—— *La Révolution du 31 mai et le fédéralisme en 1793.* 2 vols., Paris, 1886.

WALTER, G. *Histoire des Jacobins.* Paris, 1946.

Index